The Pledge

The Pledge

ASA, Peasant Politics, and Microfinance in the Development of Bangladesh

Stuart Rutherford

OXFORD
UNIVERSITY PRESS
2009

OXFORD
UNIVERSITY PRESS

Oxford University Press, Inc., publishes works that further
Oxford University's objective of excellence
in research, scholarship, and education.

Oxford New York
Auckland Cape Town Dar es Salaam Hong Kong Karachi
Kuala Lumpur Madrid Melbourne Mexico City Nairobi
New Delhi Shanghai Taipei Toronto

With offices in
Argentina Austria Brazil Chile Czech Republic France Greece
Guatemala Hungary Italy Japan Poland Portugal Singapore
South Korea Switzerland Thailand Turkey Ukraine Vietnam

Published by Oxford University Press, Inc.
198 Madison Avenue, New York, New York 10016

www.oup.com

Library of Congress Cataloging-in-Publication Data
Rutherford, Stuart.
The pledge : ASA, peasant politics, and microfinance in the development
of Bangladesh / Stuart Rutherford.
p. cm.
Includes bibliographical references and index.
ISBN 978-0-19-538065-1
1. Microfinance—Bangladesh—History. 2. Peasantry—Bangladesh—History.
3. Rural poor—Bangladesh—History. I. Title.
HG178.33.B3R88 2009
332.1—dc22 2008025284

9 8 7 6 5 4 3 2 1

Printed in the United States of America
on acid-free paper

Dedicated to the search for better financial services for poor people

Foreword

In December 2007, *Forbes* Magazine published a list of the world's top 50 microfinance institutions. With the list, *Forbes*—best known for its annual list of billionaires—turned its focus to the other pole of the world's income distribution.

A year earlier, Bangladesh's Grameen Bank had won the Nobel Peace Prize and made microfinance globally famous, but, remarkably, Grameen was down the *Forbes* list at number 17. Grameen Bank's signal achievement was to establish the fundamental premise of microfinance: that even the poorest villagers in one of the world's poorest countries could become reliable bank customers. Access to banks is the key to unleashing economic power, Grameen advocates argued, allowing customers to expand their businesses, start saving, and climb out of poverty.

The *Forbes* top spot instead went to ASA, one of Grameen's chief competitors in Bangladesh. The second spot went to Bandhan, an ASA follower based in Kolkata. ASA joins Grameen as another of the new breed of micro-banks, but ASA has pursued operational simplicity and massive scale with a vision unmatched in its clarity and relentlessness. By the end of 2007, ASA reported that they served nearly seven million women, whittled costs down to just 4 taka for each 10,000 taka disbursed in loans, and earned profit at a level that was 60 percent above their costs.

This part of ASA's story has been broadcast widely, and much can and should be learned from ASA's management strategies. In many ways, though, the most interesting part of ASA's story remains nearly out of sight. It is an unclear passage, a long ago life now mainly forgotten, a lost decade hardly mentioned in the glossy pamphlets and case studies. The now-hidden early years, starting soon after Bangladesh's independence and running through the late 1980s, are the story of an NGO committed to raising social consciousness in the villages—a grassroots people's organization that was optimistic, political, and subversive.

ASA's transformation into a micro-bank in the late 1980s was abrupt and remarkably thorough. Villagers once offered education and legal aid were now offered loans instead. ASA's new mode was financial: focused on giving credit, setting up bank branches, and guaranteeing on-time loan repayment rates from its poor clients. ASA became, outwardly and operationally, fundamentally apolitical. For better and worse, that apolitical affect marks all of microfinance today.

As Stuart Rutherford's remarkable biography of ASA shows, the organization's leadership never perceived a fundamental shift in their goals; the deep transformation they saw was in their tactics. ASA's story challenges decades of thinking about strategies to achieve economic and social development and throws fresh light on the role of NGOs, political mobilization, and grassroots activism in creating lasting change. These challenges don't come from theoretical dialectics but from the perceptions of ASA's leadership about what was possible and meaningful in the day-to-day experiences of the villagers of Bangladesh, perceptions that increasingly mirror the thinking of development activists today and that have fueled the growth of microfinance into a multibillion-dollar global financial sector.

The success of microfinance as a business model that promises poverty reduction has been so complete that it is increasingly hard to locate the voices of activists mounting vigorous defenses for directly combating social and economic inequalities through political action—action that may be a critical complement to the ultimate success of microfinance and similar community-based "micro" interventions. Inevitably, the pendulum will swing back, and when it does, understanding ASA's progress will be all the more important.

Fortunately, the story of ASA's early years is now being shared with a wider audience. Readers are forced to contemplate what is valued and by whom? What can be achieved with given resources? Where and when should idealism yield to pragmatism? What has been gained and lost? In ASA's story we have the history of one of Bangladesh's premier institutions, a world-leading micro-bank, and a tale of courage, failure, and bold reinvention. This book stands as part of the larger fight to expand the realm of justice and equality and of the inevitable struggle to translate compelling, pristine ideas into meaningful, practical strategies.

Jonathan Morduch
Professor of Public Policy and Economics
Robert F. Wagner Graduate School of Public Service
New York University

Preface

If you want directions to local offices of the Association for Social Advancement in the villages and slums of Bangladesh, it's better to ask for "ASA Bank." Though some of ASA's staff dislike the phrase, preferring to think of their organization in much broader terms, it is not inappropriate. ASA has a branch serving almost every village and slum in the country with *microfinance*—loans, savings, and insurance services designed expressly for the poor. At the end of 2007, *Forbes* magazine ranked ASA as the world's best microfinance organization.[1]

It wasn't always this way. ASA was formed in the late 1970s to train poor villagers to fight for their political and social rights. It deliberately avoided lending, arguing that loans distract the rural poor from their struggle with their oppressors for a more just society. This book tells how the change from rural revolutionaries to village development bankers came about.

In East Bengal (modern Bangladesh) there was a long history of outsiders stirring up political activism in the villages and a well-established tradition of intervening in rural credit markets. ASA's work has been influenced by both these trends, and this book begins by briefly tracing their development. But ASA is an NGO (nongovernmental organization), a new kind of body that came to prominence in the wake of Bangladesh's liberation struggle in 1971. To put ASA in context, chapters 1, 2, and 3 provide some highlights of the political history of Bangladesh and sketch the place of the NGOs and the men and women who created them.

These chapters are based on secondary sources and do not aim to be comprehensive or original.

The story of ASA itself, and of its energetic founder, Shafiqual Haque Choudhury, occupies the rest of the book. These chapters are based on the author's intimate knowledge of ASA and of the NGO and microfinance movements in Bangladesh.[2] They feature extensive interviews conducted over many years, starting in the early 1990s and continuing into 2008, with ASA staff and ex-staff, ASA customers and ex-customers, and with other observers, and use ASA's publications and records. The story begins with ASA's early eagerness to organize villagers to change not just their own lives but the whole social order. But hopes of sparking a village-based revolution faded, and ASA took up more conventional NGO work. It began to deliver services in the fields of health, population, and education and to provide emergency relief in the aftermath of disasters such as cyclones and floods. In order to finance these services, it took ever larger sums of money from its foreign donors. But by 1991 it had become disappointed with these efforts, and another change of focus occurred. This time, the spotlight fell on rural credit.

In the meantime, other NGOs in Bangladesh, above all the Grameen Bank, had been developing new ways to deliver credit to poor villagers. They were so successful that credit had become the single most common element of NGO programs. ASA was a latecomer to credit, but it soon showed an unusual single-mindedness in pursuing it. It became the first of the major NGOs to see in credit delivery an escape route from dependency on donors. It developed its "self-reliant development model" in which poor rural customers were to progress toward self-reliance by taking loans from ASA and investing them in small businesses, while at the same time ASA progressed toward its own form of self-reliance (independence of donor support) by means of the interest earned on the loans. As the book shows, ASA succeeded beyond all expectation in its ambitions for itself. Only some of its customers became prosperous by investing ASA loans in businesses, but for nearly everyone who used them ASA's services turned out to be more broadly useful, sometimes in unexpected ways.

Now ASA is stepping out boldly on the international stage. Backed by funding from the financial capitals of the world, it is taking its highly successful form of pro-poor banking to millions of poor customers in China, India, and Nigeria, just to name the biggest countries that are poised to learn about ASA.

In writing this book, my primary aim has been to give the nonspecialist reader an account of ASA—its historical roots, its founder, its birth and development, its people, its work, and its future. If at the same time I am able to make a contribution to our understanding of the evolution of the NGO movement in general in Bangladesh, and of the spectacular recent growth of interest in banking with poor people, my purpose will have been well served. And if I manage to engage the attention of specialists with my ideas about financial services for poor people, I shall be delighted.

I would like to thank ASA, especially its president, Shafiqual Haque Choudhury, for encouragement and help during the preparation of this book. I have enjoyed wholly unhindered access to ASA's records and its offices, and no limits have been placed on my freedom to quote from the many interviews I carried out with people from all walks of life. I would like to acknowledge the help I have had from hundreds of village people, dozens of ASA staff, and many others. Special thanks go to Jonathan Morduch, one of the few economists who really understand microfinance, for writing the foreword. Those who read the text, in part or in full, and made helpful comments include Asif Dowla, David Hulme, Margaret Kirton, Jonathan Morduch and Graham A. N. Wright; Father Timm and the late Azizul Haq for the ASA governing body; and Shafiqual Haque Choudhury, Darbesh Ali, Enamul Haque, Kamrul Hassan, Azim Hossain (who also provided much numerical data), Mustafa Kamal, Sohel Mahmud, and Sushil Kumar Roy for ASA staff. Anwarul Azim provided many important details of ASA's early history. S. K. Sinha not only acted as my assistant and helped with many of the interviews, but also made translations from Bengali to English. My understanding of ASA and its place in microfinance has been refined over many years by correspondence and discussion with countless colleagues whom I would also like to thank: the writings of some but by no means all of them are listed in the notes. Any errors of fact or judgment are entirely my fault.

I should disclose that in 1994 I was commissioned by ASA to write an account of its early years, *ASA: The Biography of an NGO,* published by ASA in Dhaka in 1995. Parts of the present book are based on that earlier work. For four years, from 1996 to 1999, while I was living in Bangladesh, I served as a member of ASA's governing body. I hope that readers will agree that I have nevertheless maintained an independent view of the organization, aware of its weaknesses as well as of its many strengths.

Contents

The Pledge

Prologue

March 1978

The Rest House belonging to the Roads and Highways Department at Uthuli, a village near the town of Manikganj on the main road running west out of Dhaka, the Bangladesh capital, is a modest, nondescript building. But something unusual happened there in March 1978. On a hot, dry night, well after midnight, seven silent but excited young men approached the single-storied building, and then stopped in its garden. Each knelt and touched the earth with one hand, holding the other to his breast. They made a pledge, committing themselves to brotherhood and to a new form of organization to fight rural poverty. The short ritual marked the birth of ASA, the Association for Social Advancement.

Then they made their way back to their lodgings. The training course that had brought them together had finished. The next day two of them returned to Dhaka, where they were trainers employed by the Bangladesh Rural Advancement Committee (BRAC), a private voluntary organization (or "nongovernmental organization," NGO). Another, a government worker who had links to an underground left-wing political party, went back to his office nearby, as did a local college professor. Two more who worked for CCDB, the Christian Commission for Development, Bangladesh, also took a bus back to CCDB's headquarters in the capital. The seventh, Shafiqual Haque Choudhury, stayed on, in a small office almost directly opposite the Rest House, where he lived and worked as a program director for CCDB. The fevered conversations that led to the nighttime pledge had taken place in Shafiq's rooms, and he was the acknowledged leader of the group.

Like many other thoughtful young citizens of Bangladesh, a new country that had gained its independence only six and a half years earlier, they were disappointed by the new state's failure to establish justice and progress. Their late-night debates had convinced them that not just the government and the largely discredited political parties, but even the dynamic new nongovernmental organizations, such as BRAC and CCDB, were seriously flawed. Their bureaucratic structures, they believed, would render such organizations incapable of bringing about the kind of change that would propel Bangladesh into the progressive, egalitarian, exploitation-free phase of development that, in their view, it so sorely needed.

The pledge was to develop an organization that would have its base in the countryside; would recruit and train ordinary villagers, rather than rely on the educated minority for staff; and would enjoy a shared, nonhierarchical leadership structure. Its role would be to set off a process of rural change that would mature into a broad-based, nationwide, political force that could take over the reins of power within a decade. Its uniqueness would lie in its democratic roots in the villages, where 80 percent of Bangladeshis lived, and its power would derive from its ability to express the real aspirations of the rural poor.

This book is the story of what happened in the thirty years that followed. But first, we have to look back in time to have some sense of the historical backdrop to Bangladesh and to ASA.

Chapter 1

Bengal's Peasant Rebels

By the time the British took over Bengal in 1757, this low-lying land of peasant smallholders had already absorbed, over a period of more than two thousand years, Hindu, Buddhist, and Muslim values. Early resistance to British rule was led by pious local Muslim leaders who were as concerned with spiritual matters as they were with political ones. But in 1831, one such peasant movement was bloodily suppressed by the colonial administration, sparking a tradition of peasant activism that has continued into modern times and that is reflected in ASA's earliest ideals. In the final years of Britain's rule, peasant leaders led revolts against taxation and against exploitation by landlords and moneylenders. "Communalism" (Hindu–Muslim hostility) was stirred up both by British attempts to divide and rule and by the Muslim and Hindu leadership, who increasingly appealed to their coreligionists for their own political ends. The result was that when the British finally left the subcontinent in 1947, their leaving was marred by sectarian bloodshed. Bengal was split along a religious divide, and East Bengal became the eastern wing of a new Muslim country, Pakistan. But when East Pakistan came to resent the western wing's domination of the state and their lack of respect for Bengali culture and language, the Bengalis rediscovered their sense of nationhood, and Bengali nationalism replaced Islam as the rallying cry most often used by East Pakistan's peasant leaders.

This led, finally, to the break with Pakistan and the emergence of Bangladesh in 1971.

March 1947

In March 1947, Md Abul Hussain Noman Choudhury had much to look forward to and much to worry about.[1] He had just learned that he could expect his second child by the year's end. He was a prosperous Muslim landowner in rural Habiganj, a part of Sylhet in the northeastern corner of greater Bengal, and had married a woman from a similar background. They were not *zamindars,* the elite class of landlords on whom first the Muslim Mughal emperors, and then the British, relied for collecting taxes from the peasants,[2] but they were *choudhuries,* occupying a less important but still respectable place in the landowning hierarchy. Choudhury's land amounted to a mere sixty-five acres, but it was good paddy land and its rents had paid for him to go to college, where he had dabbled in politics. Their home, a masonry structure, dominated the village and was easily the biggest house in an area where most people lived in simple huts. Choudhury was a pious man, and conservative without being illiberal. He tolerated independent views in others, such as his urbanized cousins, some of whom held senior government positions. But he kept no books in his own home except for a few religious texts and the Koran itself, in the original Arabic. He disliked Bengali translations of the Koran because he felt that translation robbed the text of its majesty, and led to anxieties about the meaning of the book that might threaten one's faith. He was a strong supporter of the Muslim League, the party of India's Muslims whose policy by then favored a separate state for Muslims when the British finally bowed to the inevitable and pulled out of their South Asian empire. Only the previous month, on February 20, 1947, the British had declared their intention to leave India (which then included the whole of Bengal) by the middle of 1948. But it was already clear that the transition would not be peaceful. There had been unprecedented and bloody rioting between Hindus and Muslims in Calcutta (now known as Kolkata) and in eastern Bengal during 1946.

Choudhury's child was a boy, formally named Shafiqual Haque Choudhury but more familiarly known as Shafiq, who went on to become ASA's founder, chief executive, and president. As it turned out, Shafiq was conceived in British India but born just after his home had become part of East Pakistan. The Muslim League leaders had carried their case, and the last act of the British had been to consent to the creation of two new independent nations, India and Pakistan. Pakistan, the Muslim state, was made up of two wings separated by a thousand miles of Indian territory. Pakistan's eastern wing consisted of the eastern part of Bengal, which had a Muslim majority, whereas western Bengal, which included the important city of Calcutta, the old capital of British India, became the new Indian state of West Bengal. The district of Sylhet, where Choudhury's home was, had been in Assam rather than Bengal proper, but had been governed by the British as part of greater Bengal. In a referendum, its predominately Muslim population voted to join East Pakistan rather than the Indian state of Assam.

At independence in August 1947, as Bengal was broken in two, perhaps as many as a million Hindus poured out of East Pakistan into Indian West Bengal, as a lesser tide of Muslims came in from India. Even so, just after partition East Pakistan retained a large minority of Bengali Hindus—as many as 22 percent of the population according to official census figures. And Hindu-dominated India, with its massive population, remains today the home of more Muslims than live in Bangladesh.

Three Religions

Bengal lies on the broad estuarine floodplain of two of the world's greatest rivers, the Ganges and the Brahmaputra, that between them channel the rainfall and snowmelt of much of the Himalayas into the Bay of Bengal. A land of rivers and swamps, Bengal was always extremely difficult to travel in, but the land was always fertile, and agriculture probably has more than a three-thousand-year history there. Not a great deal is known about those ancient farmers, but they must have fallen under the domination of Aryan invaders from the north and west some time in the second millennium before the Common Era. They then had to absorb a new religion and a new language—Hinduism and Sanskrit—and find a role within the caste system of social organization introduced by their new masters. If, as some writers believe, many original Bengalis fell within the lower castes, or even outside the caste system altogether as *untouchables,* that may be a reason for their attraction to the new ideas of the Buddha, whose birthplace was just a little to the northwest of Bengal. His vision was of a classless society in which each individual strove for release from worldly suffering by living a life of purified thoughts and deeds. Many of the Aryan elite, too, turned to Buddhism, and for some twelve hundred years until about 1000 C.E., Buddhism extended its influence over the whole of greater Bengal.

Later, a resurgent and reformed Hinduism regained dominance. But soon another new religion appeared as Muslim traders, saints, and warriors from Central Asia moved through the Khyber Pass. Islam had arrived in the subcontinent, and spread swiftly. Within two hundred years it was being taken up in Bengal with enthusiasm, above all in the east, in the wetter, less populated land of small, rice-cultivating peasant landholdings.

Pirs and the People

The Islam that spread through Bengal in the thirteenth century was a modified version of the Prophet's original message.[3] It was interpreted to the Bengalis mainly by *pirs,* or Islamic saints who belonged to the mystic tradition of Sufism.[4] The pirs, often men of great personal warmth who were believed capable of performing miracles, settled among the villagers, lived simple lives, and achieved their conversions to the new faith by their sympathetic understanding of the harsh lives of the peasants rather than by force or fear. They were happy to incorporate local beliefs into their version of Islam. Often whole villages would convert to Islam together. In this way, the ideal of neighborhood solidarity, in the face of frequent hardship, fostered by a revered but sympathetic outsider, became part of the character of Muslim Bengal.

The tradition of peaceful persuasion persisted. Many years later, in the British period, Muslim reformers who wanted to bring a "purer" form of Islam to Bengal chose to adopt the proselytizing approach used by their Sufi precursors. Haji Shari'at Ullah's *Fara'izi* movement,[5] for example, enjoyed the mass support of rural villagers by spreading its ideas through a spokesman who lived and worked alongside the peasants.[6] Later, the movement would organize villagers in parts of eastern Bengal into "circles" of 300 to 500 households, anticipating by 150 years the group formation strategy pursued by NGOs in our own time. Shari'at Ullah himself was from a small, rural landholding household and could persuade the peasants to see him as "one of us." He was an early example of the Bengali peasant leader—a charismatic, pious, and educated man from a rural background.

The *Fara'izi* movement is sometimes presented as one of ignorant fundamentalism, but despite its roots as an Islamic reform movement and its attempts to clean Bengali Islam of its Hindu elements, its leadership was rarely hostile to poor Hindu peasants,[7] and may have enjoyed the support of many Hindus who also felt oppressed by British and *zamindari* interests. Under Shari'at Ullah's son Dudu Miyan, who took over the movement after his father's death in 1840, grassroots solidarity and activism were linked, perhaps for the first time in eastern Bengal, with national level politics, and the *Fara'izi* movement became strongly identified with the struggle of the peasants against oppression by British planters and Hindu zamindars. Well-to-do Muslims by and large shunned it. Already in western Bengal a *Fara'izi*-inspired movement led by Titu Mir had come to a violent end when it openly challenged the state and was bloodily suppressed by the colonial government in 1831. Bengali politics was discovering its characteristic expression: an assault on the power of the state by a charismatic and nationalistic leadership enjoying a diffused but widespread following among the rural poor, and forging temporary alliances between Muslims and Hindus. "Peasant politics" was later to make an important contribution to the end of British rule.

The British

The British had come to Bengal in the seventeenth century as one of several European powers who set up bases on the Indian coast, attracted by what was then a prosperous agricultural land. British traders founded Calcutta, now the capital of the Indian state of West Bengal, in the 1690s. With their superior sea power, they gradually gained the upper hand against French and Portuguese competition, and sealed their dominance in 1757 when Robert Clive defeated a Muslim army at Plassey, just outside Calcutta. Clive ended 550 years of Muslim rule by taking over Bengal in the name of the East India Company, a modern trading conglomerate based in the City of London. Bengal remained Britain's main interest and main base in India right up to 1911, when the colonialists' capital was transferred to Delhi, mainly to reduce the power of the (largely Hindu) educated Bengalis who were becoming ever more restless within the imperial embrace.

For the late eighteenth and much of the nineteenth century *India* effectively meant *Bengal* to the British. Her main agricultural products—jute, indigo,[8] rice, and, later, tea—enriched generations of British traders and planters and, especially after Britain destroyed Bengal's vigorous handloom production, Bengal provided a market for the new, automated cotton textile industry of northern

England. Despite deep rural poverty Bengal was perceived as rich, perhaps the richest part of the British overseas empire. Up to 1943 she produced an agricultural surplus and exported it around the world. But in that year a terrible famine (caused by an administrative muddle while Britain fought on the subcontinental front in the Second World War) killed millions. Bengal has yet to return to prosperity.

Later Peasant Movements

The type of peasant activism pioneered by such men as Dudu Miyan and Titu Mir continued through the nineteenth and on into the twentieth century. Between the end of the First World War in 1918 and independence in 1947, village leaders throughout Bengal led struggles fed by local grievances against exploitative landlords and moneylenders and, increasingly, against government taxes and other impositions.

Typical of these was Mukhlesur Rahman, who had a religious education in a *madrassa*—an Islamic school—in his native Comilla district in eastern Bengal, and earned the title of *Maulana*, or learned student of Islam. He had then come under the influence of Communists in Calcutta. Returning home, he worked as a Communist organizer, but continued to be seen by the villagers as a pious man and as one of their own kind. In the 1930s he organized violent attacks on moneylenders, believing this to be the only way in which poor peasants could fight back against oppression. He was finally arrested on a robbery charge, but he, and others like him, had unnerved the authorities, who began to take the threat of a Communist-inspired insurgency seriously.

As political parties became more developed, the work of such men could be drawn into the wider political scene. In the 1940s, for example, the Communist Party of India (CPI) was able to mobilize many thousands of peasants by working with local leaders.

Their call was for resistance to the Japanese advance from Burma, but they also stirred up anti-British and anti-landlord sentiment, using techniques that included theater groups, singers, and musicians—techniques commonly used by today's NGOs. Other left-wing political groups such as the Congress Socialist Party and the Revolutionary Socialist Party also worked through local peasant leaders. The CSP tried, without much success, to get starving peasants to attack police stations and food stores during the 1943 famine.

The Tanka and Tebhaga Movements

Sharecropping is a system of land cultivation under which poor farmers who lack land, or the capital to rent it, farm others' land and pay their landlords a share of the harvest. It was, and still is, widely used in South Asia. North-central Bengal is home to several non-Bengali peoples who suffered from a particularly iniquitous form of sharecropping under which their landlords were able to claim not merely a share of the harvest, but a fixed quantity, so that in years of poor yields the sharecropper could end up with virtually nothing, or even with a negative share, which pushed him into even deeper debt with his landlord. An uprising against this so-called *tanka* system broke out in the late 1920s, rumbled on through the 1930s and, with CPI support, flared up in the 1940s. Its original leaders appear to have emerged spontaneously from the villages, and it may represent the most sustained example of genuine peasant activism that ever took place in Bengal. The CPI came late into the picture, but produced, in Moni Singh, a classic example of a peasant leader. He was the educated son of a *zamindar* family who, having been politicized by a spell with the CPI in Calcutta, lived in a village with the peasants and inspired Muslims, Hindus, and *tribals* (as non-Bengali indigenous peoples were and often still are called) to fight together against the government forces who had been drafted in to quell the rebellion, depicting them as agents of the exploitative colonialists and their rich local henchmen. The movement died down after 1950 because the communities most involved had been divided by the partition of British India and many of the activists fled to West Bengal. But the tanka system was later formally abolished by the Pakistani authorities as part of the reforms of the *zamindari* system, and replaced with new leasehold arrangements. Moni Singh himself remained active well into the Bangladesh era as president of the Communist Party.

Although the tanka insurrection was confined to a particular area, the *tebhaga* movement of the 1930s spread all over Bengal, and may have sprung up independently in various districts. *Tebhaga* means "three shares," and the movement's aim was to raise the share taken by the sharecropping farmer from one-third (or one-half) to two-thirds of the crop. There were many clashes between police and mobs of sharecroppers and many assaults on landlords, organized with or without the backing of left-wing or other political parties. Again, leaders well-known and respected by their local populations played a decisive role. In Jessore (in south-central Bengal), for example, Syed Nausher Ali emerged as another pious Muslim from a modest background who joined a formal political party (Congress) but maintained his independence as a local peasant leader. He supported local Muslim and Hindu peasants when they began to withhold rents due to their zamindars or refused to make interest payments on loans due to moneylenders. These movements, however, never gained sufficient momentum to exert a decisive influence on the authorities, who tended to treat each incident as a case of local banditry. Although restitution was eventually brought about by constitutional means, when a later regime changed the law, many landlords still extracted more than their legal share, without much resistance from their sharecroppers. In such matters local custom exerts more influence than distant lawmakers.[9]

The Emergence of National Muslim Leadership

The growth of political consciousness among Muslims brought about by pious local leaders during the nineteenth century came to fruition at the beginning of the twentieth with the founding of the All-India Muslim League in December 1906 as a nationwide political voice of the Muslims. In the previous year, the British, alarmed at the rising prestige and influence of the Bengali Hindu elite, had divided Bengal, and made Dhaka the capital of East Bengal. Muslims, led by Salimullah, the Nawab of Dhaka (a Nawab is a hereditary Muslim leader or prince, approximately equivalent to the Hindu *Maharaja*) saw this as an opportunity to assert themselves, and the foundation of the league took place in Dhaka.

Thereafter, Bengali Muslim leaders began to emerge into prominence at the national level and to exert their influence on formal politics. Such leaders took careful account of local peasant activism, and tried to gain some control over it. Fazlul Huq, "the tiger of Bengal," a lawyer from Barisal in southern Bengal, and Abdul Hamid Khan, better known as Maulana Bhasani, the "Red Maulana," from Sirajganj in what was then part of Pabna district in the central north, both grounded their politics in the call for a transformation of the lives of the rural masses, and built up grassroots followings. Huq, born in 1873, was active in politics right through to Pakistan times—he died in 1962. A protégé of Nawab Salimullah, he was present at the foundation of the Muslim League and served a spell as its president at the same time as being the secretary of the Indian National Congress. Bhasani's greatest years, as we shall see later, were those of the Pakistan period: 1947–71. Both in their time founded formal political parties, and Huq became chief minister of Bengal in the British administration and, later, governor of East Pakistan, but they were careful to have themselves popularly perceived as peasant leaders. Bhasani kept a village home, a straw-roofed hut, and wore peasant clothing, and many of his followers thought of him as a pir. Both leaders appealed to Hindus as well as Muslims by emphasizing economic issues and calling for the unity of the rural poor, and by stressing the Bengali rather than the Muslim character of their movements.

Nevertheless, before the departure of the British in 1947 both men, in tune with most of their educated contemporaries, had become convinced that the interests of the Bengali Muslims would be best served in a separate Muslim state, and both therefore favored the creation of Pakistan. In 1940 Huq drafted the Lahore Resolution, the document that expressed the Muslim League's commitment to Muslim autonomy in postcolonial India. Huq himself would have preferred a separate Bengali Muslim state rather than the United Pakistan that emerged in 1947, and argued for it at Muslim League meetings. But the all-India leadership of the league (who were mostly West Pakistanis) was eager to create a state big enough to challenge India.

In many respects this represented a failure. It acknowledged the inability of leaders such as Huq and Bhasani to maintain the unity of the peasantry throughout Bengal and to stem the rising tide of *communalism*—politically inspired manipulation of the natural tensions between Muslims and Hindus. Both the British authorities and the all-India leadership of the two main pro-independence movements, the Hindu-dominated Congress Party and the Muslim League, had something to gain from inciting communalism. The British slyly promoted a policy of divide and rule, and fomented religious disharmony as a way of distracting attention from the struggle against their own rule. Congress and League leaders settled for partition partly out of a belief that that was the best on offer, and partly to secure their own ascendancy in their respective communities. In doing so, both the authorities and their opponents sought to influence public opinion through the many local peasant leaders. This led, as Taj Ul-Islam Hashmi shows, in his book *Peasant Utopia*,[10] to the steady communalization of peasant politics and an attempt to redirect it away from the local peasant grievances toward the two large issues that dominated national level politics—the struggle to end imperial rule, and the struggle for a united independent homeland for India's Muslims.

Pakistan: Poverty, Peasants, and the Rise of Bengali Nationalism

The history of Bengal contains some strange contradictions, none more so than the story of the rise of Bengali nationalism, which intensified only after Bengalis had given their consent, in 1947, to the division of the Bengali nation.

Pakistan could not have come into being at all in eastern India if, on the eve of independence from Britain, political leaders (both imperial and native) had not placed more emphasis on what divided Bengalis, their two religions, than on what united them, their language and culture. The British had shown how to divide the Bengalis in the 1905 partitioning of Bengal, which infuriated the Hindus (then the dominant Bengalis) but gave quiet satisfaction to many Muslims in eastern Bengal. On that occasion the Hindus finally had their way, and the partition was revoked in 1911. Undeterred, the British snubbed Bengal by moving the imperial capital from Calcutta to distant Delhi and by beginning their campaign of divide and rule, in which they encouraged communal tension, or at least turned a blind eye to it. The result was the mounting sectarian hostility that led, during the 1940s, to Hindu–Muslim riots in Calcutta and eastern Bengal and finally to the second partition of Bengal and the creation of Pakistan.

But a united Pakistan lasted a mere 24 years, from 1947 to 1971. In looking for explanations for this failure, some historians stress the sheer unsustainable absurdity of a single country sharply divided, not only by language and culture, but by a thousand miles of alien territory. Others have pointed to the fact that West Pakistan, despite its smaller population, dominated commerce, industry, and administration, treating the unindustrialized eastern wing as an internal agricultural colony (most of Bengal's industry, above all, the jute factories around Calcutta, had fallen into the Indian part of Bengal). But for millions of ordinary Bengalis, two issues stood out above all others: Pakistan failed to respect the dignity of Bengali language and culture, and failed to address poverty in the villages. It was these themes, cultural imperialism from West Pakistan and rural poverty and injustice, that dominated the speeches of East Pakistan's leaders as they grew slowly more disenchanted with Pakistan.

This marks a big change from British times. In the pre-independence period, peasant politics, as we have seen, had been corrupted by communalism. Hindu–Muslim hostility had been so effectively stirred up that even well-intentioned leaders such as Fazlul Huq had to couch their appeal to peasants in the language of communalism. But with the emergence of Pakistan (and especially after the abolition of the *zamindari* system and the departure of yet more Hindus) anti-Hindu feeling could no longer be used as a means of stirring peasant passions. In eastern Bengal, later East Pakistan, and now Bangladesh, Bengali nationalism took its place.

The Awami League

The now aging Fazlul Huq was quick to appreciate this. He gave his support to Bhasani and to a younger politician, Sheikh Mujibur Rahman, when, as early as 1949, just two years after the formation of a united Pakistan, they formed the Awami League, destined to become, in time, the strongest voice of Bengali nationalism. At first it was called the Awami Muslim League. The dropping of the Muslim tag (in 1955) shows the fading value of communalism as a vote catcher but also shows how league leaders anticipated support from East Pakistan's Hindus who could be encouraged to fear West Pakistan's distant leadership. The Bengalis' language, Bangla, found a place at the center of Bengali national feeling when the Muslim League government failed to recognize it as a state language alongside Urdu, a language spoken in West Pakistan. Then Muhammad Ali Jinnah (the West Pakistan Muslim League leader who became Pakistan's governor general) announced, during his first visit to Dhaka, that Urdu was to become the sole official language of the whole of Pakistan. When in 1952 Pakistan's Prime Minister Nazimuddin tried to introduce legislation to this effect, students in Dhaka demonstrated and a number of them were killed by police firing. This made the language movement the symbol of conflict between East and West. To this day the anniversary of the killings, February 21, is kept as one of Bangladesh's most important holidays. Other more practical and perhaps more serious grievances, such as the domination by West Pakistan of government employment, lacked the emotional appeal of the language issue.

Maulana Bhasani, the Awami League's first president and the hottest head among its leadership, quickly seized the initiative. He accused the ruling Muslim League of turning against Bengal and of attempting to consolidate power in the hands of the "*Paschimas*" (the "westies"—an intentionally insulting turn of phrase). Later, and famously, he called for outright independence for Bangladesh (literally, "Bengal-land"), saying that if Pakistan couldn't improve the lot of the Bengali peasantry, then the Bengali peasantry would have to "say *a-salaam-aleikum* (good-bye) to West Pakistan."[11] In this way he managed to blend nationalistic fervor with peasant demands. His Krishak Samity (Peasants' Association), like other peasant parties then being organized and directed from Dhaka, relied on inspiring and recruiting educated young local men who organized groups of peasants at village level and led them in large-scale protest rallies and marches, much as NGOs, including ASA, did in the 1970s and 1980s. Proshika, for example, a large, national NGO, long used the frequency of marches and rallies as one of its indicators for the monitoring of the quality of its group formation work. Nijera Kori, another NGO, still does.

Group members of many of the Pakistan-period parties used to make subscriptions into a pooled fund to pay for the costs of such manifestations: and again, as we shall see, groups formed by

ASA and other modern NGOs were to do the same much later. There was no shortage of peasant demands. The direct economic interests of all small farmers could be appealed to with a call for lower land taxes, reform of the system of leasing markets and *ghats* (riverside quays), and more and cheaper credit. Sharecroppers could be relied on to support calls for reform of the system under which they got an unjust share of the crop. The landless, whose numbers were beginning to grow as the population swelled, could be appealed to with calls for land reform.[12] After this appeal to the pocket, their emotions could be aroused with more abstract demands: Bangla as a national tongue and, after Pakistan turned to military rule in 1958, the restoration of democracy.

Fazlul Huq did not join the Awami League, but left the Muslim League in 1950 to found his own fiercely nationalistic Krishak Sromik (Peasants and Workers) Party. In 1954, in Pakistan's first provincial elections since the foundation of the country, the new parties joined forces (under the name United Front and led by Huq and Bhasani, among others)[13] and swept the Muslim League from power in the eastern wing's provincial assembly. The United Front's Twenty-One Points, its manifesto for the election, has the recognition of Bangla as a state language as its first point.[14] These events established the popularity of Bengali nationalism and confirmed West Pakistan's view of the disloyalty of the eastern wing. But the Twenty-One Points also contained several peasant demands, including the abolition of rent on land, the distribution of surplus land to the landless, the introduction of cooperative farming, and the improvement of irrigation. Though the provincial government that was formed lasted only a few months, and ended with a murder in the Assembly House in Dhaka, from then on it was only a matter of time before growing Bengali pride and resentment came to a final clash with West Pakistani intransigence.

In the meantime, fresh ideas, many of them from abroad, found their way into the thinking of the Bengali leaders. Bhasani, for example, was drawn to the revolutionary strategies of Mao Zedong, and in time became identified as the leader of the pro-Chinese

Communists, whereas other leaders continued to espouse Russian versions of Marxism, or favored Western European or even "scientific" socialism. Although these developments reinforced the generally left-leaning flavor of Bengali nationalist and peasant-activist thinking, they served to splinter the movement into many fragments, each headed by a strong and often charismatic leader. At moments of crisis (the 1954 election was one, and another even greater one arrived in 1970–71) East Bengal acts together. But when the dust settles again, it tends to separate into its many different constituents.

Thus, for example, on the eve of the independence struggle, Bhasani and Sheikh Mujibur Rahman were to be found in separate rival political parties. Mujib had consolidated his leadership of the Awami League by his Six-Point Program, which called for a federal Pakistan with most powers (including taxation, currency, and control of separate militia) reserved for the two provinces, and only defense and foreign affairs dealt with by the center. This was in 1966, after which his Awami League was identified with the call for Bengali autonomy, though not yet for outright independence. Bhasani had by then formed his own rival National Awami Party as a vehicle for his own more radical agenda of socialist reform. Later, NAP itself split into various factions.

Apart from those who held an unassailable belief in the idea of Pakistan as a united and indissoluble home for the subcontinent's Muslims, the majority of East Pakistan's Bengalis supported the fight for independence when it finally came. They did so out of a belief that West Pakistan both exploited and denigrated the eastern wing, and that Eastern Bengal would prosper better as an independent (or at least as an autonomous) state. But exactly how the new state was to organize itself for progress and prosperity was not clear. There was no shortage of ideas, and they were often held with conviction. They competed vigorously in the anarchic years that followed the creation of Bangladesh, and among them, as we shall see, was the time-honored tradition of radical reform through peasant mobilization. ASA's work was not without historic roots.

Chapter 2

Credit and Poverty in Bengal

For more than a century, intervention in the provision of credit has been seen in Bengal not just as a matter of finance but as a weapon to fight natural disasters, poverty, ignorance, and exploitation. The British first introduced subsidized loans to help poor farmers survive droughts, floods, and cyclones, and escape from moneylenders. Then credit cooperatives, first tried in the opening years of the twentieth century, were designed to organize and educate their members as well as give access to financial services. But apart from some private local initiatives, formal credit cooperatives never worked well. A famous attempt in the 1960s to revive cooperatives (the "Comilla experiment") failed, in the end, to get the true principles of cooperatives—self-reliance and self-management—accepted at national level, because the authorities preferred to use the cooperatives as a way of pumping subsidized credit into the countryside. The Pakistan government set up state-run banks to serve poor farmers, but these failed to reach the targets. Shafiqual Haque Choudhury worked for a while at Comilla, but it was the success of a new initiative—microcredit as developed by Grameen Bank and BRAC—that was the model for ASA's later turn to credit.

March 1956

Under a 1950 bill Pakistan abolished the *zamindari* land tenure system, which had been a major symbol of oppression and injustice, and placed caps on landownership. Shafiq's father, Md Abul Hussain Noman Choudhury, feared that he would lose much of his land. But because the law was delayed and then softened by compensation clauses and other devices to allow land to be retained, nothing happened until March 1956, by which time he had sold off some of his land. By reinvesting in a transport business—at one time he owned three buses—and by leasing his remaining acres out under carefully supervised sharecropping contracts to small farmers, he was able to maintain a comfortable home and to educate Shafiq, two other sons, and three daughters.

It was an austere upbringing. Shafiq's father's demeanor was stern. If he loved his son—and Shafiq does not remember feeling loved—he did not express it warmly. This was not a household of hugs and caresses. His father's chief concern was to bring up his children to be pious Muslims and to maintain the status of the family. To that end, he discouraged any contact with neighboring children, most of whom were poor. Although he went to the local primary school, Shafiq came straight home and wasn't allowed to bring playmates with him, and his father arranged for tutors to come to the house to coach him. His mother supported his father's view of the world: it was better to avoid the difficulties that mixing with lower status families might bring. Shafiq did not rebel against this. He was an obedient child and took it as the way things were meant to be. Even now, Shafiq has told me, this class consciousness is still with him: he would not object to, but equally he would not expect, any show of familiarity from his own domestic helpers, for example.

At the age of nine, Shafiq moved to the nearest town, Habiganj, to attend a government high school, and never again lived at home. In Habiganj he stayed in a house owned by the family, was chaperoned by cousins, and took his meals with his grandfather. His father didn't want him to stay in the school hostel for fear he would be led astray by his fellows and fall into bad habits such as visiting the theater. On occasional trips home on weekends, Shafiq would have to explain his scholarly progress to his father. Happily, Shafiq wasn't a bad student and managed to stay in the top ten in his class. Later in a two-year college, also in Habiganj, he did better still, often standing second to a brighter cousin. There, he discovered politics in a small way, and joined in parochial battles: once they even managed to have the principal of the college removed for showing favoritism, though Shafiq was not the ringleader.

In 1965, Shafiq entered Dhaka University, to take a bachelor's degree and then a masters in sociology. He also sat the first-year examinations for a law degree, fancying a career as a lawyer and then as a member of parliament. The reading he did as a sociology student helped him challenge for the first time the precepts that his father had drummed into him. He began to see that religion was a matter of history and debate, as well as of faith, and though he never rejected Islam, he became skeptical of the willingly uncritical attitude to faith that his father practiced. Fellow students don't remember him for any religious views he may or may not have had: to them he was an affable character with well-lined pockets who often stood poorer friends to a meal. He was good at organizing things. For example, though he was a poor sportsman, he arranged football tournaments and the picnics that followed. He was not noted for being a brilliant student, but he was quick to understand things, read widely, and always enjoyed a debate.

The late 1960s was a time of intense politicization of students, and Shafiq found himself drawn, like most students of the time, to left-wing movements. Along with many of his classmates he joined the East Pakistan Student Union, the most popular student body, which had a Marxist coloring. But at the same time he became an admirer of Maulana Bhasani, the national politician-cum-peasant leader whom we met in the previous chapter. He was impressed by Bhasani's pro-Chinese (Maoist) stance and its stress on improving rural conditions. He began to understand, as he told me recently, "that my own background was feudal." Mao's ideas for a rural revolution seemed to him appropriate to conditions in East Pakistan—more so than Marxism with its focus on industrializing states. But it was not until he completed his degree and took his first job at a rural research institute that Shafiq began to understand the rural poor's perpetual struggle against the harsh economic, political, and demographic forces that beset them.

Shafiq was one of only two students in his batch to get a full-time job immediately after graduating. He answered a newspaper advertisement for a position in an institute he had barely heard of—PARD, the Pakistan Academy for Rural Development. PARD had been organizing small farmers into cooperative groups to promote improved agricultural techniques that could lead, it was thought, to higher incomes and a better quality of life. This work drew, to some extent, on the tradition of grassroots activism that, as we have seen, goes back deep into Bengal's past. But by arranging loans to poor peasants through the cooperatives and offering training, PARD's most important work contributed to another tradition with a rich past and a richer present—intervention in the credit market for the poor.

At the academy, Shafiq worked first as a research assistant, editing an English-language newsletter, but he needed help from colleagues to patch up his rather poor command of the language. Later he was made an assistant instructor, working under PARD's second director, Azizul Haq, who became a minister of agriculture in Bangladesh and was an active governing body member of ASA until his death in 2002. Haq remembered Shafiq as "not the brightest but certainly one of the most curious and enquiring of the young assistants, one who didn't take things at face value."[1] What engaged Shafiq's attention in the late 1960s was the experimental work in group-based agricultural credit going on at PARD. That work needs to be seen in the context of Bengal's long experience with rural credit schemes.

Peasant Credit

Fazlul Huq had been chief minister of Bengal under the British in the 1930s and 1940s, a time, as we have seen, when peasant leaders were stirring up movements against rural moneylenders, leading to the deaths of some creditors and of more debtors. One of the measures passed by Huq's administration was the establishment of the *reen shalishi* (debt settlement) boards. This was an attempt to intervene in the informal credit market by putting in place village courts with the power to cancel or modify unreasonable credit contracts.

Huq's ordinance was the latest of many government measures designed to moderate what was seen as an excessively exploitative and oppressive informal credit market in Bengal. British administrators in the nineteenth century had become increasingly worried about the level of debt into which they believed small peasant cultivators were falling. They saw this indebtedness as a major cause of the periodic famines that struck Bengal and other parts of India. The Great Famine of 1878, which may have killed as many as 5 million in British India as a whole, was followed by legislation that brought together the existing patchwork of legal measures dealing with credit, debt, and poverty.

The Agricultural Loan Act of 1885 built on an old Mogul period tradition by making formal legal provisions for *taccavi* loans in Bengal—loans for peasants struck by natural disasters.[2] From the start, these loans were thought of by many administrators as a form of relief, and repayment was not always enforced. The system lasted into the 1970s, and the view that it was morally wrong to insist that the poor repay loans (let alone pay real rates of interest on them) did not begin to change until the late 1980s, and is still widespread in the region. In Bangladesh, for example, after the severe cyclone of November 2007, microcredit clients in the affected areas were encouraged by local politicians, human rights activists, and newspapers to "demand" the cancellation of their debts and the right to new loans.[3] In India, in early 2008, the

Congress administration's budget provided for massive debt cancellation for India's peasant farmers, partly in reaction to newspaper reports about the growing number of suicides committed by indebted farmers. Allister McGregor, in a fascinating but as yet unpublished paper, describes the "heady mixture of theory, morality and ideology, rather than purely rational economic analysis" that has characterized attitudes to credit in Bengal since British times.[4]

The belief that moneylenders oppressed the poor through exorbitant interest rates gained momentum from the peasant movements from the *Fara'izi* through to Fazlul Huq and Bhasani. Because such movements were in part anti-British, British lawmakers came to see that improving peasant conditions would be one of the best ways of persuading peasants to remain loyal to the government. Thus legislation came to reflect the tone of moral disapproval of moneylenders, sometimes in the very titles of the acts. In 1918 came the Usurious Loans Act and in 1933, the Bengal Money Lenders Act, which set interest rate limits of 15 percent per year for secured and 25 percent for unsecured informal cash loans, and also set limits on rates charged for loans in kind.[5] The Bengal Agricultural Debtors Act of 1935 set up the debt settlement boards, based on an experiment carried out in Chandpur in southern Bengal (now Bangladesh) and passed under Fazlul Huq's ministry.

Cooperatives

The British had faced a problem that is still with us—how to make sure that credit designed for the poor actually reaches them. In 1904, they tackled this problem by passing India's first Co-operative Societies Act, setting up a legal framework for village-level self-help, user-managed societies, organized around personal savings. These *thrift and credit cooperatives* (also known as credit unions) had been developed most actively in Germany; in England, emphasis had been placed on producer and consumer cooperatives rather than financial ones. They are based on a simple idea rich in potential for development and growth. Essentially, a group of people come together in a free and equal association and pool their regular savings. From the fund so created, some members can take credit, on which they pay interest, which feeds back to the savers in the form of interest on their savings deposits or as a regularly distributed dividend. In Germany in the nineteenth century, as in other parts of the world since, they were seen as offering basic financial services to poorer groups of people who lack access to formal banks. In the experience of managing their own pooled resources, the organizers hoped their beneficiaries would learn the benefits of a range of wholesome values—reciprocity, mutual respect, trust, equality, and (of course) discipline and sound bookkeeping.

The credit cooperatives that the 1904 act fostered were intended to "improve" the peasants by teaching them thrift and cooperation (and even telling them how to farm) at the same time as making credit available. McGregor quotes a government report that insisted that "it must be credit which shall be so obtainable that the act and effort of obtaining it shall educate, discipline and guide the borrower."[6]

Part of this guidance, for example, was that consumption loans are wasteful and therefore morally wrong, and this is another idea that has persisted well into our own times. Indeed, as we shall see, the combination of credit and education for the guidance of the ignorant rural poor was continued by the microfinance movement, including ASA's program in its early years.

But by the 1930s the cooperatives were in trouble. Indeed, from soon after their inception, the authorities became aware that they were not working well, and many attempts were made to improve the legislation and execution of the schemes. The general view was that illiteracy made it difficult for the peasants to manage the schemes, that the official character of the movement distanced it from its grassroots users, and that many members were interested only in private profit and misunderstood or rejected the principles of cooperation. More likely, as we now see, the authorities themselves undermined the whole ethos of the cooperatives by failing to trust the cooperators to manage their own affairs, and by using the cooperatives as a means of pumping cheap credit into the countryside. But there were also external reasons for the failure. The Depression of the 1930s and the disruption it caused in agricultural markets brought widespread default and the collapse of many cooperatives. The social and political upheaval of the partition of British India in 1947 then dealt the movement a second blow. As Shawkat Ali writes, "At the time of partition there were 26,664 agricultural credit societies in East Pakistan most of which were on the brink of liquidation. By 1956–57 over 24,000 of these societies were under liquidation."[7]

Pakistan: Government Agricultural Banks and the Cooperatives

After 1947, the independent Pakistan government—like many governments around the world at that time—tried a new approach to rural credit, by setting up state-owned specialized banks to deal with agricultural loans. In 1952, the Agricultural Development Finance Corporation (ADFC) was set up, followed in 1956 by the Agricultural Bank of Pakistan (ABP). The two banks had similar loan conditions, and each had only a handful of branches in East Pakistan. The main difference between the two was that the ABP had a statutory duty to give preference to small farmers and sharecroppers, a stipulation that demonstrates that the bank was intended to be an instrument of social reform and rural development rather than merely a financial institution. But the early years of both banks were disappointing. Not many loans were advanced, and those that were given went mainly to wealthier farmers. Repayment rates were low. A commission in 1959 concluded that the banks had failed to make any impact at all on the rural credit situation.

In 1961, the two were merged into the Agricultural Development Bank of Pakistan (ADBP). The move was accompanied by legislation to simplify disbursement procedures, especially in the use of land as collateral. In the eastern wing this led immediately to more loans being disbursed, but the numbers were still small, and declined as time went by: just over one hundred thousand farmers received loans in 1961, but fewer than sixty thousand in 1968. The amount of money disbursed, however, grew over this period, as the bank moved steadily away from giving seasonal loans to small farmers and began to favor larger and longer term loans for the richer landowners. Recovery rates throughout the 1960s were never better than 82 percent—not bad by international standards but less than had been hoped for. The new form of banking was neither profitable nor able to provide useful financial services to poor farmers and sharecroppers on any meaningful scale.

Meanwhile, the cooperative movement continued to decline. The number of primary cooperative societies fell to below two thousand and their combined membership to less than fifty thousand by 1957. In the early 1960s the government tried to revive their fortunes by injecting more money into the system and by encouraging the formation of much bigger multipurpose societies at the level of the union, the smallest elected administrative unit in the countryside.[8] Membership grew again, and reached almost 2 million by 1970, but with an average membership per village-wide society of only 81 it became evident that the movement was not achieving mass coverage in the villages and that its members were drawn from a small group close to centers of influence. Even these members appear to have had little faith in their cooperatives. Savings deposits by primary societies (the village-level groups) into the secondary bodies (consisting of representatives of the primary societies, formed to offer banking and administration services) fell throughout the 1960s, as their reliance on outside finance grew.

The key idea of a credit cooperative is that it allows its members to create their own fund and manage it to their mutual advantage.

But by 1969 less than 2 percent of their loan capital came from member deposits, the whole of the remainder coming from government, banks, and donors such as the Asian Development Bank. The annual reports of the Co-operative Directorate clearly reflect the sense of failure: in 1962–63, for example, only 61, or 1 percent, of the 7,354 societies were classified as "thoroughly good," whereas 6,322 societies (86 percent) were deemed "unsatisfactory." They had become shells through which a lucky few hoped to get access to outside money on favorable terms.

The PARD (and Other) Cooperatives

The idea behind the new *multipurpose societies* had been to create much bigger entities than the tiny, village-level cooperatives of earlier years. The hope was that bigger would mean stronger and that this strength would be enough to overcome the illiteracy, petty mindedness, and tiny financial capacity of the old societies. But when PARD was set up in 1959 as a government financed academy in the fertile and densely populated countryside near Comilla, to the east of Dhaka, it revived the ideal of small cooperatives with regular face-to-face contact between members who would "learn to save and to amass their own capital," to quote Akhtar Hameed Khan, its founder and its first and most celebrated director.[9]

When Shafiq first arrived at PARD in early 1970, Khan was still the director. He was not a Bengali: he came from Agra in what is now northern India and after an education at Cambridge, England, joined the colonial Indian Civil Service and was posted to East Bengal. But he spoke some Bangla and sometimes dressed in the costume of a Bengali peasant, which is what the young Shafiq took him for in an embarrassing first encounter with him in the meeting room at PARD. However, Shafiq never got to know him well. Shafiq was very much a junior, and, in any case, within a year Khan was gone, advised by the army to leave East Pakistan as tension between the two wings brewed. Khan later split his time between the University of Michigan and his "Orangi" project, which sought to improve life in the biggest slum in Karachi, Pakistan. He died in 1999.

At PARD, working with foreign consultants supplied through the government's Cooperative Department, Khan had decided to set up small groups of 30 to 40 villagers, all of whom knew each other and all of whom were farmers. They were to hold weekly meetings at which attendance and the deposit of savings would be compulsory. They were to select candidates from among themselves for training courses offered by PARD, in both cooperative management and in other social matters that were encapsulated in the "Ten Commandments" that members learned and recited—aphorisms that drove home messages of cooperation and successful village life and development.

All this points both backward and forward. The return to small societies and the stress on integrating education and credit places PARD's works clearly in the subcontinental tradition and links it with old style European cooperative thinking. But the weekly meetings, with mandatory attendance and savings, anticipate the conventions used by the modern credit NGOs, especially Grameen Bank and its many imitators. The "Ten Commandments" are the ancestors of Grameen's "Sixteen Decisions" and of BRAC's "Seventeen Promises." PARD also experimented with credit for women, something else that has become standard current NGO practice. PARD's officer dealing with credit for women was Taherunnessa Abdullah, the first woman from Bangladesh to win the prestigious Magsaysay Award—and currently the chairperson of ASA's governing body.

Moreover although the original cooperatives of the British period were intended to defend poor farmers from exploitative moneylenders and avert famine (and, as we have seen, to dampen the fires of rural revolt against British rule), PARD's objectives, like those of the modern NGOs, were clearly developmental in character. However, the PARD work was aimed at increased agricultural production by allowing farmers to invest in technology and improved inputs, whereas the modern NGOs are aimed at the development of landless or near landless households by providing them with capital to set up off-farm enterprises. This reminds us that massive landlessness is a problem of modern Bangladesh, and that as recently as the 1960s five in six rural households had farmland, compared with fewer than three in five now. PARD cooperative loans were always secured against land, whereas most modern NGOs lend without physical collateral.

Khan had a particular vision of how the new cooperatives were to hasten agricultural development. Households should work together in joint farming projects financed by cooperative loans. In part this was for a practical reason, because he argued that no single household, even with loans, could afford to invest in the mechanization that modern farming requires. But it was also a matter of ideology. Khan was a believer in the cooperative approach, and for him collective enterprise was a social good in its own right, one that addressed the problem of rural exploitation. He writes that he told the villagers over and over again, "You are being crushed by the power of capital. The same power will release you if you learn to possess and control it."

But as Hasnat Abdul Hye clearly shows in his monograph, the PARD cooperatives were only partly successful, and their greatest disappointment was that this vision of village groups "possessing and controlling capital" never came about. Rather, as time went by, savings rates fell so that after 10 years per capita equity was dismal, at about 30 taka per member (less than five dollars in today's terms) and the proportion of members' equity in the loan fund was rarely more than 13 percent, the balance coming from generous government support. Instead of engaging in joint farming enterprises, members strove to get access to loans to finance their personal projects. As time went on, loans became monopolized by an elite minority, and default became a widespread problem. The new cooperatives appeared to be succumbing to all the faults of the old ones: misuse by the authorities as a vehicle for distributing subsidized farming inputs such as fertilizers and irrigation, and capture by the better-off.

PARD was not the only organization trying to revive the idea of the true credit cooperative. In Bangladesh, as in many other developed and developing countries, there are private groups fostering cooperatives. In Bangladesh it was mainly the very small Christian community that benefited, when priests brought the message and the experience of credit unions from other countries. In the 1950s, for example, a number of Christian villages to the north of Dhaka started credit unions with monthly savings as low as fifty *paisa*, a very small sum.[10] To this day, monthly mandatory savings have remained as low as 5 taka (about $.12 U.S.), but funds have grown to the point at which loans of up to 150,000 taka (more than $2,000) are on offer. In some villages the credit union offers a wide range of services, with two or three savings plans (basic plans with open withdrawal, and term deposits with higher interest rates) and several loan types, including immediate-access emergency loans of up to 4,000 taka. The credit union has become institutionalized as a part of village life: at village weddings the couple visits the credit union office after the church service, so that the bride (who has come from another village) can open an account in her husband's union and transfer her own deposits from her own account—which she has held since childhood. All this has been accomplished (not without problems along the way) without any outside funding, and the success of such programs points out the inadequacies of the top-down official policies.

The Informal Samity

There are many references in the literature of the British period to moneylending and to moneylenders. Civil servants appear to have been fascinated by them. Much less noticed are the voluntary savings associations and clubs of friends or of businessmen that must have existed in the colonial era but about which we know little. Maloney and Sharfuddin Ahmed, whose *Informal Savings and Credit Groups in Bangladesh* remains a good, if now dated, survey, believe that they may be a recent phenomenon, resulting largely from the example of the cooperatives and, later, of NGO microcredit groups.[11] Certainly they are usually called *samities*, the same word that was used for a cooperative society and, later, an ASA microcredit group. Maloney and Sharfuddin Ahmed acknowledge that the apparent novelty of samities may be due to the fact that most of them—by design or accident—are short lived, so that it is rare to find examples of individual samities that have been going more than a few years. But the tradition of such samities may be very old.

Local samities use the same elements as the credit union: people get together to pool their savings, store them somewhere safe (preferably in a bank, if one is available), and allow members (and sometimes outsiders) to borrow from this fund, usually with interest. Virtually every bazaar in rural Bangladesh has a number of such samities run by traders: those trading in rice and other bulk food commodities may have one samity, building materials retailers another, and so on. Current participants speak of having learned about them from their fathers. Many youth groups also run saving samities, and away from the bazaar they are common among ordinary village folk, both men and women. I have found them existing within NGO microcredit groups: their great virtue is their flexibility, and NGO customers in difficulty with the rigid repayment schedules imposed, for example, by the Grameen Bank, find it useful to have a separate pool of cash at hand for use in times of stress. But this very flexibility can manifest itself as a destructive casualness. As a result, there is frequent abuse: in an oft-repeated scenario a wealthy village leader starts such a samity and invites his dependents to join. Because he is the only literate one, the proper functioning of the samity depends entirely on his enthusiasm and on his maintaining proper records. Often he doesn't keep good records, or he "borrows" from the fund and forgets to repay. His dependents are too polite to remind him too often of his debts. The samity erodes away.

There has recently been an upsurge of interest, internationally, in a particular form of savings club, the ROSCA, or rotating savings and credit association.[12] In these, a group of people agree to deposit an equal amount of money at a predetermined interval, and to do so as many times as there are members. Each member (in turn, by lottery or by auction) takes the total periodic deposit—the "prize"—once. For example, ten of us may agree to save $10 every week for ten weeks. Each week one of us gets $100. ROSCAs have been found on every continent, show a bewildering number of local variations, and appear to be of great antiquity. Maloney and Sharfuddin Ahmed failed to find ROSCAs in Bangladesh, despite their popularity in other parts of the subcontinent, especially in the south. However, when I urged a Bangladeshi colleague, a development economist, to look, he soon found them: there are, in fact, many ROSCAs in the country.[13] The ownership of rickshaws in Dhaka city, for example, is being transformed by the ROSCA, as men, driven by rural poverty to find employment in the city, begin by renting a rickshaw during the day to drive as the only readily available source of work, and thus become part of an informal network by means of which they soon learn how to put some of their earnings aside each day in a ROSCA formed with other men from their home district. There are men who came penniless to Dhaka five or ten years ago who now own fleets of rickshaws, or have graduated into owning motorized rickshaws. There are also ROSCAs among garment workers and suburban housewives, and increasingly, among market traders in rural bazaars. Some ASA samity members also run ROSCAs, and they are found among NGO workers.[14]

ROSCAs have a number of virtues. They are extremely effective at the basic intermediating task of mobilizing savings and transforming them into useful amounts of capital, because the savings go directly from the pocket of the saver into the hands of the borrower without any middlemen or banking delays. They are so cheap to run that they are virtually cost free: no paperwork is needed, just a tally of who has, and hasn't, yet received the prize. They are flexible: as soon as one cycle is over and everyone has deposited regularly and received the prize once, they can be reformed with new members, a new savings amount, or a new time interval. They are fair: everyone puts in and gets out the same, and choosing among the three ways to decide who gets the prize first (by consensus, by lottery, or by auction) smoothes out problems of timing. They are also totally owned and managed by their users, requiring no outside input of management, equipment, or funds.

Microcredit

Microcredit, which was to be the immediate influence on ASA's credit work, emerged in the 1970s, by which time East Pakistan had become Bangladesh, and we will look at it in greater detail in later chapters. But for now it is worth noting that a microcredit loan performs the same basic task as a ROSCA: it matches a series of small, regular, frequent payments against a single, large sum. Curiously, this aspect of microcredit—the frequency and smallness of the repayments—has been less noticed than others, such as the focus on women users, and on the use of loans exclusively for microenterprises. But the worldwide ubiquity of ROSCAs, which rarely prescribe the use to which the prize must be put, suggests that their users find value in this simple basic function of turning a series of small, regular payments into one, usefully large sum. It may have been a very big factor—perhaps the biggest—in the success of microcredit. We shall turn to this idea again.

Chapter 3

Bangladesh

Bangladesh's War of Liberation, or War of Independence, led in late 1971 to the emergence of a new country with a homogenous, Bangla-speaking population.[1] But the war had torn society apart, and the 1970s were marked by civil disorder and political chaos. Underground parties tried to mobilize and control villages through persuasion, intimidation, and violence. But at the same time, a new kind of organization appeared that was destined to be more important for addressing the grievances of the rural poor. This was the nongovernment organization, the NGO, whose appearance and growth coincided with and, to a great extent, depended on the massive influx of international aid. The NGOs tapped cash and ideas from abroad, and attracted energetic and idealistic men and women at home. Many were keen to try out new ways of organizing and "conscientizing" the rural poor, inspired by the writings of Paolo Freire and guided by a secular, professionalized (and salaried) approach to project planning and implementation. Early NGO work in credit focused on setting up production cooperatives, but these were often unsuccessful. But by the late 1970s, new ways of lending to the poor were being devised, notably by the Grameen Bank and the NGO BRAC. Meanwhile, the government nationalized the banking sector and tried, on the whole with little success, to revive the formal credit cooperative system.

March 1971

Sushil Kumar Roy, now one of ASA's four executive vice presidents, was born into a large, middle-class Hindu family in the Old City of Dhaka. As a college student he had caught a mild dose of the political fever that had swept through East Pakistan's student community in the late 1960s, and was attracted by the ideas of the Communist Party of Bangladesh (CPB), though he never became a member and later became disillusioned with party politics. But at the end of March 1971 he and his family suddenly found themselves obliged to flee, along with many other Hindus, to a village outside Dhaka, where they stayed until February 1972. Sushil and his older brother hawked cigarettes to keep the family alive.

On the night of March 25, 1971, the Pakistan army responded to what they saw as an insurrection in the eastern wing with a savage attack on Dhaka and other major cities. Intellectuals in the universities, and units of the armed forces considered unreliable or disloyal, were their immediate targets. The troops soon moved on to a bloodbath designed to crush all supporters of the Awami League, the popular voice of Bengali nationalism. The Old City, the slums, and Hindu communities like Sushil's, were especially vulnerable. The Awami League's leader, Sheikh Mujibur Rahman, was arrested and flown to confinement in West Pakistan. This marked the beginning of a fierce struggle between Bengali freedom fighters and the Pakistan army and its supporters, which lasted until November. It ended, following the intervention of the Indian Army, in a humiliating defeat for Pakistan, and in the emergence of a new country—Bangladesh.

Ironically, it was the West Pakistan leadership's attempt to exploit the factionalized Bengali political scene that led to the independence of Bangladesh. In the late 1960s a weak national government in Pakistan was brought down by rioting and anarchy in the western wing and replaced in March 1969 by a military government under Yahya Khan. One of Yahya's most pressing tasks was to quell Bengali nationalism in the eastern wing while he restored order in the western. To this end, he called a general election in late 1970, the first and the last full national election in united Pakistan's history. He believed, or hoped, that the Awami League would emerge as just one of many parties with seats in the East. But many rival parties, such as Bhasani's NAP, either abstained from the vote or allowed their supporters to vote tactically for the League, and as a result the Awami League won 167 out of three hundred seats in the all-Pakistan National Assembly. It also made a clean sweep of seats in the eastern wing's Provincial Assembly, but won none at all in the western wing's.

This extraordinary result was a paradox. The league had emerged at one and the same time as a purely Bengali party and as the majority party of Pakistan as a whole, with the right to form the next national government. It was the West Pakistan leaders' rejection of this unpalatable right that led, inevitably, to conflict, and to the emergence of Bangladesh.

Chaos and Novelty

After the surrender of the Pakistan forces to the Indian army and the Bengali freedom fighters in November 1971, Sheikh Mujibur Rahman returned from imprisonment in Pakistan as the new country's most popular politician and took the position of prime minister in an Awami League administration. He was the very embodiment of Bengal, and his personal appeal was greater than any leader before him. But he could not bring unity of purpose to the new country, and his spell in power was marred by steadily increasing lawlessness, the worst famine in 30 years (in 1974) and a decline in the public's respect for Mujib himself, his Awami League party and for politicians in general. Mujib created a pro-Awami armed militia, known as the *Rakkhi Bahini*, but it stirred up resentment against the government.[2] In the end, its members terrorized the countryside. In this they were in competition with groups of disaffected freedom fighters who were angry at not being given a big enough share in Mujib's government, and with underground political parties, some of whom may genuinely have believed in armed insurrection mounted from the countryside as a legitimate political strategy, but many of whom were little more than hoodlums. In 1975, when Mujib shifted from pluralist politics to one-party rule, one of his justifications was that three thousand Awami League workers had been murdered. By 1975 the vision of an independent democratic order for the new state had been lost and politicians and bureaucrats had been discredited. This allowed the regular army to begin to see itself as the only remaining disciplined institution left working for the public interest,[3] and in such a situation it was not long before a minority element within the army made its move. On August 15 1975, Mujib, and most of his family, were gunned down in their home in Dhaka by junior officers, and after several more months of anarchy, an army-backed government emerged.

An ASA Member

In March 1971, just as the war was breaking out, Kulsum Bibi, who later became a member of an ASA credit group, was born into a landless family in the southern Bangladesh district of Patuakhali. Kulsum's father, Yusuf Ali, told us that his wife gave birth to Kulsum, as to all their children, lying on a mat on the earth floor of their home. A relative had allowed them to build a one-room straw hut in the courtyard of his house. Kulsum was their third daughter, and a fourth was born before the first son came along. Yusuf Ali remembers Kulsum's infancy as the most difficult period of his life:

> It was not just that my family was young in age and I was the only earning member to feed five of us. Also the whole country was in a mess. We used to live on government land near the

> river where I got work being crewman in a fishing boat. But it was a very remote place and also very lawless. That means, the ex–freedom fighters were very active and they started fighting with the Rakkhi Bahini to control the area. For which we were so frightened, my cousin told me to come and live in his *bari*.[4] He was solvent but as a result of famine many of his poor relations like us took shelter with him finding no other help. One of my own brothers got no work, he left the area with his family taking them to Dhaka instead of passing his days here in starvation. We have got no news of them. They must have died.[5]

Yusuf Ali's predicament was shared by millions all over the country. According to tables published by the World Bank, Bangladesh's per capita income in 1974 was the lowest in the world bar that of Rwanda. It is estimated that in the 1970s, 80 percent of the rural poor were in the "extreme poor" category, characterized by frequent food shortages and chronic poor health and malnutrition.[6] A decade later that proportion had dropped to 60 percent, and by the turn of the century to less than one-third. Some of that improvement can be attributed to the role of international aid and to Bangladesh's remarkable NGOs.

Aid and the NGOs

Against this chaotic background, new forces were emerging that were to become influential in the political and social development of Bangladesh. Yusuf Ali remembers that

> there was advantage of living in my cousin's bari as he had better relations with the local administration; hence we received some relief food and goods. The NGOs were beginning their activities, and the officers of these NGOs visited my cousin's bari too, to get him to help them with their work. Several landless laboring people became involved with these NGOs. We built many houses and repaired roads, being paid cash or wheat.

> Also we got some relief goods. As for example, at one time I was involved with an NGO, they leased land and gave it to the landless group for joint rice cultivation. That project did not function well—maybe it was our fault. But it seemed that they tried to do their best and work nicely and for this reason I did not raise any objection when Kulsum sought my suggestion about joining ASA.

Soon after the war ended, international donors began to support Mujib's government with ever larger amounts of aid, in cash, credits, and commodities including food. However well-intentioned and necessary this was, it had the effect of aggravating the incipient anarchy, as different groups strove to get their share of this international bounty. The Awami League government was quickly seen to be incapable of (or indifferent to the need for) regulating fairly the flow of aid, and aid-related scandals featured strongly in the many accusations of corruption thrown at politicians and officials at all levels.

Among the recipients of this aid were private initiatives that had sprung up in response to the chaos and suffering of the war, and the devastating cyclone in the south of the country that killed up to half a million people in November 1970, on the eve of the struggle. Access to assistance from abroad allowed some of these initiatives to move from purely spontaneous and voluntary action to become permanent, professional entities. At first, Christian groups featured prominently, because churches were among the international donors who preferred to disburse their aid privately through their own local partners, rather than through government. As early as 1972, the World Council of Churches helped coordinate the efforts of its members in Bangladesh by organizing the Ecumenical Relief and Rehabilitation Service. This ran programs in the countryside with an annual budget of around 50 million U.S. dollars, and fielded up to fifty foreign volunteers and administrators. Yusuf Ali, for example, may have been a recipient of help organized by the Christian Commission for Development, Bangladesh (CCDB), which, in partnership with Caritas, a Catholic organization, ran a program in Patuakhali District at that time. BRAC had been started by a Bengali employee of the multinational firm Shell, and began work in the refugee camps in West Bengal while the war was still raging.[7] Contacts with various western donor agencies allowed it rapidly to build up funds and tap into their worldwide experience, so that by 1975 BRAC was an NGO, as they came to be called. The growth of these local NGOs soon outpaced that of the Christian organizations, and since the 1980s, most of the biggest and best-known NGOs have been wholly secular, and locally owned and staffed, even if much of their funding continues to come from abroad.

A Freedom Fighter

Darbesh Ali is now an assistant director in ASA's head office in Dhaka. But when the Pakistan tanks started rolling in 1971, he was a 16-year-old high school boy. After the March 25 onslaught the schools closed, and Darbesh went back home to his village in Manikganj, west of Dhaka. Within weeks the Pakistan army established a camp in the local administration headquarters nearby and four boys from Darbesh's village were recruited to "work" for the camp. The work consisted of making a list of Hindu families, and bore grisly fruit in the form of looting raids on Hindus by the soldiers. Darbesh's father, a mild-mannered Muslim farmer with half a dozen acres of land and four sons and a daughter to look after, was appalled and frightened, and tried to keep his family out of the struggle. But Darbesh, his second son, was a hothead: he was already secretary of a village committee he had started, and general secretary of his high school students' union. When the army bombed the bridge on the main highway and started firing on local houses, Darbesh stole a little money from his father and left the house at night to make contact with a group of freedom fighters in the neighboring district of Tangail.

Like many other such bands, his group of freedom fighters was isolated from other similar groups, poorly trained, poorly equipped, and poorly informed.[8] They harassed the army as best they could with whatever weapons came to hand, never moving far from their base. But they paid a heavy price for it: Darbesh lost an admired teacher, among many other casualties. Gradually the Pakistan army established control of the towns, and replied to the threat from the freedom fighters by setting up gangs of *rajakars*, volunteers who were given arms to oppose the independence movement. They also set up Orwellian-sounding "peace committees," gangs formed, it seems, mainly for the indiscriminate killing of Hindus. This setting of villager against villager contributed to the difficulties Bangladesh had in establishing national unity in the postwar period.

At year's end, after India's sudden and decisive intervention in the war, Darbesh found himself back home, and at a loose end. With a friend who was already working for an NGO, he started another group, this time consisting of 17 young men who dedicated themselves to rehabilitating their villages. They raised funds by begging for subscriptions in the marketplace and by cutting and selling bamboo. Their first work was to rebuild the shattered huts of people too poor to do so for themselves. Later, the local authority encouraged them by giving them some tin sheets with which they built themselves a crude office. Thus established, they called themselves the *Naba Jagaroni Sangsad* (New Awakening Association), a name that lives on as a modern NGO in the area. With volunteer labor they started building an earthen roadway to relink the village to the main road. Fuzzy photographs of their efforts in Bangla-language newspapers brought them to the notice of the local MP and, more significant, to that of Fazle Hasan Abed, the accountant from Sylhet in northeastern Bangladesh, then busy developing BRAC and looking for like-minded groups to work with. Abed met these "new awakeners" and promised them some training. In this way Darbesh Ali was exposed for the first time to new ideas like project planning and management, human development, adult literacy, and group formation. Darbesh and his association started looking for funds and obtained a little cash from other agencies. They got some wheat through the government system for food-for-work projects like road building. They even began to give out tiny, interest-free loans.

Darbesh, by then a mature 17-year-old, went back to school to retake his high school exams. He passed, but his father was now in poor health and quite unable to fund his son through college. Darbesh decided in favor of a career in social work, throwing in his lot with the newly emerging NGOs. He took more training from Oxfam, the British NGO that was one of the first international agencies to work in Bangladesh after independence. He did some voluntary work for Service Civil International, another overseas NGO. Then in 1974 Zafrullah Chowdhury started up his People's Health Centre in Savar, down the road from Manikganj, and Darbesh went there to help construct the buildings. By 1975 UNICEF, the United Nations Children's Fund, was offering training to NGO staff, and Darbesh was one of many to benefit. In that year BRAC, now well funded, gave Naba Jagaroni three years of support for a self-starter project, a cluster of village activities centering on rehabilitation, group formation, immunization, adult literacy, and pond fish culture. By now, Darbesh had joined the staff of BRAC, serving as a trainer. In BRAC he encountered a wider and more exciting range of views, and soon he was on the NGO's radical wing, pushing for projects dedicated to the landless poor in a politically more committed way. Through his duties as a trainer, he met workers from many NGOs, including CCDB. Those contacts led him to ASA, where, in October 1980, he became their second full-time employee.

The NGOs and Credit

As they came to the end of their program of immediate relief and began to turn to rehabilitation work, the NGOs identified three enormous problems facing the rural population of Bangladesh: (1) a general and desperate lack of resources, including finance; (2) massive unemployment and underemployment; and, perhaps most serious of all, (3) the breakdown of social cohesion, brought about by the divisive issues of the independence struggle, during which time many households were torn between their adherence to Islam and their identity as Bengalis, and aggravated by the failure of government to bring discipline to the social and political order.

One way of tackling all these problems at the same time presented itself—the production cooperative—and much of the early credit offered by NGOs went into developing cooperatives. This path was well-liked by many of their overseas supporters. In the West, the idea of the cooperative was going through something of a revival in the 1970s. In Britain, for example, it became an icon of a certain view about how society should be organized that was very popular among the kind of young men and women who staffed the NGOs that provided resources for Bangladesh. The British NGO Save the Children Fund (SCF), which ran its own programs in Bangladesh, responded to the 1974 famine by setting up, in a badly hit area on the banks of the Brahmaputra, a cooperative of thirty fishermen, supplying them with capital to buy boats, nets, and other equipment. SCF's team leader, a young Dutchman, wrote to the head office that "the theories say that after one year they will be able to pay back the loan" and that the fishermen were being given lectures "in which we try to teach them the most important thing in cooperation."[9] But a year later SCF repossessed what they could of the equipment. The cooperative had repaid less than a tenth of its loan. SCF's postmortem showed that the idea of the cooperative had been imposed without any real understanding of the relationships between the thirty fishermen, or of their livelihood strategies, or of the actual cash flows that characterize river fishing.

The NGOs responded quickly to these failures. Some abandoned the whole idea of credit (or never got into it in the first place), arguing that political and social reorganization was needed before the ground could be sown with credit. ASA, as we shall see, was among these in its early days. Among those who persevered with credit, two main strategies emerged, and can be characterized by looking at the work of two of Bangladesh's most famous organizations—BRAC and the Grameen Bank. BRAC organized poorer villages into large, village-wide, single-sex, village organizations (VOs) and offered them at least a year of preparation, including literacy and numeracy training, and help with management and skills upgrading, before providing credit. This was clearly in the tradition that linked credit with education that had so enthused the colonial and Comilla advocates of the cooperatives. Dr. Muhammad Yunus at the Grameen Bank took a different, more minimalist, view, arguing that poor people were perfectly capable of using small amounts of credit, and if it could be delivered to them in a simple, immediate way, they would respond with better repayment behavior than the richer recipients of more formal bank credit. This *credit-only* view was not popular at first with many people in the NGO community, who found it too materialistic. Many believed it simply couldn't work, because oppressive forces in society would find some way of cheating the borrowers out of the fruits of their loans, if not the loans themselves. However, the differences were not really as stark as they seemed, for in the text that introduced the Grameen Bank, Yunus made it clear that he, too, saw a need to "bring the disadvantaged people within the force of some organizational format which they can understand and operate, and can find social political and economic strength in it through mutual support."[10]

To achieve this, Professor Yunus and his colleagues set up the basic Grameen structure of the *kendras*—smaller groups of poor men or women who meet weekly to save, and to take loans that are paid back in weekly installments over one year. The first loans were available within a few weeks of the kendra's formation, and follow-up loans as soon as the first loan was fully repaid. The main business of the weekly meeting was to collect the savings and repayments and to build the discipline of the weekly rhythm. Members were given no skills training, although they were taught how to sign their names, principally so as they could sign the attendance register, and they were asked to learn and to subscribe to the list of "Sixteen Decisions," morally wholesome undertakings such as refusing to pay dowry or to allow their daughters to be married before the age of sixteen. And although Grameen did not dictate to its members what kind of trade or business their loans should be employed in, nor offer them any training in business skills, it did very much insist that the loans should be used for businesses and not for consumption or for relending to other people. For a long time it even frowned on loans being used for buying agricultural land, on the grounds that such purchases would simply deprive another poor household of some of its land.

It was Grameen's simpler and cheaper version of microcredit that finally won the day, and almost all of the hundreds of microcredit NGOs that were subsequently formed followed this basic pattern. After some years, BRAC followed suit. BRAC did not abandon its efforts to provide a wide range of training and other services to its members: indeed, it intensified them, but their administration was separated from the credit work, so that a BRAC weekly microcredit meeting came to look very much like a Grameen one. When ASA turned to microcredit in 1991 it claimed to have done so as a result of its own analysis of its members' needs, but its microcredit system was clearly derived from that of Grameen, though it was simplified in some respects, and, as we shall see, ASA even borrowed Yunus's words when it announced its microcredit program in its annual report.

PARD Becomes BARD

Shafiq Choudhury was working at PARD when the war broke out in March 1971. Like many followers of Maulana Bhasani, he did not take an active part in the independence struggle. Bhasani had argued that independence from Pakistan might become necessary, but that it would not of itself change the unjust structure of Bengali society nor solve rural poverty. His ambivalent relationship with Mujib and the Awami League left many of his supporters unsure of what attitude to take to the Awami-led struggle. Bhasani's open support of Chinese communism (he was very publicly embraced by Zhou Enlai during the Chinese leader's visit to Dhaka) caused further confusion when China supported Pakistan in 1971. Earlier, Bhasani's willingness to spend time and effort trying to talk Pakistan's leaders into adopting socialism had made him appear soft on the West Pakistanis in the eyes of many Awami enthusiasts. In the chaos of 1971 there were even outbreaks of fighting between Mujib and Bhasani supporters.

In the first short phase of the 1971 struggle, when the Pakistani army with its massive firepower secured the towns one by one, Shafiq returned to his home village in Habiganj. The longer middle phase of the war was a standoff between the army in the towns and the groups of freedom fighters camped in the countryside who harassed the army with guerrilla tactics. Shafiq, along with most of the staff, went back to work at PARD. His colleague Manzarul Alam remembers only one staff member leaving to become a freedom fighter: most carried on work as best they could, though the situation meant that the program of meetings in the villages had to be curtailed.[11] Khan had gone, and Azizul Haq had taken over as director. Haq, himself an admirer of Bhasani, was very much a diplomat, and skillfully protected the academy, its staff, and its large and beautiful campus.

After the sudden end to the war in November, there was considerable anxiety about what an Awami-led government might do with PARD. In fact, the new government gave it a new lease of life as BARD, the Bangladesh Academy of Rural Development, the name it retains to this day. Shafiq stayed on for another two years, learning as much as he could from Haq, and, according to his aunt, "discovering poverty."[12] When Haq left, Shafiq became restless and got embroiled in internal politics at the academy, jointly leading an unsuccessful campaign to have Haq's successor dismissed. Haq, with whom he was still in contact, remained patient with this increasingly fiery young man, perhaps because he admired his frankness, and he began to look for a more suitable place for Shafiq to employ his talents. Haq had been invited onto the board of CCDB, then one of the biggest NGOs in Bangladesh, and he introduced Shafiq to its director. Shafiq left BARD and joined CCDB as an extension officer, posted in Dhaka, in 1974.

New State Banks and Cooperatives

The new government was active in the credit market. Yusuf Ali remembers his cousin getting loans from the Bangladesh Krishi Bank (BKB), which was what the ADBP became after liberation. His cousin's loan may well have come from a special provision for interest-free credit to farmers in the southern, cyclone-hit zone. BKB inherited 75 branches in 1971, and began to expand quickly: by 1974 there were 147.[13] But the number of borrowers failed to keep pace with this increase: indeed, the reverse happened, for in 1974–75 a mere 66,000 borrowers took loans, compared to 175,000 in 1972–73, whereas the amount disbursed remained steady. Once again, it seemed that a state-owned bank was being gradually captured by a small group of bigger borrowers.

The Awami League government's economic stance, and the general temper of political-economic thinking at the time, was socialist, and state ownership of important parts of the economy was an early ambition that was applied to the banking sector. As well as retaining ownership of the BKB, the new government took over a group of private banks, which became known as the nationalized commercial banks (NCBs), and set up specialist development finance institutions (DFIs) to promote industrial growth. These, however, had little impact in the countryside.

For farmers, the government was involved in yet another attempt to revitalize the cooperative movement, this time by setting up a new chain of cooperatives to run alongside the decaying ones inherited from Pakistan times. The old system of multipurpose cooperatives (which came to be known as *traditional cooperatives*) was quietly allowed to wither. Its membership continued to decline, and the societies that survived were almost wholly for specialist trades and not for the farming poor. They will play no further part in our story.

The new approach took its inspiration from the cooperative experiments set up by Khan and the PARD staff in Comilla. The government's first five-year plan (of 1972) called for a somewhat simplified version of the "Comilla system," to be extended to 250 local authorities by 1978. The cooperatives that it gave birth to were registered with the Cooperative Department, but their supervision was entrusted to a specialist government body called the Bangladesh Rural Development Board (BRDB). The board encourages the formation of village cooperatives for the purpose of savings and credit, improved agriculture, and more productive use of labor. The societies were federated at local authority level in the TCCA—the Thana Central Cooperatives Association, which accepted and banked member savings and sanctioned loans. BRDB, with an office in the local authority (*thana*) headquarters, was asked to encourage membership among the landless and marginal farmers, as well as the richer landowners. Targeted membership, in which societies were composed of members of more equal socioeconomic standing, came later (in 1982) in response to the evident success of such homogenous groups in NGO programs.

Because many of the "traditional cooperatives" (a large number of which existed on paper only) were absorbed into the new Comilla system, it is very hard to use official statistics to evaluate the performance of the new initiative. But the position during the 1970s does not look good. Membership certainly grew throughout the decade, and may have reached 1.5 million by 1980. But savings remained as unattractive to members as in the traditional societies, with an average savings balance per member of less than 100 taka for the whole period. On-time repayment rates on loans were poor—never better than 60 percent—and even this rate may have been achieved by issuing many rollover loans.[14] The new system failed to extinguish the old attitude that cooperatives were a means to access "soft" loans from outside the village, rather than a mechanism to raise funds by the collective pooling of local cash resources.

The future did not belong to the cooperatives. It belonged to microcredit. For Shafiq, though, getting to that destination was to take him down a long and winding road.

Chapter 4

Development as Struggle

ASA was conceived and established mainly by people who worked for NGOs. But some of them felt themselves to be NGO dissidents, arguing for a more radical, people-centered approach. Others who helped get ASA going had connections with underground political parties or were on the radical left but outside the NGO movement. All shared the view that the 1971 conflict had failed to eliminate exploitation from the villages of Bangladesh. ASA began life, therefore, as something in between an NGO and a people's movement. In this, Shafiq's role was central: he was himself an NGO officer, and had been radicalized by a training course in India from which he returned eager to prepare the poor for conflict. It was he who arranged funding from some sympathetic donors. But he was among the first to see that the villagers of Manikganj, where ASA began its work, did not want unending conflict and were not responding enthusiastically to ASA's calls to take up the struggle against the exploitation of the landlord and the moneylender. ASA's heroic period as a revolutionary movement was short lived.

March 1976

In March 1976, in Manikganj District, BRAC gave its first loans to landless people organized in groups. Darbesh Ali, too, was in

Manikganj, his home district, working for BRAC as a trainer and supervising his local self-help village development group. On the other side of the country Muhammad Yunus, economics professor at Chittagong University, was concluding the experiments that led him to launch the Grameen Bank project at the year's end. Meanwhile, Shafiqual Haque Choudhury, the son of a provincial landowner, an admirer of Maulana Bhasani, an ex-officer of the Bangladesh Academy of Rural Development at Comilla, and newly married, was also in Manikganj. He was working on fishing cooperatives on the Jamuna (Brahmaputra) River as the project director for the Christian Commission for Development, Bangladesh (CCDB) in their rural development program. At the same time he was hatching plans for a new type of NGO.

Shafiq's marriage was a traditional, arranged one, not so different from that of his parents. Family members found his bride for him, and the wedding took place in Dhaka. The couple soon built a stable marriage on these foundations supplied by others. For a long time, according to his own account, his wife has been the only person that Shafiq is really close to, the only one with whom he shares all his worries and whose advice he consistently listens to. Shafiq, always affable, has always had plenty of acquaintances but few close male friends. Shafiq is always ready to move on—to new ideas, new challenges, and new friends.

The new challenge that faced him in Manikganj was how to move CCDB away from the failing fishing cooperatives, and his new friends were radical youngsters, some of them from well-to-do backgrounds like his own, now working in the new world of NGOs. The problems with the fishing cooperatives were the same as those that had faced the Save the Children Fund. The cooperative groups, with memberships often cobbled together quickly by inexperienced NGO staff members or left to a local leader to nominate, were easily captured by a richer and more aware minority who took over the assets and employed the rest of the members at low rates of pay. To many who had adopted left-wing views, this seemed to be the proof that society was inherently unfair and needed radical transformation. At a CCDB workshop, Shafiq argued vociferously that the NGO should change its strategy. If not, Shafiq thought he might have to form his own organization.

A New Set of Ideas

The group of friends and colleagues with whom Shafiq chewed over such issues in his digs in Manikganj had a rich menu of ideas to draw on. Several had been influenced by the thinking and inspired by the example of Bhasani, so that the old peasant–activist vision of peasant liberation from oppression and poverty became their fundamental ideal. From Bhasani, too, came the Maoist flavor in their thinking, especially the idea of a political restructuring originating in a peasant movement based in the countryside. Unlike people in other countries who had been attracted by Maoism, Bangladeshis had just emerged from a real revolution, and could judge for themselves how far it had changed society. Some of them felt that casting off Pakistani rule was only a first, though important and deeply symbolic, step on the road to liberation.

With the country still in some turmoil, with armed groups of ex-freedom fighters, Rakkhi Bahini, gangsters, and underground parties at loose in many districts, the role of armed struggle inevitably had to be taken into account. Shafiq's circle in Manikganj included one articulate and persuasive personality who had contacts with an underground political party and who was prepared to argue that in the end violence would prove an indispensable ingredient of radical political change. At the time I interviewed him, almost two decades later in 1994, he was a government officer, and I promised to keep his name concealed. His contacts were with the *Sorbahara* (Have-Nots) Party, a group originally led by Siraj Sikdar, whom the Mujib government had taken seriously enough to have tracked down and (many believe) killed by the police. Anwarul Azim, a colleague of Shafiq's at CCDB who went on to become a cofounder of ASA, also knew members of one of the two main Sorbahara factions, and sometimes sheltered them in his home. Occasionally, he gave them donations from his salary, as did Shafiq, who admired their courage.

From Shafiq's time at BARD came the group formation approach, in which the poor were organized for economic progress. This was reinforced and extended by the example of those NGOs who by 1976 were moving away from relief and rehabilitation toward development, largely through group formation. BRAC, for example, was putting together its outreach project, in which groups of the poor were given help to analyze the economic and political reality of their day-to-day lives (*conscientization*) and then encouraged to work together to do something about it (*social action*). Social actions may include wage strikes, protest rallies, or the collective occupation of government land that by law should have been set aside for the landless poor. Social actions are clearly in the tradition of peasant activism that we have traced in earlier chapters, but much of the language that was now used was new. For example, the influence of Paolo Freire, the Brazilian writer and activist, is clear in the use of the word *conscientization*. These ideas reached the NGOs partly through the many foreigners who worked as volunteers for local NGOs or as officers of international ones. CCDB, for example, had as many as 50 foreign nationals working as volunteers in Bangladesh at one time. CCDB itself was also moving toward what became known as the *target group approach,* in which the membership of the groups with whom the NGO worked was made as homogenous as possible, to avoid interclass conflicts of interest. CCDB's director Susanta Adhikari told me, "In 1975–76 the 'target group' approach of selecting poorer people for group formation grew out of our field experience, especially disappointment with poorly performing groups and cooperatives which mixed rich and poor. The main question became 'how to reach the poor'?"[1]

Then CCDB gave Shafiq an experience that had an enormous influence on his thinking. They sent him for a short training course to the Centre for Development Studies in Bombay (now Mumbai), in India. There he was exposed not only to a radical ideology of political transformation through peasant activism, but was shown how such ideas might be incorporated into the work of an NGO by setting up *people's organizations*.[2] He met these ideas with enthusiasm, and they had two important effects on him. First, by showing how such an agenda could be brought into the programs of an NGO, they provided a way in which hitherto disparate ideas and influences could be focused on a single activity—building an NGO—an activity with which Shafiq was already familiar. Second, they reinforced his belief in collective political and social action as the only feasible route open to the poor in their struggle against oppression, and turned him into an opponent of programs to improve the wealth of individual households through credit. Looking back, Shafiq told me, "We didn't understand credit at the time. Rather, we criticized Grameen Bank, all banking facilities, World Bank.... We said these people are exploiting us, ruining our economy."[3]

It was to be more than a decade before Shafiq began to take the potential of credit seriously.

Ziaur Rahman

Meanwhile, an important shift had occurred in the national political environment. In the immediate aftermath of Mujib's murder, power was exercised by an unstable partnership between competing factions in the army. In early November 1975, the army chief of general staff, Khaled Mosharraf, a popular ex-freedom fighter, staged a coup, forcing an acting president to resign. But within days, an uprising broke out among the common soldiers, led by another freedom fighter, the Marxist colonel Abu Taher. Taher was linked with the JSD (Jatiyo Samajtantrik Dal, or National Socialist Party), which grouped left-wingers, many of them previously

Awami League members, who sought to build a new revolutionary alliance of students, workers, peasants, and soldiers. From within the army, Taher was organizing for the JSD a radical group of soldiers, the Revolutionary Soldiers' Organisation, who believed in establishing "an exploitation-free society under the leadership of a classless army."[4] When Taher sensed that Mosharraf's coup was unpopular with the public at large, the RSO seized the opportunity to stage its own revolutionary coup, and it transferred the leadership of the army into the hands of another and even more famous freedom fighter, Ziaur Rahman, whom they thought would be sympathetic to their views.

But he wasn't. Indeed, Zia put an end to the confusion that followed Mujib's death by imposing discipline, first on the army and then on the state. In the process, Taher was imprisoned, tried, and hanged; the Revolutionary Soldiers' Organisation collapsed; and the JSD was weakened beyond recognition. The idea of a mass-based socialist revolution had had its day and popular support for such ideas began a decline that is still going on.

Zia, a general, was a household name in Bangladesh because it was he who had taken over the radio station in Chittagong in 1971 and had broadcast a declaration of the independence of Bangladesh, on behalf of Mujib and the Awami League. He was proclaimed president in April 1977, confirming the failure of civilian politics and the shift to military rule. A month later, he ordered a referendum, inviting the people to "express their confidence" in him, which the Bangladeshis appeared to do, by a big majority in a high turnout. A year later, he won a presidential election, standing against a formidable opponent, General M. A. G. Osmani, the leader of the Bangladeshi forces in the Independence War. For many, Zia was a popular president who toured the countryside and showed an interest in local government, particularly literacy and population issues. For others, he remains the head of state who usurped power and failed to bring to justice the brutal murderers of the country's founding father, Mujib. Zia founded a political party, the Bangladesh Nationalist Party (BNP), which went on to win parliamentary polls in 1979. With the end of anarchy in the countryside, many Bangladeshis began to feel that the fortunes of their new state were at last on the upturn. The mood was helped by favorable weather, improving agricultural yields, and a relatively calm international environment.

As Zia consolidated his power, the fortunes of the smaller political parties, particularly those on the left, and of rural groups of terrorists-cum-revolutionaries, continued to wane. Skillfully, he banned the underground parties at the same time as inviting their adherents to come out into the open political scene. Many ended up supporting him, including what was left of Bhasani's NAP, now a small party among dozens of small parties. Zia sought national reconciliation by welcoming all to his party, including some who had been opposed to or even fought against liberation in 1971. Rounaq Jahan, in a commentary written in the mid-1980s, thought she had identified one major change in Bangladeshi politics of the 1970s—that the masses are no longer easily drawn to political struggles and movements. In the 1930s and 1940s, religious fervor stirred the hope that a new state based on Islam would bring political and economic progress. In the 1950s and 1960s, similar hopes, based on the idea of Bengalis ruling themselves in a nationalist state, were raised. Twice disappointed, and lacking any fresh inspiration that could move them in the same way that Islam or Bengali nationalism had, the rural poor became less and less disposed to listen to revolutionary talk.

Getting ASA Up and Running

On his return from Bombay, Shafiq discussed his radical new ideas with CCDB management. Because the general drift of these ideas (away from relief and rehabilitation and toward target group formation and conscientization) accorded with CCDB's own changes in orientation, and that of other NGOs like BRAC, CCDB gave him the go-ahead to experiment in Manikganj, but warned him against stirring up conflict in the villages. Shafiq saw that as a contradiction: how can an NGO promote a pro-poor radical analysis of the village political economy if it is not prepared to support landless people in their consequent struggle against their oppressors? He had understood his time in Bombay as "training for NGO leaders which emphasizes the organization of the rural poor to prepare them for conflict with the landowners."[5]

Unable to put his ideas fully into practice under CCDB, Shafiq began to discuss alternatives with sympathetic CCDB colleagues and with local people in Manikganj. He got further encouragement from an Australian theologian who often visited Bangladesh on behalf of the Christian Conference in Asia. Harvey Perkins, who helped facilitate workshops and seminars in CCDB, saw the church's role as one of leading the poor in their struggle for liberation from poverty and oppression.

But the voices that most closely chimed with Shafiq's own thoughts belonged to the radical youngsters at BRAC. Abed, BRAC's founder, had introduced his staff not only to the "conscientization" ideas of Paolo Freire but also, among others, to the writings of Frantz Fanon and Ivan Illich. Fanon, from the French colony of Martinique, wrote his most influential book, *The Wretched of the Earth*, during the Algerian struggle for independence from France. It discussed the role of intellectuals, and of violence, in revolutionary struggles, and identified rural peasants as the class most likely to be able to lead a successful assault on colonial or neocolonial power. Illich, an anarchist writer with a talent for upsetting his readers' preconceptions, articulated a critique of institutions that some BRAC staff members adapted and used against BRAC itself, that it was growing bureaucratic and unresponsive. Because BRAC's training center in Savar was just down the road from Shafiq's Manikganj office, it was not surprising that on more than one occasion, impatient BRAC staff members whetted their revolutionary appetites with excited discussions in Shafiq's rooms.

The alternative to the stagnation of BRAC and CCDB, they thought, might have to be the creation of a new NGO, differing from existing ones in several important respects. First, it would be based in the countryside, where its work was to be concentrated, and not in the capital. This was because its role would be merely to promote people's organizations. Its own structure should remain lightweight and impermanent, and it should not get trapped—as BRAC and CCDB had, so the argument went—into institutional aggrandizement. Consistent with this, its staff members should be drawn mainly from the villages, rather than from the pool of educated sons and daughters of the urban better-off who would be unlikely to share the aspirations or understand the lives of the oppressed poor. Its management would be nonhierarchical and cooperative.

In other circumstances the obvious course would have been to form a political party. But this was never seriously considered. Political parties were discredited, disorganized, and short of funds. These were hard times, and the availability of foreign donor funding made NGOs a much more attractive proposition. In any case, Shafiq and others were, by then, established NGO officers. Why not use NGO techniques, and donor funding, to build people's organizations instead of fishing cooperatives?

The people's organizations would be built from the bottom up. At first, a small number of dedicated volunteers would be needed to promote village-level groups. Group members would learn from the volunteers how collective social action could bring access to resources, correct injustices, and promote unity among the poor. They would also be taught to use savings to build up a commonly owned fund to support their social actions and allow them to weather adversity and stand up to the economic power of their oppressors, as Bhasani's groups had sought to do. A number of mature groups in an area would then federate at the union level, then *thana* (subdistrict), then district, and finally at the national level, at which point their strength would be expressed as a political force able to take power through the democratic process (though there were those who insisted that an armed struggle would be required at some point). By the time this national level empowerment had been reached, and they were bold enough to set the tentative target date of 1985, the NGO itself would have withered away.

ASA was conceived according to this formula, but its emergence was a slow process. Serious discussions started at a CCDB workshop in Barisal in late 1976 or 1977 when CCDB staffers Shafiq and Golum Chowdhury talked to Harvey Perkins about how Bangladesh needed an NGO with a radical philosophy. The definitive moment almost certainly came in March 1978 when the pledge described in the prologue was made and the name ASA was chosen. As well as being an acronym for the Association for Social Advancement, *ASA* is a homonym of *asha,* the Bangla word for "hope." The name was the idea of Anwarul Azim, Shafiq's colleague at CCDB who became an ASA board member and then an ASA senior staff member until 1990. He, too, had been a Bhasani follower, and was the general secretary of a NAP subdivisional committee for a time in his native Cox's Bazaar.

After that things moved more quickly. The original pledgers each put up 10 taka, and a bank account was opened in the name of ASA. Shafiq and Golum Chowdhury, the fellow CCDB staff member who was closest to Shafiq at the time, were the account signatories.[6] By courtesy of pledger Sushil Bhowmik, a professor of Bengali (Bangla) and a member of Shafiq's contact group in Manikganj, a room in a local college there was used as the ASA office from August 1978 and a signboard erected. Immediately, Shafiq began to recruit volunteers and to send them into the villages to start forming groups. In a final step, ASA was formally registered as an NGO, under the Societies Registration Act, on May 19, 1979.

That same day, Shafiq's wife gave birth to their first son, Ashraful Haq Chowdhury, nicknamed Tanvir.[7]

The First Groups

Shafiq later described the first years of ASA as a "foundation phase" with "the vision of creating an enabling environment to establish a just society."[8] He has also spoken of making a political version of the work of BARD. He began, as most NGOs did (and still do), with group formation.

Memories of those first groups were still alive in the mid-1990s when I went to interview the (by then) middle-aged men who had composed them. Mongol Sheikh's account of how he came to be a member is typical. He met a neighbor, a young schoolmaster called Akhtar, who had volunteered to work for ASA. Akhtar suggested that Mongol join a *samity* (group).

> I asked, what would my benefit be? He told me unity of the poor will be increased, that they'll get a just wage, free treatment from government clinics, proper justice, and a chance to save. Without all this I would never be able to stand on my own feet, he said. The more poor people who joined, the bigger the effect would be, and the poor could have their own leaders. Then the rich would be no longer able to interfere in our lives.

A few days later Mongol went along to a night-time meeting with about twelve other men.

> Akhtar was glad to see us but said we had to motivate more people. At the next meeting there were twenty of us and Akhtar inscribed our names. We paid five taka each into the savings pool and promised to meet each fortnight and save another five taka each time.[9]

At Akhtar's suggestion, they formed a three-person managing committee for their samity: a chairman, a secretary, and a cashier. Akhtar then led a discussion, which Mongol remembers as consisting of advice about

> the proper use of the savings fund, how to get the rich to pay us more for our labor, the need for unity among us, and about how the rich managed to dominate the poor. He also talked about literacy—most of us couldn't read or write—and about getting the use of government land.

But his most vivid recollection is of the training course that they were then sent on, at the college where ASA had its one-room office.

> We had to take an oath. In a darkened room, we had to place one hand on our breast and the other on the earth floor and swear to form and join the samity. After that, I felt bound to join.

This secret-society atmosphere also has a precursor in Bengali politics. At the time of the first partition of Bengal (1905–11) there were numerous secret organizations in Calcutta that cemented their brotherhood by such ritualistic means. As we saw in the prologue, ASA itself started with a similar pledging ceremony.

When we visited Manikganj in 1994 and met Mongol, we found that Akhtar was still living and teaching in the village. He is from a prosperous peasant family: indeed, Mongol told me that Akhtar "was from a rich family and his elder brother disapproved of his being associated with the samity." In his account of how he became an ASA volunteer, Akhtar explained that one day an older neighbor told him that CCDB was giving out loans in the next village and that "if an educated person like you goes along they'll probably listen to you: then we could get loans in our village too."

Partly to please the old man, partly out of curiosity, and partly out of hope that he might get a better paying job, Akhtar went along to the CCDB office, and was admitted to a room where Shafiq was discussing his favorite topic: how to form a new NGO. Three months later he got a letter from Shafiq inviting him to attend a training session for volunteer workers at the ASA office at the college. The training focused on what was known at the time as "awareness building of the backward people," and on organizing the poor into samities, savings, adult literacy, and the unity of the poor.

Back in his own village, Akhtar began to recruit people in the way that Mongol describes. The first time he tried it was a failure.

> I talked to some people in my own village and they decided to form a samity. The meeting they held included some rich people and against my advice one of them was nominated for cashier. I think the poorer members thought that they should have a better-off, more educated man for that post. That *samity* lasted only eighteen months. The cashier suggested to the other members that they should lend out their savings at a high rate of interest to some local rich people. Unfortunately they didn't repay: I think they were friends of the cashier. Anyway, after that the samity collapsed.

Mongol Sheikh's samity, on the other hand, lasted almost six years, and he was extremely hopeful at the beginning. One day, he told me, "I had a dream. In that dream, all our members made great strides and became very rich. But we never achieved this in reality."

His samity also ended in disappointment:

> In the third year of our samity, a rich man, Azad Miah, wanted to join us. Since he was related to one of our members it was hard for us to say no. Later, he became our chairman. Some time after that we heard about some abandoned land that had been illegally occupied by rich people. We knew from what we had learned in the samity that such land was meant for the landless poor. Encouraged by ASA, we ploughed that land and sowed wheat. But at harvest time the rich men hired a gang of roughs and cut our wheat. They also filed a case against us. We fought it for over two years, but finally we ran out of money: we spent the whole of the money in our savings fund, and most of us paid more out of our own pockets. By that time ASA was no longer interested in supporting us. Reluctantly, we closed down our samity. Our chairman had deceived us, and that caused us great pain and suffering.

Many of the stories we heard followed a similar pattern: great hope followed by disappointment as social actions failed and interest waned, or rich men captured the samity, or quarrelling broke out, or, so we were told in one case, an ASA volunteer worker "mismanaged" the savings fund. Nevertheless, there were success stories, too, as Sushil Bhowmik, the college professor, recalled. One samity of rickshaw drivers formed in 1979 was still going strong fifteen years later.[10] Some government land—Bhowmik estimated it at around 25 or 30 acres in the Manikganj area—was taken into use for the landless poor as a result of samity initiatives, but nearly always through patient use of the formal application system backed up by persuasive advocacy by senior ASA staff members, rather than through impromptu invasions. There were many court cases, and not all of them were lost. Numerous small battles, such as getting the full payment of wheat in a food-for-work project, were fought by samity members, backed by ASA, and won.

But ASA had failed to "prepare the landless poor for conflict with the landowners." As another former member, Poran Ali of Sibrampur village recalls, "there was talk at the meetings of us going on movements, strikes, *gheraos*,[11] and all that sort of thing, but we never wanted to do any of that. We were so few."

Shafiq himself, looking back on those days in informal conversation with me in the mid-1990s, was quite candid:[12]

> We realized that maybe we were doing the wrong thing—not only theoretically wrong, even practically wrong, because people didn't like our advice. When we said to them "please come for fighting with a moneylender or with the landlord" they would say, "no why, why? They are helping us in some way at least. But you are not helping, you are giving only sermon or lecture." Then we thought we are really.... These are stupid things we are doing. How can we change that? Then gradually we thought, no, we will organize the people only for bargaining, not for struggle or conflict with the landlord, not thinking for changing the structure, etc. There will be bargaining, trade unionism. We can take some small issue and we can get them some benefit. When we talk about systems, about changing society, people are not listening to us, they are not thinking us their good friend.

As a result of such anxieties, ASA's activities gradually became more structured. In addition to the original emphasis on consciousness-raising leading to social actions, two further programs were identified: legal aid and teaching basic knowledge of the law, and training for rural journalists.

Getting Funds and Going Public

In 1981, CCDB transferred Shafiq from Manikganj back to Dhaka. He believes CCDB did this because they were anxious that he was leading their program in too radical a direction, though this was not confirmed to me by CCDB. Back in Dhaka, Shafiq found that "that time I was really crippled: I could not do a lot of work by sitting in Dhaka. But part of my job was to write to donors on behalf of CCDB. So I told them I had already formed and registered an Association."

Two CCDB donors, whose representatives had visited Shafiq in Manikganj, had already taken a sympathetic view of his aspirations. The Australian Council of Churches (ACC, the group that Harvey Perkins was associated with) sent a first tranche of 76,000 taka as early as 1978 and followed up with larger grants later. Then in 1981, HEKS, a church organization based in Switzerland, gave ASA half a million taka, and from then on donations came in a growing stream. For the super-tolerant CCDB, all this was the last straw, and they finally, though reluctantly, got around to telling Shafiq that he'd better choose between CCDB and ASA. He chose ASA, and left CCDB in 1982.

By that time, ASA had rented a small liaison office in Mohammadpur, Dhaka, not far from the present headquarters at the ASA Tower in Shamoli. It was staffed at first by two or three workers who serviced the seven or eight volunteer field staff members in Manikganj. The family rented a home opposite the office. Tanvir, Shafiq's firstborn, whose earliest recollections are of that home, remembers it as a small "studio house." Shafiq based himself in the office, with frequent trips to the field, at first to Manikganj, but soon to many other districts where ASA set up shop as donor funds flowed in and ASA expanded. This period of rapid growth turned out to set a pattern: the "ASA way" ever since has been to mull over options and then act swiftly and decisively, emphasizing growth above all else. Small-scale piloting is simply not their way of doing things.

Shafiq energized, dominated, and enjoyed this huge workload. Others who were named in the registration documents as board members—some of those present at the pledge in the Uthuli Rest House and others drawn from BRAC's young tigers or from CCDB colleagues—were less involved. Most of the BRAC radicals, after eyeing ASA as a possible vehicle for their aspirations, in the end turned to other organizations. Khushi Kabir left BRAC to reform the NGO Nijera Kori ("We Do It Ourselves") and dedicated it to empowering very poor rural women and their families. Nijera Kori still runs, as we shall see later. Kabir's husband Kamal Uddin went on to start at least two NGOs (the Community Development Library and ARBAN—again, both of these are still running). A few pointed out that the Dhaka office and its salaried staff, paid for by the abundant donor funding, seemed at odds with the original ideal of a rural-based movement run by the landless for themselves. An election to ASA's governing body began to sort out these issues, although, as we shall see, ASA's constitution still had weaknesses that later led to further modifications.

ASA's constitution called for a general council composed of representatives—one staff and one samity member—from each thana (subdistrict) where the movement was operating. This council, in a plenary session every three years, was to elect the chairman and members of a nine-person governing body to be legally responsible for ASA under the terms of its registration. In 1983, a plenary session, with representatives from thirty-three thanas, voted overwhelmingly for the faces they knew—Shafiq and the team he had picked, worked with, and trained—rather than for names they had merely heard of. Shafiq was elected chairman, but only two of the original founders joined him: Anwarul Azim (the author of the name ASA) and college teacher Sushil Bhowmik. Nelson Rema (now a director in the ASA head office) was elected to represent the staff, and there were two landless group representatives, hand-picked by Shafiq and Azim. With just six members elected, they had the further privilege of co-opting the three vacant places, and they chose three well-known public figures to join them, including Father Timm, a teacher and human rights activist from the United States but long settled in Bangladesh, and Taherunnessa Abdullah (from BARD), who both later became chairpersons of the governing body. They also chose as their patron Ataur Rahman Khan, who as well as being a sympathizer of ASA's aims was a prominent figure well chosen because he was close to the country's new political leadership. Indeed, he became prime minister a year later. Shafiq, ASA's founder, was firmly in the saddle. In just a few years, ASA had grown from an idea in the minds of a few youthful radicals, to a well-funded and hyperactive NGO with links to the famous, the talented, and the politically powerful.

ASA appointed a public relations officer as early as 1981. Kamrul Hassan, who first filled that post, had a degree in journalism and, like Darbesh Ali, had worked for a spell under Shafiq's friend Zafrullah Chowdhury in the latter's radical, health-oriented NGO, GK (People's Health Centre).[13] When he applied to ASA, Kamrul was taken to Manikganj and shown an ASA samity meeting in progress. He liked what he saw.

> There was no fixed agenda nor text, but a free ranging discussion, after dark, about government-owned land, wage rates, access to public resources and family matters like divorce and dowry. Social actions were planned—mostly gheraos, processions and rallies, and strikes for better agricultural wages.[14]

Under Kamrul's editorship, ASA began to publish an occasional Bangla-language newspaper, *Gramer Khabor* (Village News).[15] It contained upbeat stories about successful social actions and was intended to encourage field staff and samity members.

Writing about ASA's field work increasingly came to take on a life of its own. Long after ASA leadership had begun to recognize the practical problems in the samities—poor attendance and dropouts, declining interest in social actions, capture by better-off groups, mismanagement of savings funds, and so on—ASA went on publishing an account of its work that made only a passing reference to these difficulties.

The tone of ASA's publications at that time can be appreciated in ASA's first-ever formal report on its work, which came out in 1983. Titled *ASA Annual Report 1982–83,* it in fact covers the period since its inception in 1978–79. ASA is presented as "a development organization whose decision-makers are the downtrodden people themselves" and which believes that the root of poverty is social injustice that will not go away until there is "a basic change in the social structure." With help from ASA in the form of group formation, training, social awareness-raising, and the promotion of group actions, "people will determine and regulate their own destiny [and] participate in the process of structural transformation."[16]

The next formal report, *The Counterlinkage, ASA Activity Report 1985,* is much fuller, but equally confident of the power of the village samities to transform society. Shafiq writes in the foreword that "the focal point of ASA's efforts in development is the emergence of a people's movement based on awareness and solidarity among the rural, landless peasantry," which the editor, Anwarul Azim, puts in an entirely political context, writing that "development is thus essentially a problem of transferring power to the majority of the people," and he goes on to describe how this will be brought about by the steady building up of a federal structure of people's organizations.

A theory of *counterlinkage,* a phrase derived from discussions with Harvey Perkins, is expounded: helping the poor to develop mutually supportive links to counter those that the rich form among themselves and with government officers. This may be a reference to a classic text, *The Net*, published by BRAC in 1980, which detailed the links between the rural powerful (and criminal) in a handful of villages as discovered and traced out by BRAC researchers Andrew Jenkins, Anjan Kumar Dutta, Manzur Hasan, and Khaja Zahurul Islam Khan.[17] By revealing the divisions and alliances in a typical village, *The Net* did much to help turn NGOs toward the target group approach and away from community-wide associations that appeared to be vulnerable to capture by a privileged few. It remained the dominant approach used by NGOs, and is only now being challenged and refined by, among others as we shall see, BRAC itself.

ASA's 1985 report went on to explain how progress at the grass-roots level was to be measured mainly by the number of social actions that samity members carried out. This is clear not only from the statement that "social actions are considered as the only tangible outcome of ASA development education efforts"[18] but from the presentation of tables of social actions as the main evidence of progress in this and subsequent reports right up until 1989. The 1985 report uses a sevenfold categorization of social actions and plots the incidence of each category against each of the main geographical areas where ASA was working. Categories included strikes, rallies, gheraos, and other means of achieving better wages, better shares in sharecropping, access to government-owned land, and a fair share of wheat in food-for-work programs, as well as the holding of "people's courts" (*shalish*) to settle disputes without the interference of the wealthy elite, and lobbying for women's rights. These are all techniques used by the peasant activists of the 1930s. (Food-for-work is a phrase of the 1950s and later: in the 1930s such programs were called "gratuitous relief.")

By 1985, ASA had organized 92,000 men and 24,000 women into (separate) samities, serviced by 340 "volunteers" (actually paid, but not given formal employment status). Some of the 29 branch offices were much keener on social actions than others, but even in the most active there was rarely more than one action each year per samity. Away from these active branches, the average ratio was very much lower, and 8 out of 10 samities engaged in no social actions at all during the year.

A flaw in the presentation of tables of social actions is that there is no clear indication of how many of these actions had successful outcomes. There are no surviving records of the success ratio in the ASA office today, and this information was probably never well known. There is very much a sense of the inherent, existential value of the social action exercise—that the very doing of it was a good in its own right, irrespective of its outcome or of who gained or who was hurt by it. This is another attitude that has stood the test of time: as late as 2008, an officer in a bilateral aid office in Dhaka told me that funding support for an "empowerment" NGO could be justified in part because such work was "worthwhile in its own right," even though it is horribly hard to measure the outcomes. As we saw earlier in this chapter, our own delving into the memories of former ASA members suggests that the success rate was not high. The 1985 report states that 87 samities had been active in trying to get hold of government-owned land, and had, between them, gained 42.5 acres, but there are no other outcome statements beyond generalities.

ASA's publications evidently lagged behind ASA thinking, because senior staff members were well aware of the many difficulties that beset the program of social actions, and were already devising new activities for the samities, as we shall see in the next chapter. Shafiq told me,

> We found we didn't always have work. Once a year in a samity we might find one social action to carry out, or one issue to bargain over. Then we thought, "how will we survive?"—because donors may start asking awkward questions: "only one issue, two issues?—how are you justifying your salaries?" Then we thought we should have to do some continuous work in the samities—service delivery, preventive health, legal aid....

Despite Shafiq's concern, ASA continued to be well supported by its donors. Their number had grown to eight by 1985. HEKS was still lending support, and there were three more European backers: Miserior of Germany, Dutch Interchurch Aid (DIA), and CEBEMO of Holland. From Australia the Asian Partnership for Human Development and the Australian Freedom from Hunger Campaign sent funds. In several cases these were CCDB donors whom Shafiq had gotten to know in the course of his work there. None had permanent representatives in Bangladesh, but most sent staff members on occasional visits, and Shafiq grew to know and like many of them. Many were young and some, on the left politically, believed that poverty in countries like Bangladesh was the direct result of an unjust international political and economic order dominated by Western commercial interests, though ASA itself in its publications never subscribed to the theory that poverty in Bangladesh arises from international conditions, nor have I heard Shafiq express that view. There were also several groups in the developed world who lobbied against conventional aid to poorer countries on the grounds that it merely perpetuated their poverty. They argued for direct support to radical local people's organizations prepared to fight for their rights. For Bangladesh, BIAG (the Bangladesh International Action Group) was one such organization.

Staff in the funding agencies were attracted by the image, fostered by ASA's publications, of an NGO dedicated to helping the world's poorest people fight back against international oppression and injustice. Rick Davies, now a leading researcher of monitoring systems, but in the early 1980s a staff officer at the Freedom from Hunger Campaign in his native Australia, remembers being excited by the ASA reports about social actions.[19] The mood in his office was "this is the kind of thing we should be supporting." Rick gave a lecture at Flinders University in Adelaide called "Development as Struggle," illustrated with ASA stories. It went down well.

Are Unity and Social Action Enough to Develop the Poor?

Looking back on that period, Shafiq sees "positive—but unsustainable—impact." Many of the groups withered away: they just didn't have the strength or the will to keep going against adversity, which might come in the form of government harassment, capture, or cheating by the wealthy, natural disasters or ill health, sheer grinding poverty, or a feeling that they simply weren't making progress. Organization at any higher level proved impossible: there was little effective networking among groups, and the idea of federating the groups in apex bodies never got off the ground.

But at the time, ASA mounted its own evaluations, which came to different conclusions. At least two were done in partnership with donor representatives. *Is Unity and Social Action Enough to Develop the Poor?* was carried out and published in 1984. It was headed by senior ASA staffer K. M. Jahangir Alam (later of the NGO Mouchak) and Manfred Statzer for HEKS, one of ASA's oldest funding partners. It interviewed members and staff in 20 groups in two geographical areas, including Manikganj, where the first samities were formed. It notes that most of these early samities fell apart quickly, but finds that the newer ones, supported by better-trained staff, were performing well—attending meetings regularly and depositing savings on time, for example. Other positive findings were that ASA had "succeeded in making its members non-relief minded," that the members "wholeheartedly believe in ASA's ideology," and that most of them "are taking social actions." But these conclusions are at odds with the findings in the body of the report that reveal other trends. The local staff reported that members find financial and employment problems much more pressing than political ones, and constantly ask for loans from ASA. Local staff strongly supported this demand, arguing for at least some kind of income-generating projects even if outright loans are not possible. Curiously, the report concludes that "workers have succeeded in convincing members that loans are bad for them" although noting that other organizations like BRAC and Proshika "are creating problems by distributing loans to the poor people... it becomes very much disturbing and takes a lot of time for a worker to overcome this kind of situation."[20]

The workers, given their say, complained of poor salaries, poor logistical support, and poor personal security—especially the risks associated with getting involved in any kind of confrontational social action. Local people, who were not samity members, described ASA's work to the study team as "insignificant and in decline, with workers demotivated and prone to use the samities for their own ends."[21]

The Moving Spirit

Harvey L. Perkins, whom we have already met, wrote the booklet *ASA: Hope for the Landless* in January 1985, a sort of eulogy-cum-evaluation of ASA. He was an early and very strong influence on Shafiq, who has described Harvey as "the moving spirit behind ASA." His booklet opens with a historical analysis of Bengal's poverty that stresses the injustices of the British land tenure system and the curse of the moneylender—precisely the same two themes that were given prominence by peasant leaders in British and Pakistani times. He sees a return to communal use of land for irrigated rice cultivation as the only answer, something that can be approached only through awareness building for the landless. He ran a workshop for ASA that stressed collective economic projects at the village level, nonhierarchical management structures, and collective decision making. He reached the conclusion that ASA's samities "do look like the early stages of the emergence of a landless people's movement," and says of the ASA women's program that "women share a vision of communal ownership of land."[22]

Such conclusions seem a world away from the ASA of that period that has been recalled for us in our conversations with samity members and staff, but a closer reading of Harvey's booklet shows that he was sensitive to the tensions that grassroots-level staff members were experiencing. He was aware of the disappointingly low incidence of social actions and of the strong demand for economic programs coming from the membership: "What seems to have hindered [things], however, was a desire to get on with some form of economic gain ... [and] the training of the *shevaks* [fieldworkers] did not enable them to handle these motivational problems." He puts this down, in part, to ASA's weak political analysis and lack of clarity in its awareness raising work: "The cause [of why I am landless] must be identified, the power factor uncovered, the oppressive power named."[23]

Without abandoning his vision of communal rice farms, Perkins recognizes that samity members face acute employment problems, and looks for ways of answering this within the ASA program. He insists that "an ASA program in the village must never start with an economic project," on the grounds that such projects may distract the poor from their search for justice, but recommends a policy of supporting economic projects for mature groups as long as the projects (1) arise out of the collective search for justice, (2) are collectively owned and run, and mobilize local resources, and (3) use proceeds for collectively determined uses.

But ASA was already moving away from collective action and continued to do so.

Chapter 5

Development as Delivery

ASA suffered an internal conflict in the mid-1980s that came close to breaking Shafiq's control of his creation. It precipitated a reorganization after which ASA stopped pretending to be a "people's organization" and settled down as a conventional NGO. At the same time, ASA was looking for a new role for itself in the villages and took up a variety of programs then popular with donors, including, for example, Women in Development. A serious cyclone in 1985 and devastating flooding in 1987 and 1988 allowed ASA to increase dramatically its cash support from international donors and to establish itself as a major mainstream NGO. Some of the cash was given as loans to cyclone or flood victims, and the borrowers' propensity to repay took management by surprise. By 1990 ASA was ready to recognize that, for better incomes and reduced poverty, "there is no alternative to credit."

March 1982

President Zia was brutally murdered in 1981 by army officers opposed to his policies, and the country plunged into autocratic stupor for the decade of the 1980s. In March 1982 General Hossein Muhammad Ershad, who had been deputy chief of army staff to

Zia, assumed power in Bangladesh as chief marshal law administrator. Ershad had a background quite unlike that of Zia, the popular nationalist hero. Ershad was in the army in West Pakistan and confined to barracks for the duration of the liberation struggle, so he had not been a freedom fighter and was not well known to the general public. Though he proved a skillful administrator, he was by no means a charismatic figure (though he was something of a poet), and was quite unable to convince the peasants, or any other sector of the community besides the army, that he had their interests at heart. He, too, offered the voters a referendum, but by and large they ignored him, and his overwhelming majority was of an underwhelming number of votes. He, too, founded political parties, but in his increasingly desperate quest for legitimacy he only once persuaded a political leader of note to run against him, and his elections became sad affairs with low turnouts and systematic riggings. It was Sheikh Hasina, one of Mujib's only two surviving children and leader of the Awami League, who once agreed to stand against Ershad. She was not forgiven for this by the voters, who rejected her in favor of her great rival, Khaleda Zia, the widow of General Ziaur Rahman, in the 1991 elections that took place after Ershad was forced from office.

Nevertheless, Ershad's stay in power lasted for nine years, with the result that he was able to achieve much in areas where Mujib and Zia had been able only to plan or to make a small start. Under Ershad there was steady progress in national infrastructure, decentralizing reform of local government, and improved management of food stocks. His response to flood emergencies was impressive. He pushed along the privatization and decentralization of the economy started by Zia, and was not afraid of bold controversial measures, such as the drug policy that banned the sale of expensive fancy products and stabilized the production and price of basic drugs.[1] By and large, NGOs enjoyed his support and were able to continue to grow throughout the 1980s. Despite the further institutionalization of corruption (it was around this time that Bangladesh started to earn its reputation for being one of the most corrupt countries in the world), donors did not find Ershad difficult to work with, and they stepped up their assistance—a good thing at the time for the Bangladeshi people, perhaps, but one that undermined later efforts to tie aid to democratic standards.

The Ershad referendum took place in March 1985. I was touring southern Bangladesh at the time, and I was curious to see how the poll was organized. Early in the morning, pretending to be Mark Tully (the BBC India correspondent who became well known and well loved in Bangladesh because of his informed reports on the progress of the war in 1971), I persuaded a village policeman to let me look inside the polling booth. There were two ballot boxes, one painted white and marked "yes" (meaning, "yes, I support General Ershad") and the other painted black and marked "no." Perhaps to help the voters make up their minds, the white box was considerably larger than the black.

More Politics

ASA, too, was having a little difficulty with elections. ASA's first governing body, composed of the self-elected group, some of whom had taken part in the nighttime pledge at Uthuli, was, as we have seen, changed in the 1983 election when the samity representatives, who came to the general council meeting with little understanding and somewhat in awe of the ASA leadership, could be relied on to vote as directed. All this was much to Shafiq's satisfaction.

However, by the mid-1980s, ASA's staff numbered about four hundred. Most of them were low-paid, village-level semi-volunteers. For some time resentment had been building up among them, caused by what they saw as their own tiny rewards for the long hours they put in compared to the comfortable offices, vehicles, and salaries of the Dhaka-based officers. Among the latter was an ambitious and skillful rival to Shafiq who saw an opportunity to use ASA's own rhetoric and constitution against him. Jahangir Alam used his popularity in the field to gather support from the junior staff, firing them with the original vision of a rural-based coalition of volunteers and samity members and portraying the ASA leadership as having betrayed the cause. He reminded them that ASA's constitution reflected a belief in a powerful confederation of landless folk to whom ASA related as a junior partner with the limited task of supplying ideas and helping to organize the groups. At an ASA staff meeting held at BARD in late 1985, Jahangir proposed that the NGO ASA should be folded into a (yet to be formed) federation of samities to make a single organization led from the villages by samity members and their volunteer helpers. Shafiq read that proposal as a bid to use the idea of the federation as a means to grab ASA's assets (above all, its access to foreign donations, which had increased sharply). He resisted fiercely and, for the time being, the idea got nowhere.

But the next meeting of the general council was scheduled soon, and Jahangir began to lobby skillfully for support for a bid to oust Shafiq as chairman. In a preemptive strike, ASA management dismissed him on a technical irregularity. The matter went to the governing body, which set up an inquiry to look into the matter and into accusations of corruption against Shafiq before deciding, narrowly, in favor of the management. Jahangir responded by taking over a group of ASA offices in the Narsingdi area, northeast of Dhaka. ASA had to resort to a court injunction to get them back. But up to 150 staff members followed Jahangir out of the organization. Jahangir went on to run the NGO Mouchak.

I have told this story from ASA's point of view, but of course Jahangir had every right, under ASA's constitution, to mount an organization-wide campaign for chairman.[2] The point was not lost on the ASA management, and changes to the constitution were introduced. At the general council meeting in June 1986, it was agreed to transfer the executive power of ASA wholly into the hands of the governing body. They were given the power to expel any members whom they believed to be "acting against the interests" of ASA, and replace them with people of their own choosing. Later, the two peasant representatives on the governing body (one of whom had been a staunch Bhasani activist for many years, and seen by management as a supporter of Jahangir) were quietly dropped.

As a result of all these changes, ASA stopped presenting itself as a people's organization and acknowledged that it was in fact an NGO with a conventional management structure. It remains so today.

The story represents both a continuity and a break with the past. Earlier people's movements had been chronically prone to division and subdivision as individual leaders faced up to each other. Usually such splits led quickly to oblivion, because what had bound people together was irrevocably lost. But under new post-1971 conditions there was something other than brotherhood to make it worth holding the organization together—foreign funding, both current and anticipated, and manifested in offices, vehicles, a large and permanently salaried staff, and in prestige and public attention. Given the inherent instability of the original structure and the pattern of internal coups and countercoups so common among the voluntary organizations in Bangladesh, it was easy to argue that ASA's move from people's organization to conventional NGO—from brotherhood to hierarchy—was a step that ASA had to take to prepare itself for a more professional future.

Reform

The incident closed the transition from ASA's "foundation" phase to its "reformative" phase, to borrow ASA's own language.[3] Reforms were not limited to ASA's organizational structure: its work in the field also continued to evolve. But although it is quite clear what it was evolving away from—confrontation, political indoctrination, and social actions—it is much harder to say exactly where it was heading. Shafiq's own *ASA in Transition* claims that the new reformative phase was characterized by an "integrated approach," but a harsher judge might conclude that ASA was, in fact, in danger of disintegration during this period, as it dabbled in a long list of programs borrowed from other NGOs or inspired by its donors' wishes. This was the least satisfactory period in ASA's history, and there must have been many sighs of relief when, around 1991, ASA took a fresh grip on itself, pulled away from a motley collection of schemes, and settled for developing its financial services work.

One very important way in which this period differed from the "development as struggle" phase is in the quantum of funds provided by foreign donors. From the first receipts up to and including 1984, ASA had been granted a total of 6.7 million taka (about $335,000 at the rates then prevailing). Receipts during 1985 alone were twice as much as that, with HEKS providing over 11 million taka during the year. Receipts then fell back in 1986, to recover in 1987, and to go on growing for the following three years. This can be seen clearly in figure 1.

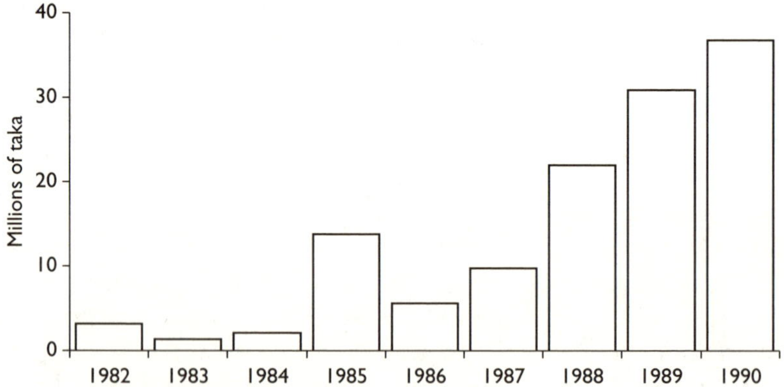

FIGURE 1 Grants received from donors, by year.

ASA never had fewer than seven donors during the 1985–90 period, and it usually dealt with each of them on an individual basis. As a result, its field program showed considerable variety, for ASA often set up in a new area, or modified a program in an old one, to suit a particular donor. This affected both the content and the size of the programs. Some districts were left plodding along with a milder version of the old social mobilization program, whereas others moved on to deliver services in irrigation or water supply, health, or nutrition, or took up "women's development," the dominant paradigm of rural development in the mid- and late 1980s.

However, the main causes of the sudden increase in funding receipts in 1985, and then again in 1987 and 1988, were natural disasters: first, a cyclone (known elsewhere in the world as a hurricane or typhoon) and then two years of flooding.

Ill Wind

On the evening of May 24, 1985, I was on the southern Bangladesh island of Bhola, busy taking delivery of plastic piping from UNICEF for use in a program of domestic water tube wells for poor rural neighborhoods.[4] The work was paid for by supporters of ActionAid, a U.K.-based NGO, and I was there as their representative.[5] In those days, international NGOs commonly ran projects in the villages: it would be another decade before they changed their strategy and contracted local NGOs to carry out projects while their own Dhaka offices turned to "advocacy" work. But the older system suited me: I could travel through the countryside and notice the work that other NGOs, such as ASA, were doing.

The launch from Dhaka carrying the material was late, and by the time the truckload of pipes reached ActionAid's field office, in the south of the island, it was dark and raining heavily. The radio had been broadcasting the likelihood of a cyclone for some days, but like most of the local inhabitants, we NGO workers had grown used to such warnings and took little notice. But when rickshaw-mounted loudspeakers started touring the roads, we went to the local administration office to find out what the Red Cross Red Crescent radio had to say. The news was serious: this was a big cyclone, and it looked to be heading straight for us.

Bhola had been in the eye of the biggest cyclone ever recorded, the one that delayed the 1970 election, when up to half a million people died. Memories of that night were still strong among ActionAid's local staff and their families. In 1970, there were no protective embankments, and the wind pushed a wall of water up to six meters (almost twenty feet) high across the level landscape and then, a little later, sucked it back again in the opposite direction. We were now surrounded by an earthen embankment, but it had never been tested. We headed to a solid masonry building, a local orphanage, for shelter. As the evening wore on, hundreds of people, mostly women and children, joined us, and this flow continued until about 8 o'clock, when it was impossible to move about outside.

The cyclone's course shifted a little to the east. For us the wind peaked at three in the morning, but there was no flood. The morning dawned clear, cool, and bright, revealing uprooted trees, scattered roofing sheets, and collapsed homes and schools.

Our relatively good luck meant disaster for others, of course, and we learned from the radio that it was the tiny silt island of Urir Char in nearby Noakhali District that suffered the direct hit. Some four or five thousand people died. But on the morning after the disaster, things looked a lot worse, and by the third day, one of Dhaka's English-language daily papers was headlining: "Death Toll Crosses 50,000."[6]

The national response to this, the worst cyclone in the new country's 14-year history, was enormous. Everyone remembered that in the November 1970 disaster the Pakistan authorities had made themselves even more unpopular in Bengal by being slow to respond. Maulana Bhasani had, famously, dropped his political work and gone to Monpura, the worst affected part of Bhola, where he comforted the bereaved and railed against Pakistan's hard-heartedness. So in 1985, by contrast, the authorities were quickly on the scene: Ershad was hosting a meeting of SAARC (the South Asian Association for Regional Co-operation) at the time of the cyclone, and he took some of his SAARC guests, including heads of state, with him on a well-publicized visit to Urir Char.

The International Red Cross Red Crescent had been quick to alert the world to the emergency, and international public and private donors responded generously. Among them was HEKS, who sent more than 9 million taka (about $550,000 at that time) to ASA. This was more money than ASA had received in the whole of its six-year life, and the organization was faced with the challenge of spending it on a new activity in which it had almost no previous experience: it had helped mop up after floods in 1984, but had never encountered a cyclone. In terms of ASA's programs, the 1985 cyclone, more than anything else, marked the start of the new phase of "development as delivery."

ASA was the only NGO to set up a permanent camp in the cyclone affected area, and it sent its cofounder, Anwarul Azim, to run it (after some indecision, Anwarul had left CCDB and joined ASA two years earlier). But because the extent of the disaster had been unwittingly exaggerated, there were problems spending the money. Though no one dared admit it in public, there was simply too much relief and rehabilitation cash chasing too few opportunities to spend it well. But to have refused the money, or to have sent it back, would have been impossible: it would have seemed an insult to the five thousand dead and to their bereaved survivors, and it would have been an admission that NGOs lacked the skills to spend money wisely. To have held the money back until productive opportunities to spend it arose would have been risky, too, leaving ASA open to the accusation that it was sitting on money that should have gone to the bereaved and distressed.

Finally, housing was identified as the best way of using the money: it was obviously a medium-term investment of value to local people, it was desperately needed, and it could be done fairly quickly. Several thousand bamboo dwellings were erected and handed over to villagers. The job was not without its problems. Getting supplies in bulk to a remote island area was not easy. Transactions that have to do with land and with building, in every country, are among the shadiest parts of an economy, and in dealing with officials and others, things often had to be "managed." There were hints of corruption. Nevertheless, the organization emerged from the experience with its reputation among other NGOs enhanced: it had moved from a rather obscure position, somewhere out on the "left," to prominence as one of the major operators with one of the biggest budgets in rehabilitation work. ASA stayed on in the neighborhood, establishing a permanent program there. In 1991, after the very severe cyclone of April 29, ASA sensibly restricted its relief work to the area, where it had staff and knew its way around.

Tossing on the Waves

Bangladesh, as Francis Rolt remarks in *On the Brink in Bengal*, is not so much *on* the Bay of Bengal as *in* it.[7] During an ordinary summer monsoon, seasonal shallow floods cover one-third of the landmass, irrigating the rice and jute crops. Roads and buildings are placed on low mud embankments and mounds. In a bad season, the peak snowmelt from the Himalayas carried by the two great rivers, Ganges and Brahmaputra, reaches Bangladesh from the west and north at the same time, and combines with heavy rain to raise the flood level above these mounds.[8] This happened in 1984, was worse in 1987, and catastrophic in 1988. A decade then passed before the next extremely severe flood of 1998.

The 1988 floods stand out especially clearly in the memories of Dhaka's inhabitants for two reasons. They went on for many weeks, and they affected central Dhaka like no previous or subsequent flood. In its wake, Ershad raised money to build an embankment that was not breached, even in the equally deep 1998 floods. My own office in 1988 was across one of Dhaka's main thoroughfares, the Mirpur Road, from ASA's office. Within a few days, the road went from being busy with trucks, buses, cars, and rickshaws, to being almost equally busy with speedboats, rowboats, and old inner tubes or anything else that could be pressed into service as a vessel. Carpenters used to making chairs and tables had a heyday turning out crude boats, fetching fancy prices. Householders strung nets across especially fast-flowing channels of water to catch fish, freed from overflowing rural ponds and rivers. I took a speedboat to Tangail town, some seventy kilometers northeast of Dhaka, and did the trip in a straight line, over the tops of submerged roads, dodging roofs and the upper branches of trees.

ASA again received special funds during and after the 1987 and 1988 floods, and was more careful about how it used the money. There was more house construction and reconstruction, especially in 1988, when work was concentrated in just three districts, corresponding to the areas funded by particular donors. But much of the money was used to provide flood victims with rehabilitation loans, usually in kind, but including some small cash loans. ASA had done this in a very small way after the 1984 floods, and it hadn't gone wholly unnoticed. Rob Gallagher, in a report prepared for the British agency War on Want, on the use of 1984 flood rehabilitation cash, pointed out that although most NGOs gave "food for work," ASA "stood out as an agency that did no cash for work but concentrated entirely on giving special emergency loans."[9]

I had read the Gallagher report and been struck by his comment. My observations after the 1985 cyclone had been that there was something odd about the conventional NGO reaction to emergencies. Their first instinct was to load up trucks or launches with rice and lentils from Dhaka and ship it down to the affected area, and then arrange to have these goods handed out in small, daily quantities to the victims. That might have been sensible if the local markets had been wiped out, but such wipeouts were rare. Bangladesh has a huge internal market in grains, and in normal times, millions of tons move around the country every day, and there are tens of thousands of experienced traders and carriers. After a disaster, wherever an NGO could take a truck or a launch, you could be sure that the normal distribution system would have beaten them to it. Rather than duplicate this normal trade, it seemed to me that NGOs would have been much more efficient if they had simply handed out cash to families. I had put this idea to a few NGO workers and been told that if the victims had been given cash they might have spent it on something other than food. The idea that distressed people might have needed things other than what NGOs were prepared to give them did not seem to be taken seriously. I had seen beneficiaries of such handouts taking their grain to the market to sell it in order to buy medicines or clothes or construction materials and, later, I saw the same thing after the 1997 and 1998 floods and the 1991 cyclone. So I liked what I read about ASA, and that is what led me to visit a few ASA branches when I was in the field, to see their work for myself. As it happens, I wasn't impressed: ASA in the mid-1980s, judged by a few casual visits, looked to me chaotic, ill-administered, and aimless. Grameen Bank, I thought, with its disciplined lending system, was years ahead.

In that ASA experiment with emergency loans after the 1984 floods, the loans were given to ASA samity members in affected areas, and were supposed to be repaid into the samity-owned bank accounts, to be recycled for the benefit of other members. Because ASA was not expecting to get the money back (and nor were its donors), not much is known about what actually happened. But because many of these group-owned accounts were not well maintained, and because members saw the loans, correctly, as disguised grants, the suspicion is that in most cases the money didn't revolve.[10] Moreover, Shafiq was still vociferously expressing anticredit views in 1984, and was unlikely to have paid much attention. As late as the 1986–87 ASA report (*The Counter Linkages*), Shafiq could still write in the foreword "ASA could organize about 1.3 million people in nearly four thousand groups and provided no financial inputs yet they remained steady and unwavering."[11]

The 1985 cyclone produced no further experiments with post-disaster loans because ASA had no previous presence, and so no samities, on Urir Char. The situation was quite different much later, in the disastrous "Sidr" cyclone of November 2007, as we shall see.

But the 1987 and 1988 floods saw further rounds of lending, and the experience changed ASA forever. If you ask ASA old-timers, "What was the most significant thing that happened to ASA in the 1985–90 period?" you will almost certainly be told about how flood victims repaid the loans they took as part of the flood recovery work. This took the organization—at least at its upper levels—by surprise. And so it becomes clear that ASA's antipathy to credit was based not only on the ideological premise that credit diverts the masses from their revolutionary destiny but also—and perhaps more so—on the fear that they wouldn't repay. When this fear turned out to be unfounded, ASA was ready for credit, as we shall see in the next chapter.

Meanwhile, ASA was trying out a wide range of other programs. A former staff member told me that at this time ASA was "tossing on the waves," and one of the governing body members remarked to me on ASA's worryingly "deep-seated lack of philosophy" at this time, and wondered aloud what the final goals were. If we seek an answer to that question by reading the successive annual reports, we find that the goals were evolving in a fairly steady direction. The vision in the 1985 report was, as we have seen, of "transferring power to the majority." By the time of the 1986–87 report, this had been softened to the "collective resistance against injustice and the gradual improvement of human rights for the downtrodden masses of the population."

The 1988–89 report repeats this formula, but in the preface Shafiq softens years of talk about confronting the powers-that-be when he writes that ASA is "engaged in rural development activities to supplement *and complement government programs* in diversified fields of upliftment for both the men and women of landless and marginal families" [my italics].[12]

As in earlier reports, there are descriptions of social actions carried out. But ASA now tries to play down their confrontational character, captioning a list of social actions by workers in the Habiganj tea gardens with the comment that "what was most remarkable was that all the bargaining or achievement took place peacefully with mutual understanding and good employee-employer relationships." Clearly, ASA was equally carefully maintaining its own peaceful relations with government and business.

A look through one of these reports reveals the diversity of programs that was going on. As a catchphrase, "mass education" replaces "social mobilization," and in *ASA in Transition* "development education for empowerment" is given pride of place in the description of the work of this period. Thus we find a Mass Education and Nutrition Improvement Program in one district, a Mass Education and Women's Development Program in another, Mass Education: Empowering the Powerless in yet another, and even Mass Education: Landless Laborers Development Program.

What this meant in practice was that ASA continued to use the group formation approach as its basic forum for interacting with the villagers, most of whom participated during their regular meetings in literacy classes and adult education. From each group of twenty to thirty men or women, five members would get a five-day training course in basic skills, such as cattle rearing or sewing. But only two members would go on to the consciousness-raising course (three days), the leadership course (four days), or the group management course (also four days).

Apart from this, members had access to whatever special program was being run in their area. For example, Australian Freedom from Hunger Campaign funded a women's program in eight subdistricts from 1984. The 1985 report introduces it with a quotation from Mao Zedong and described its aim as "overturning the passive, unequal role for women."[13] Elsewhere in a few subdistricts a conventional primary health program, financed by another donor, ran for a few years. A legal aid project was set up. Another donor gave money for "rower pumps," small portable pumps that can be operated by one person and can lift water from a canal or pond onto cropland: these were offered to marginal farmers on a credit basis. In addition, of course, there were the postcyclone and postflood recovery programs.

When, in the mid-1990s, we went to Narsingdi, northeast of Dhaka, to talk to staff and members, we listened to what ASA workers remembered of those days. Azizunnahar was one of six children of a middle-income farming household who married, when she was 12 and still in high school, a jute mill supervisor. She joined an ASA samity and soon became its chairperson, because she was the best educated. This meant that she went to the ASA office for training on samity leadership, and this in turn gave her the chance to apply for a job. She became an ASA group motivator in 1988. She looked after five samities. They had weekly meetings during which she helped the members learn to sign their names and discuss issues like women's rights and "the importance of unity." There was no credit, but she was supposed to get them to make a weekly subscription to a samity-owned fund, out of which the members could have taken loans. But management was poor, she says: both staff and members attended samity meetings irregularly, and the subscription cash was sloppily handled and accounted for.

Her colleague Shirin Akhtar, who joined ASA in 1986 agreed: she said that there were no clear rules or directives for the samities and as a result attendance was poor, and dropouts and samity closures ran at a high rate. Some closed because they simply couldn't rely on ASA handling their subscription funds safely. After the 1988 flood there was a new sense of purpose: ASA handed out relief and this, as Shirin put it, "helped members gain more confidence in ASA."[14]

There was little attempt to get people interested in social actions, and Shirin and Azizunnahar's recollections of the ASA of the late 1980s do not paint the organization as one committed to peasant-led rural revolution. During our conversation, though, one chilling echo from the old days cropped up. Azizunnahar told us that, a year after joining ASA as a staff member, she received a letter purporting to be from the Sorbahara (the "Have-Nots") Party warning her to resign from the job or face the consequences. Sorbahara denied it came from them, and Azizunnahar believes it may have come from a conservative religious group or from a jealous neighbor. She continued working.

Nurunnahar Begum, a samity member since early 1988, remembers her samity getting involved in protests. In one case, her samity chairperson managed to arrange a *shalish,* an informal public hearing chaired by village elders, as a result of which the husband of a fellow samity member apologized in public for beating her. In another incident, trainees in a sewing program, which included some ASA members, wrote to the deputy commissioner of the district to complain that they were getting less than their prescribed training allowance of wheat and cash.[15] The DC investigated, and they got compensation.

Nurunnahar ascribed these successes to the influence of her samity but she, too, complained of poor attendance by workers who rarely stayed for more than a superficial discussion about social issues. But her samity survived. It began to take loans, at first small ones at unpredictable intervals, and then, finally, in a more systematic way. It was running well when we spoke to her in 1995.

Azizunnahar, Shirin, and Nurunnahar were looking back from a position, in 1995, of considerable organizational strength. They may therefore be guilty of exaggerating the indiscipline of the period around 1988. But most of what they say rings true. Elegantly written prescriptions for Freiresque techniques of consciousness raising may look very convincing when they are read in the comfort of the head office of the NGO in Dhaka or by the donors in Geneva or London. But in the Bangladesh countryside, poorly trained, poorly paid workers who have just tramped through thick mud for an hour may be forgiven for a certain lack of subtlety in their approach. They will make sure that the measurable parts of their job get done: getting the women to sign their names, filling up the passbooks, and so on. The more ineffable parts of the conscientization process may not receive quite the attention that a thoughtful reader of Freire might like. Anyway, the children are wailing and the women have to get home to cook lunch. And so does the worker.

No Alternative

Credit played an increasingly important part in most of these programs, so that by 1990 there was a patchwork of different credit systems, in kind and in cash, for men and for women, with varying interest rates and repayment schedules. Meanwhile, there had been enormous growth in Bangladesh's specialist, credit-giving NGOs, above all, Grameen Bank and, to a lesser extent, BRAC and Proshika. The BRDB, helped by some foreign donors, was restructuring its cooperatives in many districts, imitating Grameen Bank practice and in some places getting close to its quality. A "samity" came to mean a group of borrowers from an NGO or government quasi bank. Among these, ASA's were weak and lacked discipline. Its members knew it, and ASA came to know it, too. In commenting on this phase of ASA's history, Shafiq's final remarks focused on the poor quality of its credit program. The "integrated" approach, he wrote, "takes much time for preparing the group members. Over and above this, there was no provision for a minimum standard [loan] amount for all group members. Several thousand group members waited for several years to get credit." Against this had to be set the fact that "people realize there is no alternative to credit intervention for increasing their income and thus reducing poverty."[16]

More to the point, ASA itself realized there was no alternative. What ASA did about it is told in the next chapter.

Chapter 6

The Turn

ASA moved quickly, though at first a little awkwardly, to microcredit. To soften the abrupt transition, credit was initially combined with development education. But after clear signs of success with microcredit, education soon fell by the wayside. Instead, ASA's motto became "self-reliance"—self-reliance for its group members through loans, and self-reliance for ASA through income from lending. ASA broadly followed Grameen Bank's microcredit system, but devised procedures that were simpler and more standardized and transparent, and that drove growth more relentlessly. Samity membership rose quickly, with little opposition from elite or conservative groups within the village. Branches were soon able to show that within a year, they could cover all their costs from loan interest income. ASA began to move away from grant support from donors toward more commercial forms of funding. By the end of 1996 ASA had half a million borrowing members and a billion-taka loan portfolio. Its transition to microcredit was complete but—more than that—ASA had found a program of action that suited it. Microcredit under ASA is simple, practical, measurable, and busy, characteristics that fitted snugly with the temperament of its founder.

March 1991

President Ershad struggled on through the second half of the 1980s, never managing to persuade Bangladeshis that he had become a true democrat despite a referendum and two parliamentary elections. In 1988, by amending the constitution to make Islam the state religion, he disappointed some who wanted to turn Bangladesh into a full-blown Islamic state and infuriated many more who were appalled at the move away from the secularism enshrined in the original constitution. Civic groups began to step up their campaigns for women's rights, and trade unions called for strikes to protest Ershad's privatization of state-run businesses. Bureaucrats, who resented the influence of the army, were apt to go slow on Ershad's projects.

Finally, in 1990 the student bodies of the two main parties, Sheikh Hasina's Awami League and Khaleda Zia's BNP, put their differences aside and combined in a vigorous and at times bloody assault on Ershad's regime. Ershad declared a state of emergency as vehicles blazed on the streets, but it was too late. His fall was brought about neither by a rural-based mass movement nor by bullets from army machine guns, but by an urban coalition of students and professionals and a lack of open support for him from the army. When he stood down in December 1990 the political parties, learning cooperation from their own student wings, agreed that a former chief justice should form a neutral caretaker government to oversee elections. The idea worked well. A vigorous campaign was fought, though to an outside observer it looked curiously as if the election was being contested by two dead men, for Sheikh Mujib's photograph was the main icon used by the Awami League on its posters, and General Zia's on those of the BNP. The election was held in late February 1991, and on March 1 it became clear that the BNP under Khaleda Zia, President Zia's widow, had triumphed. It was the fairest election in Bangladesh's short history and attracted massive interest and a high turnout. Irrespective of its outcome, its very success as an electoral exercise impressed many, and restored faith in parliamentary democracy.

The result surprised those observers who thought that the Awami League's superior organization in the rural areas would give Sheikh Hasina the edge. But some of Awami's policies had become less attractive over the years, and the league quietly began to downplay its commitment to socialism and to soften its perceived antagonism to business. Meanwhile, the Awami MPs accepted the results of the election, albeit grudgingly, and took up their seats in parliament to work with the BNP to pass a constitutional amendment providing for a parliamentary form of government. Bangladesh had good reason to feel pleased with itself, and for some months the country enjoyed a functioning democracy.

No Lack of Enthusiasm for Credit

ASA, too, was making a fresh start. In 1991 ASA became a microcredit provider. For an organization that began as a promoter of peasant power and had railed for years against credit, it was an astonishing turn. As late as 1994, Shafiq was still racked with doubt. In August of that year he told me,[1]

> You know, my heart still aches for those early days, when we dreamed of a peasants' movement that would take political power.... After the 1971 struggle most of us were primed for a socialist approach. I now find I am confused about these issues: am I a traitor? But I had no alternative. Financial services have proved to be easily the best way to help the poor. That means, easiest and cheapest to deliver on a really massive scale.

Faced with "no alternative," ASA turned to credit. As Shafiq remarked in that same conversation, "Being able to change course quickly was always our secret weapon. ASA has always shown an ability to adapt. But this has not always been appreciated as a virtue: I have often been accused of being an opportunist."

These misgivings were echoed by some senior staff members, though others were pleased. Darbesh Ali, the freedom fighter from Manikganj whose views we will hear more about later in the chapter, left ASA for a couple of years, to return in 1993. Sushil Kumar Roy, who had had to hawk cigarettes to keep his family alive during the 1971 struggle, had worked at BRAC before moving to ASA and had absorbed the public service ethic that began to prevail there. To him, the idea of delivering a basic service like credit appealed much more strongly than trying to foment civil disobedience in the countryside.

Shafiq himself made up his mind in 1989, and as usual his views soon carried the day. ASA convened a special workshop that year, and one of those who attended told me that Shafiq "didn't allow any lack of enthusiasm for credit."[2] After the workshop the move to credit could be justified on the grounds that it responded to genuine demand from grassroots workers and samity members. This was not a hollow claim: the Jahangir-Statzer evaluation way back in 1984 had articulated these demands, and although at that time management had been, as always, ready to listen, it had not yet been ready to act.

Now it was. To soften the abruptness of the change in direction, microcredit was initially presented as a supporting service for the existing development education programs. But at the same time, the phrase *self-reliance* was becoming important in ASA's discourse. We can get a glimpse of ASA's internal debate by observing the language used in successive reports. The report that covered the 1989–91 period was still largely couched in the old vocabulary of social mobilization and there were the usual lists of social actions. But for the presentation of ASA's objectives, the words were taken (unacknowledged, and slightly misquoted) from Professor Yunus's 1982 paper, *Grameen Bank Project in Bangladesh,* and begin with Yunus's oft-quoted objective of creating "a system to break the vicious circle of low income, low saving, low investment, to more credit, more investment and more income," putting credit firmly at the spearhead of the attack on poverty.[3]

In the next report, for 1992, there are no lists of social actions, and ASA's overall objective is restated: "to help the grass roots communities be self-reliant and make ASA a self dependent organization." Then the 1993 report appears to take a step back, readjusting the balance somewhat in favor of collective action, when it declares that "the individual capacity for self-reliance cannot be achieved without collective efforts."[4]

But in 1994 ASA's work is presented almost entirely in terms of credit delivery, self-reliance for samity members by using their loans in small businesses, and institutional sustainability for ASA by covering its costs with the interest earned on loans. It discusses the samity only in terms of its convenience and its capacity to guarantee high recovery rates on loans through the use of peer pressure: "Group lending among the poor is advantageous in many respects, such as group pressure, attending in one place regularly, lower cost of lending." The report went on to concede that "after several years of involvement with the poor ASA as well as its group members realized that their development is delayed," and worse still, "many ASA members decided to leave ASA and join Grameen Bank or other NGOs who are providing credit ."[5]

Clearly, something had to be done.

Microcredit

What, exactly, was it that these ASA samity members were attracted to when they deserted ASA to join microcredit providers like the Grameen Bank? Here, we will reconstruct how microcredit was understood at that time.[6] Later, we will discover other ways of looking at it.

When modern microcredit started—and most observers agree that Muhammad Yunus's 1976 experiments outside Chittagong in southeast Bangladesh that led to the foundation of the Grameen Bank mark that moment—its objectives and strategy were unambiguous and its working methods clear. It was created to end poverty. It was to do so by enabling poor households to enrich themselves by borrowing to finance the establishment and growth of small businesses.

The focus was very much on poor *households* rather than poor farmers. Grameen, rightly, did not assume, as most previous rural credit programs had, that villagers were farmers needing support for their agriculture. Landlessness was spreading fast in the villages, and many households supported themselves, precariously, through day laboring on other people's land or in nonfarm jobs in the market or in publically financed construction projects. Some ran small services, carrying people on rickshaws or small ferry boats, and others scratched out a living from small-time production of local goods—processing rice, making mats from reeds, or producing packaging from paper waste. Rural markets were full of tiny shops and stalls, and many poor men and women bought a few goods from a bigger trader and squatted on a mat in the marketplace to sell a handful of tomatoes, or cigarettes by the piece.

Because lending to nonfarm poor households had previously been thought too difficult, it hadn't been much tried: most experiments had been charitable and therefore impermanent and small in scale. Microcredit was to be different: it was to recover as much of its costs as possible by charging an affordable rate of interest on the loans and by discovering methods that would make its delivery cheap and its performance, in terms of the success it had in recovering loans, better than conventional banking norms. This could be done by collecting the poor into groups and requiring group members to cross-guarantee each other's loans. Material collateral was not taken—the landless poor simply didn't have acceptable assets to offer as collateral.

Grameen staff selected households for membership of a borrowing group by applying a means test based on land ownership and income. This was done to ensure that only poor households participated. A representative from the household joined with four others, all from different households, to form a five-person cell, and was trained to understand the rules of the bank. Eight or 10 such cells (40 or 50 people) met together weekly in their neighborhood in a gathering called a *kendra* (center), to which the bank sent a field worker. There were separate kendras for male and female members. Grameen began with as many male as female groups, but it found, as others soon did, that women made the best borrowers: they were available at home during the working day, and appeared to take their obligations to attend the group meetings and repay their loans more seriously than men. Soon almost all members were women. Each week, they made a tiny compulsory savings deposit, which was held in a joint account and could be used by the group members to help each other out of difficulties.

The main purpose of the group was to borrow. In each five-person cell, two members were selected to borrow a modest sum, usually not much more than a month's household income. If repayments flowed in as planned, then soon two more members and finally a fifth member would take similar loans. They borrowed as individuals, directly from the bank, but agreed to see to it that their fellow cell members repaid the loan in full, together with interest, on pain of having their next loan withheld or delayed. The repayments were weekly, and stretched over a year, so the installments (which included an element of interest at a rate that worked out to a little more than 20 percent a year) were very small and rather easily manageable, at least as long as the disbursed loan amount remained modest. As soon as a loan was repaid in full, the borrower became eligible for another loan, usually somewhat larger.

All loans were to be invested in small or "micro" businesses. That was repeatedly drummed into borrowers, though the bank left them to decide which businesses to invest in, and offered no training in business methods in general or in skills specific to particular businesses, though it did teach its members to sign their names. With repeated annual injections of capital, a little larger each time, the idea was that the businesses would grow, and eventually produce enough income to push the household up above the poverty line. Meanwhile the bank, if it was careful, could cover all or at least most of its costs from the interest income.

Subtly Pleasing

The keywords of this new antipoverty device soon entered the development dictionary. They were *loans, small businesses* (or "microenterprises"), *groups, joint liability* (or "peer pressure" or "social collateral"), and *women.*

Yunus's vision of microcredit had many features that made it attractive to development workers and donors, and he had promoted it skillfully. To donors, the program offered amazing value for money: grants given to fund the loans would revolve endlessly among the borrowers, with each dollar potentially reaching dozens of poor women. Compared to other possible areas of investment, it would be easy to monitor. Its use of capital to invest in businesses was reassuringly aligned with conventional (capitalist) economic theory, while at the same time its claim to be helping the poor to "organize" themselves to work for their own development was attractively "pro-poor," "participatory," and "bottom-up." The discovery that women made the best borrowers was a stroke of great good fortune: it allowed microcredit to be presented as very much in line with the "women in development" thinking then current. Better still, women, it was argued, are more likely than men to reinvest profits from their businesses in the family and its children. Its appeal to poor villages turned out to be immense, though, as we shall see in a later chapter, not quite in the way that was expected.

ASA's version of microcredit, when it eventually arrived in the early 1990s, a latecomer by Bangladeshi standards, followed this general prescription, even as it simplified and standardized it.

All Change

At ASA, as soon as management makes up its mind, things move quickly. The organization does not believe in agonizing or in piloting. There were two stages. In the first, in late 1989 and 1990, lending practices that had developed within ASA following the 1987 and 1988 floods were stepped up. Seniors were given big disbursement targets. Some, like Enamul Haque, now one of ASA's most energetic vice presidents, took up the challenge with confidence. Others, like Darbesh Ali, were less comfortable. But things quickly went awry, on two fronts. The good repayment rates that they had expected failed to materialize, and ASA began to run short of funds.

So disbursements were stopped as suddenly as they had been stepped up, and things stood still for some months as ASA restructured itself. Expenditure was pruned, and ASA staff saw even their provident funds tapped to ensure enough liquidity for the organization to run day to day. The predominantly male samity membership, the nighttime meetings, and the predominantly female semi-volunteer workforce were identified as the main problems. Accordingly, local semi-volunteer women workers were largely replaced by full-time, better-paid men recruited nationally and sent to work in areas away from their home districts.[7] The reasoning was that a man from out of town would be better able to counter opposition from the local village elite, and would not be able to abuse his position by favoring his own relatives and acquaintances with loans.

With a new workforce in place, ASA asked its male samity members to stop attending meetings and to send their wives or daughters to the next meeting, which would be held during the working day, allowing each worker to service up to three samities each day. This was in line with Grameen's discovery that women can be easily reached close to home during the day, and make better microcredit clients than men.

At the same time, management worked to remodel the microcredit product and delivery system. In this Shafiq took the lead role, and many of the early formats were drafted by him. There were departures from the norms set by Grameen, helping ASA to claim that its version of microcredit was entirely of its own design.

The changes were all in the direction of simplicity and standardization, with the aim of reducing costs and accelerating growth. This affected the composition of the borrowing groups, the loan product, the management system, and the logistical arrangements. Grameen's five-person cell, on which the main pressure of joint liability fell, was ignored by ASA. Shafiq, rightly, could not see the point of this complexity and went instead for smaller but seamless twenty-woman samities. (ASA retained the name *samity* for its borrowing groups rather than call them *kendras*, as Grameen did).

ASA greatly simplified both the loans and the savings. It standardized loan values to multiples of 1,000 taka. For each 1,000 taka borrowed, clients made 46 weekly payments of 25 taka. This totaled 1,150, including 150 taka of interest at the nominal rate of 15 percent (something over 30 percent annually), higher than Grameen's rate of 10 percent nominal but on a par with most other credit NGOs. Each weekly installment was thus a whole number and a multiple of five, and Shafiq correctly supposed that this would make bookkeeping easier and cut down the number of transcription errors. Savings were compulsory and standardized at 5 taka per week, and could not be withdrawn until the member left the scheme. All members were required to borrow the same amount, starting with an initial loan of 3,000 taka (about $75 at that time). The effect of this was that at each meeting each member paid the same amount: 80 taka for a 3,000-taka loan (including loan interest and savings at 5 taka). This helped to make the collection process transparent as well as speedy, and bookkeeping easy. Each evening the branch manager would chalk onto a blackboard the amount of money that each of his loan officers would be required to collect at samity meetings the following day, and loan officers would have to explain themselves if they failed. The blackboard is still in use today, an icon of ASA's trademark brand of simple commonsense innovation.

ASA upset critics by not having an accountant at the branch, and by not observing accountancy's traditional preference for separating the handling and the recording of money. But doing without an accountant saved money and contributed greatly to ASA's efficiency, and in the end even the severest critics were won over: to this day the situation remains the same. Shafiq, who is not an accountant, devised an extraordinarily simplified and elegant bookkeeping system that guides loan officers and branch managers smoothly through the accounting routines, including sending reports each month to head office.[8] The various cash- and check-handling tasks were shared out among the branch manager and his loan officers and revolved periodically among them. Loans are disbursed in the branch in the presence of all the staff, and each signs the disbursement document as evidence of their shared responsibility.

An ASA branch had a manager, four loan officers, and a peon (a messenger who may also cook), and each loan officer looked after more than three hundred members, going to two or three samity meetings each day for a six-day week. ASA branches serve fewer clients than do those of Grameen. Branch staff members are therefore closer to their clients, all of whom can normally be reached in a 10- or 15-minute bicycle ride. This has proved a considerable advantage in following up poor payers. The branch itself is a modest rented building, and its furnishings are specified down to the smallest detail in the ASA manual. A branch is allowed just one ceiling fan (type and cost specified), hung centrally above one table (timber type, size, and cost specified), around which everybody sits, including the manager. Normally, one or two rooms are set aside as dormitories in which the whole staff reside.[9] As a result, they don't need to employ a night guard.

ASA has maintained a very flat hierarchy. Whereas Grameen developed area and zonal offices that need buildings, furniture, and support staff, and generate paper of their own, ASA has always had just two levels: the branch and the head office. There are intermediate posts—regional and district managers—but they have to share their offices with a branch.[10]

Light in Our Dark Society

Although I had observed ASA's work for some years, I didn't meet Shafiq until late summer 1993. He was looking for funding partners, and I was called in by one of them to comment on his ideas for a self-reliant microcredit system. I was not very enthusiastic: the plans looked too mechanical to me, too dependent on villagers conforming, in their borrowing behavior, to a script too tightly written for them by ASA. But I liked the business-like ideas that lay behind the plan: that there were many opportunities to make cost savings in microcredit that had been overlooked by its pioneers, so that microcredit might become profitable without raising the loan interest rate above what was then commonly charged by most credit-giving NGOs, and in the end allow the NGO to fund its own growth through profits, freeing it from dependency on donors. So despite this unpromising beginning, we kept in touch. A few months later I accepted an invitation to take a closer look at his system, promising Shafiq that if I was convinced by what I saw, I would write an English-language account of it.[11]

A year later, in early October 1994, my assistant S. K. Sinha and I went to see ASA's Patuakhali program in southern Bangladesh. There we met Darbesh Ali, back in ASA and looking after one of ASA's biggest work areas, funded by Danish bilateral aid.[12] Darbesh's early life is described in chapter 3: he was the schoolboy from Manikganj during the Independence War who became one of ASA's very first staff members. He had come to ASA from the radical wing of BRAC, where he had pushed for more politically committed policies for helping the poor, so I was curious to know what Darbesh thought of ASA's new approach. His reply was thoughtful—this was something he had spent a lot of time pondering. He told me that the shift into credit was in response to the realization that social actions cannot be sustained by the poor if they lack the basic economic security that loans can provide. For him education and social action remained the fundamental tools that ASA should continue to use to bring about social transformation, with credit merely a means to an end. Still, he was clearly disappointed that the number of social actions had fallen off so sharply.

Darbesh introduced me to Shah Alam, a 27-year-old who had been recently promoted to branch manager after joining ASA some 18 months earlier and working as a loan officer in the north. Alam was only 4 when the 1971 war ended, and the perspective he brought to his work was quite different from Darbesh's. He had no politics in his background. The son of a fairly well-to-do farmer in central Bangladesh, he was educated at a local college and had a brother who worked for BRAC. When I asked him about ASA's goals, he said that their main work was development education, reflecting the orientation he had been given when he joined. As examples of this education work, he told me about the rising school attendance among the children, especially the daughters, of ASA members, and the increase in tree plantation by the members themselves. I nodded, knowing that under ASA's rules at the time, evidence of these two activities were conditions for obtaining a loan. He said, enthusiastically, that he thought that these improvements, especially girls' schooling, would have "a big impact on society." He thought poverty arose mainly from ignorance and underemployment. Oppression and social injustice found no place in his analysis, and he'd never heard of Freire, Fanon, and Illich. He knew little about his organization's history, but had heard that "originally, there was no loan program: instead, there was just adult literacy, the main purpose of which was to teach people to sign their names."[13]

ASA still teaches members to sign their names, but in Shah Alam's time in Patuakhali, his staff members were issued a book produced by ASA, *Jibon Gorar Notun Pat* (New Ways to Change Your Life).[14] It was composed of short messages attached to alphabetically arranged keywords. The first entry gives the flavor:

> R rights R I G H T S
> Women do not enjoy equal rights in society. To bring about your rights take up popular development education. Become conscious, make a movement, and make new laws for women's rights. When women and men are equal the country's development will be easy.

Other entries are rather more prosaic:

> A area A R E A
> Bangladesh's area is 143,998 square kilometers.

Reading aloud at least one of these messages, and getting the members to discuss its ideas, was a mandatory part of each weekly samity meeting: this comprised ASA's development education at that time. Alam admitted that it wasn't always easy to get members excited by these messages—members might tend to sleep or chatter through a session on Bangladesh's land area, for example. And because the credit work was so much more pressing—getting the repayments in and recording them, then moving on to the next samity meeting—loan officers (community organizers, as they were still called in those days) did not always give the readings from the book the highest priority. Their branch manager didn't push them: Alam thought that members were getting bored with the book.

Later that month in Gazipur, in central Bangladesh, I asked member Shamsunnahar if she felt that development education was the main function of her samity.[15] She didn't. "Credit is the most important part of our *samity* work. I've had three loans, of 2,000, 3,000 and 5,000 taka, and have benefited by buying a cow, goat, poultry and so on. No one else would have given me a loan."

But she wasn't completely dismissive of development education. Later she said, "As well as getting loans, the illiterate members have learned to sign their names. ASA helped them. The book is important: we have learnt about marital violence, dowry, illnesses and cures, immunization, and how to overcome crises by increasing our income, and so on." And her neighbor, Anwara Begum, remarked, "I have learned much from the book. We are more conscious of the state of our society.... The book gives light in our dark society."

Nevertheless, by 1996 reading from "the book" was on its way out. Members had tolerated it rather than demanded it, and there was no outcry from them when it went. Staff members found other aspects of their job much more demanding. And as the head office gradually gained confidence in credit, it no longer needed the "development education" fig leaf to cover its embarrassment at moving so firmly in a direction it had for so long opposed.

Shah Alam's Branch

But we are running ahead of ourselves. We need to see how ASA staff set up these new-style samities in the first place. In 1994–95 Shah Alam kindly let me follow him around and ask questions as he developed a new branch in Konokdiya village, Patuakhali. Konokdiya is a small market center with, then, a very poor road network linked mainly by canal to the outside world. Alam had been sent by Darbesh to find a suitable building to rent for the office, and he was living in it along with just two loan officers, because ASA, economically, waits for the workload to build up before sanctioning additional staff. Despite Konokdiya's remoteness and poor roads, ASA did not have the territory to itself. About a kilometer away from the branch, on the other side of the market, stood the Grameen Bank branch in its own purpose-built brick building.[16] At first, said Alam, there were some misunderstandings with the Grameen Bank folk that he generously attributed to his own inexperience: "I should have consulted them earlier: I didn't go and see them until we had two groups up and running. Some people told Grameen Bank that ASA workers were saying bad things about Grameen in order to get members. It wasn't true but it made things difficult."

Shah Alam had an excuse—he was very busy. He and his two assistants had spent their first month getting to know the surrounding villages. They had found several neighborhoods where Alam thought there were at least twenty-five "target" households: households that were poor, with less than half an acre of agricultural land, with some prospect of running a small business, and with a woman aged between 18 and 45 who could become the samity member.[17] He told me that he avoided the absolutely poor, such as those with not even homestead land, because such people "are too poor to engage in economic activities and they could become badly indebted to ASA. Besides, other members don't like to include them, for fear of repayment problems."

From Gazipur-based member Shamsunnahar I heard this same idea put the other way around—members were told by staff to avoid the poorest households because staff members fear repayment problems. Telling us about how her samity came to be formed, Shamsunnahar said,

> ASA field worker Khadeza urged us to form a samity. . . . She said the women in the next village had done so and had already had loans and had benefited from them. She said it would be good for us, too, and after making savings for a few weeks we would get loans and make much progress in life. She also suggested we picked members who are "not very rich and not very poor." A month later we made a *samity* with twenty women.

Shamsunnahar was married to an unskilled but regularly employed laborer and they had two-thirds of an acre of land. By the standards of her village, and even of Bangladesh, she was not very rich and not very poor.

Though he avoided the very poor, Alam was prepared to take some households headed by women—as long as they had a male relative to help them: "They can make good members. We advise them to use their loans for making things like mats that can be sold to people in their own *bari* who can then re-sell them in the market. Of course, if they have no male relatives to do this marketing then we can't take them."

At the end of their first month in the area Alam and his staff signed up their first samity of 20 women, each from a different household. One of them was Kulsum Bibi, the daughter of Yusuf Ali, whom we met in chapter 3. After that things speeded up, and they were able to form samities, from first encounter to registration, in less than 10 days. They had 40 samities, with 760 members, by the end of 6 months.

At the start of a samity's life, Alam set about persuading its members to behave in conformity with ASA norms. That meant getting them all to attend the weekly meeting on time, and a considerable amount of development education went into getting that straight in everyone's mind! Appeals were made to samity unity, ostensibly to further the common interests of the poor, but made more urgent by the workers' need to get everyone there on time each week so that the repayments could be collected and the busy loan officer could go on to the next samity and still get back to the office in time to write up the books.

When the first samity had been saving for two months its members became eligible for loans, and Alam was rewarded by being sent a further two loan officers. Then, as now, the decision to grant a loan was made in the branch by the branch manager, who had no predisbursement procedures whatsoever to clear with his superiors before he handed out the cash. Often, he delegated his decision to a loan officer, but because disbursement rules were cut and dried, there was little responsibility to delegate. As we have seen, loan sizes were fixed, as was the repayment schedule, and the rate at which subsequent loans increase in value. Savings were fixed. All members were eligible to borrow—indeed, were required to borrow. There was no loan underwriting (calculations designed to see whether the loan is a good commercial risk).

This unusual combination of extreme decentralization with extremely limited discretion is one of the cleverest aspects of the ASA version of microcredit: it allows ASA to employ staff members with modest educational backgrounds and without needing to give them more training than they can absorb in a 10-day on-the-job apprenticeship at one branch before being sent off to start real work in another. In 1988 when ASA gave loans in the wake of the floods, Shafiq signed off on every loan. Three years later young people with no more than high school diplomas were selecting borrowers and disbursing loans to them in cash as a matter of daily routine.

Good for This World

By 1994–95, when S. K. Sinha and I were visiting ASA's branch areas to talk to staff and members, there was already a rich literature on microcredit groups, which raised many intriguing questions about them. We wanted to hear for ourselves what ASA's members said about their samities—what they were for, why they were composed solely of women, and what the neighbors said.

Sitting and watching those early samity meetings, I often noticed how matter-of-fact they were. Member Shamsunnahar described a typical samity meeting like this, "During the meeting I first pay my *kisti* [her loan repayment: *kisti* is the Bangla word for installment] and savings, and they fill in my passbook. Then they read out the book for about fifteen minutes. Then I put my signature to the attendance register and come home."

Shamsunnahar's brisk description of her samity at work struck me as exactly right. These meetings are not social events, nor are they occasions for planning peasant revolution or female emancipation. They are business meetings, concerned with the getting and repaying of loans, and keeping records.

Members I spoke to had the simplest of answers to my question as to why they were composed only of women: it was what ASA wanted, and was the same in Grameen and other NGOs. Some went a bit further and explained that it was easier for women to attend than men, who were supposed to be out earning a living for the family. Almost everyone confirmed that they were careful to gain the consent of their husbands before joining a samity, and some said they had joined at their husband's request. Shamsunnahar's neighbor Rahima Begum told me, "The present chairwoman started our samity: I don't know the details of how she did it. I joined with the consent of my husband. The samity is useful for us because we can save and take loans. I have had three loans. . . . The kistis are paid out of my husband's income or by selling milk and eggs: there has never been any problem."

Her husband confirmed this: "I gave my wife's name for our economic development in the future. Before she joined I had heard about ASA from neighbors: that they give loans and you can make weekly savings. Though some people said the samity is not a good thing, I thought the loans would be good for increasing our income. So I let them write my wife's name on condition there would be loans."

Another husband who uses the loans his wife brings home and is anxious not to lose this convenient source of finance told us that "though I don't attend the samity meetings I keep an eye on it to see that no conflicts arise between the members."

Sometimes men were happy to take advantage of their wives' membership of the samities. One told us, "I felt it would be good for us if my wife joined the ASA samity: we would get some money and I wouldn't have to work so hard." But women members often made the opposite observation, noting that loans were good precisely because the weekly repayments forced their otherwise lazy husband to go out and seek work.

Despite such comments the women that we spoke to expressed no resentment that their samity membership unfairly benefited their menfolk. Most accepted the fact that they were representing their household, and that as head of that household their husband would decide what to do with the loans. ASA staff, at least in our hearing, did not encourage women to take a more assertive stance. Some members, like Mina from Narsingdi District, northeast of Dhaka, are de facto household heads, clearly in charge of its management and finances. She told us "this samity is very useful for me. My husband is not good at earning money, or dealing with it at all. Without loans from the ASA samity I don't know how I'd manage our household."[18]

In other cases the male head of household may be old or infirm, or away from home, so that both the membership of the samity and the control of its loans fall naturally to the woman. Kulsum Bibi from Konokdiya was in this position: she was married by then, with two daughters, but her husband worked in Dhaka, and she still lived with her parents. Her father Yusuf Ali was old and no longer working, and Kulsum ran the household.

The extent to which women controlled the use of the loans they took, and whether it mattered if they did, and the extent that membership of credit groups empowered the women, were all discussed vigorously by observers. A paper by Anne Marie Goetz and Rina Sen Gupta based on a field survey done in 1994, at about the same time as I was talking to Kulsum Bibi, stoked the debate, by coming to some rather worrying conclusions.[19] The authors suggested that women could be left bearing the burden of repaying, out of their own very meager resources, loans that are used, perhaps unproductively, by their husbands. Worse, they thought that tension in the household resulting from disputes about loans and their repayment could also lead to increased violence against women. Replying to their paper after interviewing a large number of women borrowers at length, Naila Kabeer found that women borrowers themselves overwhelmingly rate the benefits of being able to borrow as far exceeding any disadvantages.

NGO credit groups have sometimes been the object of criticism, and sometimes worse, from conservative religious groups. They dislike the way that group-based work brings women out of the home into a public space where they meet men outside their family circle, and they disapprove of interest-bearing loans. One such incident occurred when I was with Shah Alam. In late 1994 a local newspaper in Borguna in remote southern Bangladesh reported that an ASA member's husband had committed suicide out of shame after ASA workers had forced his wife to hand over her gold nose stud in payment for an overdue loan. An official inquiry revealed the story was baseless. The ASA member's loan was not overdue, ASA staff did not confiscate her nose stud, and the husband was heavily in debt to other creditors. But by that time the story had been splashed in a religiously conservative Bangla-language newspaper, and anti-ASA remarks had been made after Friday prayers in the leading Dhaka mosque. Hoodlums presenting themselves as righteous Muslims chucked homemade bombs into the compound of the ASA head office. Sensitivity about Islamic values runs high in Bangladesh, and anecdotes of this sort are a staple of newspapers. The 2007 book *MicroCredit: Myth Manufactured* is a collection of essays highly critical of microcredit.[20] Though its criticisms are from the left rather than from an Islamist viewpoint, the book's use of local newspaper stories (in English and in Bangla) makes it a good sourcebook for understanding the anti-microcredit tone of some newspapers.

Mindful of all that, I had pricked up my ears when Rahima's husband, quoted above, had said "some people said the samity is not a good thing." Rahima's neighbor Helena Begum, who had been a member of Rahima's samity for three years and been a good borrower, told me how her husband had suddenly told her to quit ASA: "After three years my husband insisted I leave, though I was interested to stay in. Some people had told my husband that the samity was bad."

She didn't say exactly what about it was "bad," but the woman sitting beside her said, "In my view joining such a samity is good for this world but not for the next. From the point of view of Islam such samities are very bad. The money this bank gives is foreign money. As far as I know our own country is poor and couldn't give its own money through the bank in such amounts."

But hostility from the pious is by no means the rule. Joygam Bibi, from another village in Gazipur, is married to an imam (the keeper of a mosque). A well-educated man, he gave us a long interview during which he told us the following:

> Some people have raised questions about whether an Imam's wife should break purdah [the South Asian (and not just Islamic) principle of the exclusion of women from public spaces]. Some even said "Imam sahib, you have let your wife join the samity without thinking about your future afterlife." But I replied that ASA samities are like educational institutions where the members are taught by an ASA teacher. It is a student-to-teacher relationship and I find no objection from the religious point of view.
>
> The biggest benefit is the loan money which we have used for goats, poultry and rice husking [preparing rice from raw paddy]. I do the marketing for the rice and we make a good profit. Four of my children are in school, madrassa and college and I have to bear their expenses.

Though samities have an overwhelmingly female membership, they are not in the front line of any feminist battleground. The role of women as the members of the samity seems to have been accepted by them on practical grounds, based on their availability during the day, just as men are expected to be the main users of loans. ASA women members may well enjoy some improvement in their social lives as a result of meeting together weekly, for many of them, especially those who didn't attend school, may never previously have experienced membership of a nonkin formal group. But because they meet quietly within the confines of a nearby *bari,* they rarely pose much of a threat to the traditional gender-based ordering of rules and behavior. Nor would the ASA workers, most of them men, encourage them to raise such a threat.

The ASA Self-Reliant Microcredit Model

We stayed with Shah Alam long enough to get an overall sense of the place of his branch in the ASA system of microcredit. As the manager of a new branch, he was left in no doubt by the head office as to what he was expected to achieve, and the resources he would have. Working at first with a small up-front fund of 50,000 taka to cover costs for the first few months, he was to prepare enough samities to produce 480 first-time borrowers in each of months four, five, and six of the branch's life, each borrower taking a first-time loan of 3,000 taka. This came to a total disbursement in these three months of 4.32 million taka. To fund this, the head office would send 1.63 million taka, just in time for the month four disbursements. The balance of 2.69 million (actually somewhat less because a branch begins to get back repayments from members very soon after the first loans are disbursed) comes from other branches further along in the process. In due course, Alam's branch would reciprocate. Branches need only that initial investment to fund all subsequent lending, assuming that members repay on time and increase the value of their annual loans by 1,000 taka each year.

Shah Alam had four streams of incoming cash flow to fund his loans and meet his expenses: the capital from head office and other branches, then weekly savings, repayments, and loan interest. Only the interest is income, of course, but that grew quickly when loans were paid on time: by the end of the year he should have earned, at 15 percent flat, more than 400,000 taka. That would be more than enough for his total expenditures for the whole year: rent, salaries and other regular branch costs, interest owed to members on their savings, interest paid on capital, and a contribution to the head office costs.

As it happens, Shah Alam at Konokdiya missed these targets, though through no fault of his own: there was a delay in getting approval for the transfer of funds for his region from the donor to the head office, a circumstance that made ASA even more determined to become truly self-reliant.

A chart representing the cash flows through an ASA branch for its first year was to become an icon of ASA, appearing endlessly in annual reports and press accounts of ASA's work. It still does. And so it should. Like the "blackboard," it sums up the single-minded, cost-conscious, and ingenious spirit of ASA's microcredit.

But of course for it to happen, everything has to work like clockwork. Members have to be recruited and retained, loans have to be disbursed, and repayments collected. Of these three key tasks, the last is the hardest, as any loan officer will tell you. This has a wonderfully simplifying effect on staff behavior. An ASA field worker's life revolves around avoiding *khelapi*—overdues. If he succeeds, he can feel sure that his job is secure and that as ASA, on autopilot, expands, he will be promoted. Shah Alam spent not much more than year as a loan officer before he took over the Konokdiya branch.

Similarly, for the head office, there are only three field-based numbers that really count: the number of borrowers, the periodic disbursements, and the repayments. Not surprisingly, these are the numbers that people in the head office most closely scrutinize as they come in from the branches each month. Monitoring, in ASA, is not complex. In the days of social actions, as we have seen, Shafiq worried, rightly, that donors would ask questions about what staff members were doing in the field. If your job is to encourage poor villagers to pick quarrels with their landlords, it isn't hard to find excuses for inaction and poor results. Not so in microcredit. It is simply not possible to be a lazy ASA worker and survive in the organization.

Fueling the Machine

To set this machine in motion, of course, ASA needed capital. It had some donor money on hand, and one might have expected that in moving into microcredit, it was motivated in part by the promise of easier access to further donor handouts. Although 1991 was a difficult year, grants from donors did begin to grow again. In each of 1992 and 1993 ASA received about 67 million taka from donors, compared with the peak during the development-as-delivery period of 37 million in 1990. But in 1994 donor grants shrank again, to 31 million, and by that time ASA was looking elsewhere for funds.

An early hint that *self-reliance* was intended to mean that ASA could get by without any donor grants at all came in the 1992 annual report, which contained this surprisingly frank admission from Shafiq that dependence on generous foreign donors has not always been a good thing for NGOs like ASA: "Learning from experience it has been perceived that dependency on external resources reduces efficiency and quality. As the intervention of foreign fund has come to an easy exercise for the NGOs so people get wages out of less effort. In many cases people are found to feel alienated towards their responsibility."[21]

Seven years later, in 2001, ASA accepted its last, very small donor grant. The total amount of grant money that remains on ASA's balance sheet now, in 2008, is 750 million taka, less than 3 percent of all funds it uses for its lending. Donor money was absolutely critical to ASA's early survival and growth, but soon after the turn to profitable microcredit its continuing importance diminished sharply.

ASA was lucky (or perhaps shrewd), though, that its turn to microcredit coincided with a peak in microcredit's reputation as an almost magical antipoverty device. PKSF (Polli Karma Sahayek Foundation) a government financed fund, soon heavily supported by the World Bank, was set up to lend to credit-giving NGOs in 1991, just when ASA most needed support.[22] ASA was one of the earliest, and for some time the biggest, PKSF borrower. PKSF quickly earmarked a large loan for ASA, and charged the modest interest rate of 4.5 percent a year. By the time Shah Alam finished his first year at Konokdiya, ASA had already drawn down 97.6 million taka from PKSF and used it to finance 46 additional branches. Later, much more was to come from PKSF. But by then a more secure and, in the end, a much bigger source became available, as we shall see in the next chapter.

ASA also tried bank borrowing. Indeed, it was a pioneer of this, securing in 1995 the first fully commercial loan to a Bangladesh microcredit NGO by a commercial bank. It struck a deal with Agrani Bank to take 10 million taka ($250,000) priced at 9 percent a year, securing the loan with its Dhaka head office buildings.[23] This 9 percent was a commercial rate: Agrani had good collateral in the form of real estate and bore none of the risks of lending the money on to ASA's members. The deal helped to establish ASA's reputation as an especially businesslike NGO, and at the time there was an expectation of more such loans. But other sources materialized, and since 2001 ASA has had no bank loans at all in the composition of its funds.

When the World Goes That Way

In December 1996 there were more than half a million borrowing members, served by five hundred branches, and the value of loans outstanding had surpassed 1 billion taka for the first time. ASA's turn to microcredit was complete, and it was already challenging Proshika for third place in the rankings of Bangladeshi microcredit, behind the leaders, Grameen Bank and BRAC. Not only had ASA abandoned all other work, it felt comfortable with itself in a way that Shafiq had hoped for but never quite achieved since he created ASA eight years earlier. Shafiq is above all a practical man, a doer. He prizes action, output, and growth above all else. He believes in doing what can be done, rather than struggling and failing to do something that might in theory be more worthwhile. Reflecting on ASA's history, he said to me in 2008, "the problem is that—you see, Stuart, I consider myself a realistic man—if the world is going in a certain way you can remain a very good person by keeping your own lamp in your own hand, but it may not help anybody very much. So in that situation I prefer to set my philosophy aside and try to get stuck in and do something practical to help the poor."[24]

He had been endlessly frustrated and impatient at the slow progress of "social actions" and unhappy with the heterogeneity of the "delivery" strategies. He hated being dependent on donors. With microcredit he had discovered something that exactly suited his temperament, talents, and ambitions. A natural simplifier, he was suspicious of any trend to make microcredit mysterious. He would listen politely to elaborate theories about microcredit, and ignore them. He knew from his own work that poor people wanted microcredit and he accepted the prevailing view that they benefited from it. This was, for Shafiq, sufficient justification for getting on with it. A natural organizer, he resisted all attempts to make microcredit appear as if it were anything more than getting loans out and repayments in, and structured ASA to focus narrowly on success in those two key tasks.

In 1996 Shafiq was nearing 50. His second son, Ariful Haque Choudhury, had been born in 1985, and his third, Ashiful Haque Choudhury, in July 1990. The ASA governing body voted to award him a comfortable, though still modest, salary, and he had moved into a house that he had built in a mid-market residential area not far from the ASA office. He spent his days in the office monitoring the numbers that flowed in from the field, and dedicated himself full time to turning ASA into a machine for growth.

Chapter 7

The Decade of Growth

Bangladesh held on to its democracy until 2006. The 1996–2006 period was one of rapid economic growth, and poverty continued to decline. Microcredit was among the fastest growing parts of the economy, and ASA was the fastest growing of the big microcredit providers. Over the period, *microcredit* evolved into *microfinance,* as savings and insurance products began to be offered alongside credit. ASA achieved its ambition of self-reliance: it stopped taking grants from donors, sharply cut down its borrowings from PKSF, and became so profitable that its accumulated surpluses financed two-thirds of its massive loan portfolio. Virtually all of this growth was based on its unchanging core product, the simple annual loan repaid in weekly installments. But ASA was quick to learn from the behavior of its clients, and its understanding of the basics of microcredit evolved rapidly. It did away with joint liability as soon as it found it was ineffective, and developed more practical methods to ensure good collection rates on loans. It learned how to harness savings to satisfy client demand and at the same time to protect its loans. It soon understood that microloans are multipurpose credit that borrowers use for a wide range of uses. Microfinance responds not so much to a demand for capital to invest in microenterprises as to a demand for reliable ways to manage money. That is what makes it so popular, and makes the market for microfinance seem boundless. ASA thrives on it.

March 1996

The successful elections of 1991 had led people to hope that Bangladesh had fully returned to democratic politics. Particularly encouraging was the way the two main parties had used the debating chamber to discuss and pass the constitutional amendment to set up the parliamentary system. But the Awami League soon despaired of achieving anything in parliament. It boycotted its sessions and moved politics back to the streets. Claiming that Khaleda Zia's government had become illegitimate, it called for the next general election to be held early, under a neutral caretaker administration. Because the government would have none of this, Awami launched a series of *hartals*—strikes enforced by thugs that shut down the capital. Then in 1994, the Awami MPs resigned en masse from parliament. Khaleda Zia brazened it out, and it wasn't until the end of 1995 that she dissolved parliament and scheduled an election for February 1996. But the opposition parties refused to take part, and the election was a farce: very few voters turned up. Khaleda and her Bangladesh Nationalist Party (BNP) had no option but to agree to fresh elections under a caretaker administration led by Habibur Rahman, former chief justice. The February parliament met just once, against a background of continuing street disturbances, to set up the mechanism for the neutral administration.

On March 30, 1996, Khaleda Zia stepped down as prime minister and handed over to Rahman. The election that he organized was seen, like its predecessor in 1991, as credible, and this time the Awami League took most seats and formed the next government. Once again Bangladesh's democratic future looked bright. Despite months of mayhem, this had been the first transfer of power from one elected government to another, and the high turnout had shown that voters liked the idea of being able to choose between two major political parties who were fairly evenly matched.

The party in power changed, but the political standoff didn't. Soon, the BNP opposition was behaving just as the Awami League had done. It boycotted parliament and went to the streets with demonstrations and hartals. It declined to take part in by-elections and called for the general election to be brought forward. But the Awami government was as determined as the BNP had been to hang on to the end of its elected term. This time around, at least there was no "mock" election preceding the real one: in July 2001, Awami handed over to another caretaker government headed by yet another former chief justice, who arranged elections in October of that year. The electorate understood that no matter how shallow democracy becomes, at least it gives you a chance, every few years, to throw the incumbents out. It did so. Awami had to step down, and the BNP, still led by Khaleda Zia, came back to power. In another rerun of the events of 1996, the MPs on the losing side, this time Awami, alleged that the elections had been rigged, sulkily declared they wouldn't take their seats, but soon did so.

But even then, after three successive democratic elections, the two parties were unable to function as government and loyal opposition. The leadership of the BNP and of the Awami League had become more bitterly opposed than ever. So, in the aftermath of the 2001 election politics returned quickly to "normal": the Awami-led opposition boycotted parliament, took no part in by-elections, declared the government illegitimate, and called for a "movement" to overthrow it. This time there was a serious collapse of law and order, and the fact that both sides of the political divide blamed the other for patronizing gangsters seemed to confirm the public's impression that the violence was politically engineered. The government brought the army onto the streets and in 2004 created a new force, the Rapid Action Battalion, or RAB. Clothed in black, armed, and mounted on powerful motorbikes or pickups, RAB terrified, alike, the criminal and the law-abiding, though at first it was quite popular among shopkeepers and small businesspeople, who found that extortion rackets and other forms of small-scale lawlessness declined.

The good news for Bangladesh was that throughout the period of the three elected governments (1991–2006) there was economic growth. Indeed, it accelerated as time went by. A new industry, ready-made garments for export, blossomed, creating hundreds of thousands of low-paying jobs, especially for women. More and more Bangladeshis, including women, got jobs abroad, and remittances swelled, noticeably changing the look of some villages on the receiving end. Surveys showed that the number of households living in poverty was falling, with those living in extreme poverty dropping the most sharply. In the villages I no longer saw large numbers of children with the outward signs of malnutrition that I had seen when I first came to Bangladesh in 1983. Infrastructure improved, though the ports remained chaotic and the roads were overwhelmed by the rise in the number of vehicles, especially in Dhaka.

The annual improvement in the country's GDP—the value of all the goods and services it produces in each year—edged up until it reached 6 percent in 2004, and then stayed at that level. This is a pace fast enough to be noticed, and it was noticed. Dhaka had a building boom, with apartments, offices, and modern shopping centers rising all over the city, and factories spreading along the main highways miles out into the countryside. Agriculture grew, but the countryside also contributed massively to economic expansion by exporting its labor to the garment and other factories in the cities, and to jobs overseas, particularly in the Gulf area and Southeast Asia. As a result, many rural households that a decade or two earlier had been almost wholly dependent on the land, now enjoyed a mixture of income from farming, small trading, and remittances from the cities or from abroad. Villages that didn't have a tradition of sending its sons and daughters away to work began to have a bleak and old-fashioned air, and microcredit schemes fared less well in them.

The Microcredit Boom

Microcredit was one of the fastest growing sectors of the economy. Of the four biggest microcredit providers, who between them held 80 percent of the market, Proshika began to fade after it fell into political difficulties: it had let itself become identified with the Awami League, and the post-2001 BNP government pursued it, jailing its head for a time and blocking the receipt of its international funding. ASA, starting from behind, grew fastest, so that by 2007 it had caught up with Grameen and BRAC in the number of borrowers it served. In step with the economy as a whole, ASA's growth was good in the second half of the 1990s and even better after the turn of century. During the Awami government, its borrowers tripled, from half a million in 1996 to almost 1.5 million in 2001, and then quadrupled to almost 6 million by the end of 2007. Even allowing for inflation—which was quite tame in the period—members tended to borrow in larger amounts, so that the value of loans outstanding grew from just under 1 billion taka in 1996 to more than 24 billion in 2007 (equivalent to about U.S. $350 million) with an average annual growth rate of 32 percent in the years from 2001 to 2006. Savings also grew quickly. The number of branches and the number of staff members grew, but at a slower pace, showing that ASA was benefiting from economies of scale: at the end of 2007 there were 3,300 branches and a staff of 25,000. As a result, annual surpluses grew faster than anything else, from 28 million taka in 1996 to 2.9 billion taka (about $42 million) in 2007.

Throughout, these surpluses were speedily and relentlessly plowed back into growth, the habit at the heart of ASA's strategy. In 2001, the first urban branches were opened, and when it became clear that ASA's service appealed as much to the urban poor as to villagers, the number of branches in towns grew rapidly. On-time repayment rates remained at very high levels, and there were no internal events and only one external event that threatened this sustained performance: in 2004, another year of uncommonly deep flooding, portfolio growth slipped to just below 20 percent. It was a decade of uninterrupted growth.

Self-Reliant Indeed

ASA had achieved its ambition of becoming a self-reliant micro-credit provider. The extent of its self-reliance is best illustrated by examining the *composition* of ASA's funds: in other words, by asking the question, where does all that money that ASA lends to its members come from?

The composition of ASA's funds at the end of 1996, which is where we left ASA at the close of the previous chapter, is shown in figure 2.[1]

The single biggest source was the savings that ASA had on deposit from members: members were by then already the biggest financiers of their own loans. Next in value were the grants from donors that ASA still had on its books. Loans, almost all from PKSF, also contributed significantly. "Retained earnings" is accumulated surpluses (they would be called profits if ASA were a business rather than an NGO) made up of what was left of ASA's earnings from interest charged on loans to members after all its expenses had been paid for. It had just, for the first time, risen to become the

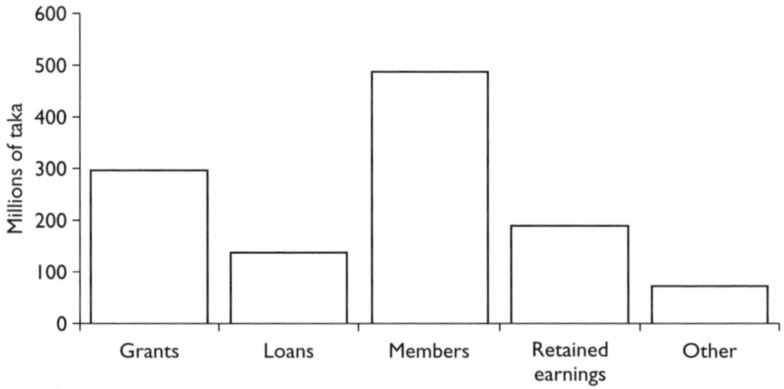

FIGURE 2 Composition of loan sources at the end of 1996. (Note that figures 2 and 3 are not drawn to the same vertical scale.)

third biggest source of funds. The picture had been transformed by the end of 2006, when it stood as shown in figure 3.

The value of grants had in fact increased, but the *share* of grants in the very much bigger total had shrunk into insignificance. The same was true of loans. Members' savings (of all sorts—including the security fund deposits that we will hear about in this chapter) had swelled by more than twelvefold. But by far the biggest component of ASA's funds was its retained earnings—its "own" money. That now stood at more than 13 billion taka—equivalent to about $193 million, financing a huge 62 percent of the 24.2 billion taka's worth of loans outstanding to samity members. To own outright almost two-thirds of a large loan portfolio is a very powerful index of self-reliance indeed.

There were several turning points in this story. One occurred in 2001, when ASA stopped taking grants from donors. ASA is, of course, still benefiting from the use of the money that was gifted to it, which is why, when its results are strictly assessed by microcredit accountants for the purpose of comparing ASA's performance with that of other providers, its profitability is adjusted down a little, to compensate for this use of costless funds. But because

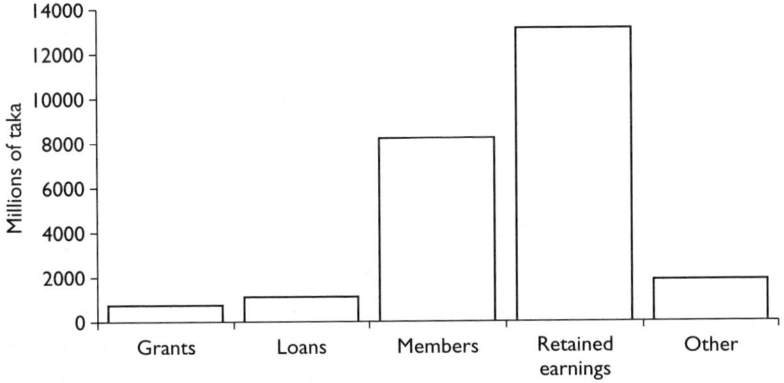

FIGURE 3 Composition of loan sources at the end of 2006. (Note that figures 2 and 3 are not drawn to the same vertical scale.)

ASA has taken no new grants since 2001, and because the fraction of grants in the composition of its funds is so small, the effect is tiny and does not undermine ASA's claim to be a fully self-sustaining profitable operator.

Another turning point came in 2003. In that year, ASA decided to take no more loans from PKSF. It could afford to. Although borrowing from PKSF peaked in 2003, at 3.5 billion taka, that was also the year in which retained earnings became the biggest source of ASA funds. The withdrawal from PKSF came after several years in which PKSF drew ever-larger funds from the World Bank, and ASA in turn borrowed more and more, though at the higher price of 7 percent per year. But then PKSF set a cap on the interest rate that its partners should charge when they lend its money on to group members. Unwilling to have its interest rate policy dictated by others (a luxury you can afford if you really are "self-reliant"), ASA decided to repay PKSF and take no fresh loans from that source. By the end of 2006 it held only a billion taka of PKSF money, and now holds almost none at all.

Supercharged by Overcharging?

If PKSF, a respected World Bank–backed microfinance body, wanted ASA to reduce the interest it charged its samity members, does that suggest that ASA was overcharging, "gouging" its poor borrowers, getting fat and profitable through usury? Not unless we believe that microcredit interest rates in general in Bangladesh have been usurious. When we were with Shah Alam in Patuakhali in 1994, we saw that ASA was charging a flat (or nominal) rate of 15 percent, equivalent to about 32 percent a year. Soon after, the rate came down to 12.5 percent flat. After deep floods in 1998 it rose again to 15 percent, and then returned to 12.5 percent in early 2007. This puts ASA on a par with most microcredit providers in Bangladesh, though the Grameen Bank has always charged less.

ASA's unusually high profitability, then, is due to other factors, above all greater efficiency, and not to abnormally high prices. In fact, Bangladesh's microcredit interest rates are quite low by international standards. In other countries, especially where labor costs are much higher than in Bangladesh, rates can be as high as 100 percent a year. At around 28 percent a year, ASA's current rate is in the range that some banks charge for unsecured loans in developed countries like the United States, and American credit card rates can soar even higher.

Nevertheless, ASA's most recent numbers are eye-catching. As it reaps the benefits of scale, with no need to make expensive changes to its system, it is able to pocket a large share of the interest income after paying for all costs. Accumulated net surpluses (retained earnings) grew by 58 percent in 2003, 48 percent in 2004, 38 percent in 2005, and 34 percent in 2006: in 4 years they had grown five times bigger. ASA's policy has always been to invest all these profits, as quickly as possible, in new branches. But at these rates of growth the time must come when there is simply no room left for expansion. That point may now have been reached, and, as we shall see in a later chapter, deciding what to do with all its money is set to become a big issue for ASA.

Learning Microfinance

Growth in ASA was not confined to its financial and operating numbers. Its understanding of microcredit also grew at a rapid pace. Some of this new knowledge was surprising, even counterintuitive, but that didn't put ASA off its sharply marked-out course. Throughout the growth period, up to today, the great bulk of ASA's business has been in its core product: the simple annual loan disbursed to women members of samities and repaid in weekly installments. ASA has used its learning to fortify this core product, rather than to modify it. Though Shafiq earned a well-deserved reputation for straight talking and for revealing in an unusually frank way some of microcredit's secrets, his public pronouncements have been consistent. Over and over again he has stressed his practical message of how to do microcredit well: how to cut costs, how to simplify and standardize, how to make sure you get the loans out and the repayments in, and how to turn a deaf ear to those who would otherwise get you to waste your time and money on unnecessary training, or complicated systems, or self-indulgent theorizing.

Unzipping

One of the first things that ASA discovered was that the idea behind joint liability is flawed. Shafiq was the first microcredit leader to go public with this truth: perhaps, as a relative newcomer to microcredit, ASA had less institutional prestige invested in its mystique and it cost it less to admit that what it had taken to be one of the very foundations of the industry had fatal cracks.

Shah Alam, the branch manager in Patuakhali, found that samity members did not include the very poorest households out of fear that they would not be able to repay their loans, and that ASA's enforcement of joint liability would threaten their own resources and their own access to further loans. Enthusiasts of joint liability would have viewed this behavior of Alam's members as an example of joint liability at work: keeping out households unlikely to be good borrowers is good for everyone. Economists saw joint liability as a way of overcoming the information problem that all lenders face: the fact that it's hard to know enough about borrowers to ensure that they will repay the loan. It costs money to gather information, and if loans are very small, earnings on them are too small to cover those costs. Joint liability, it was theorized, cleverly got around this difficulty by offloading the information problem to the borrowers themselves. After all, in a village, one's neighbors should be the best judges of whether one is honest, hard-working, and capable of running a small business. If neighbors knew that their own prospects for getting a loan depended on the repayment success of their fellow borrowers, they would take care to ensure that each other's businesses were sound. They would therefore be choosy about whom they would admit to their group, think carefully about how big a loan each member could handle, and monitor the progress of the businesses carefully. The theory was elaborated, with appropriately incomprehensible algebra, in a number of economic journals.

Joint liability was more than elegant theory. It was a straightforward idea that was easily grasped by millions of Bangladeshi villagers. In Patuakhali, Nur Banu, an ASA member in Gerakhali village, told us, "We formed the samity with women whose economic status was a bit better—that is those who would be able to repay regularly. We took M's [the ASA worker's] advice. We didn't include the very poor because they wouldn't be able to pay." Despite this precaution, "sometimes we had to pay *kistis* [repayment installments] on behalf of others, otherwise *sir* wouldn't approve us more loans."[2]

So far so good: joint liability had controlled member selection and then incentivized members to accept joint responsibility for repayment. But all this had a high cost:[3]

> These days the meeting starts late and everyone is reluctant to attend. There are many repayment problems. There is a lot of quarrelling about that. Problems began about a year ago, then became very severe in Ashin and Kartik months [the hungry season just before the main rice crop] because there is not much work then for the poor. There are only thirteen of us left now in the samity, and no-one is paying at all. I won't go any more.

Another ex-member, this time Parveen from Narsingdi, told us about her samity: "There was a rule that if any member left the samity without repaying a loan in full then we should all repay it. Three of our members left in this way and went to Dhaka. We had to pay all their arrears. We were expecting that their relatives would repay us but none of them paid anything. So then members became reluctant to attend."

Finally, the samity collapsed entirely. These were cases of what I have called *unzipping*. Members will cover for fellows in arrears if they believe that by doing so they are sure to protect their own access to future loans. Unfortunately, that threshold is reached only too quickly: if more than a few members stop paying for more than a week or so, others follow suit to limit their losses. The samity unzips.

Rajendra, the loan officer who had looked after Parveen's samity, told me, "Members don't like joint liability: they don't like being responsible for other people's business: we have lost many good members that way." This was an excellent observation. By enforcing joint liability, ASA was offending and penalizing its better performing members, instead of dealing directly with the poorly performing ones.

By 1996, Shafiq was telling international conferences that he had given up on joint liability. Staff members were told to exercise judgment in using it. They were even told that they could dispense with meetings as such, and just set up "payment points" at a fixed time each week in the village where members could come and transact. But with neither physical collateral nor joint liability to rely on, how could loan officers be sure of getting the loans repaid?

Getting the Repayments In

ASA set joint liability aside and figured out more practical ways of making sure it collected on its loans. It was very much helped by the fact that microcredit clients usually want to make their repayments. They value the service and look forward to further loans. There is prestige in being invited to participate in this disciplined, "modern" activity, and they want to show village neighbors that they, too, know how to interact with the educated folk who come from the NGOs to serve them. A microcredit group meeting is a place for repaying loans in the same way that a mosque is a place for praying and a school a place for reciting lessons: it's what one does there. This doesn't mean that every meeting goes as smoothly as microlenders would have you believe when they release pictures of smiling women happily handing over their money. There are many reasons why some clients can't or won't repay, and all sorts of behaviors are used to apologize for or justify the failure, from staying away to bluster. Loan officers have evolved ways of dealing with such situations.

Though Shafiq had said that strict weekly meetings need not be enforced, loan officers prefer to run meetings wherever they can because, even without joint liability contracts, they can still harness *peer pressure*—inducing poor payers to find their repayments by exposing them to the risk of criticism by their fellow members—and the weekly meeting is the best place to do this. At the meeting there are other opportunities to solve the problem. For example, a loan officer may be able to persuade a member who is about to receive a loan that day that, because she can afford it, she might temporarily lend money to another member who is short of cash. In the "moral economy" of the neighborhood it is hard for the better-placed member to refuse to give this help.

The meeting also provides loan officers with an environment in which they can use their superior status to good effect. Loan officers are male (most of them), educated, and middle class. Members are women, poor, and largely illiterate. Members address the loan officer as "sir," and sit on mats looking up at him as he sits at a table covered in a white cloth that the members have scrambled to put in place at the beginning of the meeting. The loan officer treats his samity members with gruff politeness, and if all the payments have not been made, he may be able to keep them sitting there until the money is produced. But what if these techniques fail? Then the loan officer has little option but to visit each house individually. For samities in which repayment problems are severe, this may be the weekly norm, for he may have lost his power to get more than a handful of members to attend the meeting. Because he has to get back to his office to take his lunch and write up his accounts, he may still be short of full repayment when he leaves the village. When that happens, he remounts his bicycle and goes back to the village in the evening, sometimes accompanied by his colleagues, and simply sits on the doorstep, embarrassing the debtor until he gets the money.

Some microcredit NGOs, especially those that have made much of "participation" and of the "solidarity" of their groups, are squeamish about this rather messy process, and prefer not to talk about it. But ASA believes that its performance depends on grasping nettles like these. Its monitoring system is designed to identify problems, and successful solutions to them, quickly, and relay them to the field. It is frank and clear when it instructs its loan officers how to use such techniques to maintain high repayment rates.

Microcredit: Something "You Can't Get anywhere Else"

When ASA turned to microcredit it believed that its members should invest their loans in small businesses. Recalling that period much later, Shafiq told me, "Oh yes: in those days we would even try to punish any member who didn't invest properly: punish means, for example, stopping her from having any more loans."[4]

ASA preached double self-reliance: ASA's via income from loans, and its members via income from loan-supported businesses. As the 1996 annual report put it: "Ultimately, ASA's 'Self Reliant Development Model' is only successful if its beneficiaries become self-reliant themselves. To achieve this, a beneficiary needs to continuously invest and re-invest in small businesses."[5]

This was followed by a table describing the cash flow of loans, investments, and profits for a typical member-run business. It was every bit as mechanical as the plan for ASA's own profitability. Escape from poverty by investments in small businesses was the standard claim of microcredit, and it has proved surprisingly resilient. But ASA's loan officers and branch managers soon found the claim hollow: they saw with their own eyes that ASA's loans were used for all manner of purposes, and not just for business investment. Management at some microcredit NGOs refused to believe the evidence of their own workers. ASA did, but kept tactfully quiet: it knew that international support for microcredit depended to a great extent on the "microenterprise loan" idea. But the next ASA report dropped the aspiration to make all its members self-reliant, and described a new kind of loan product, designed expressly for real microentrepreneurs. A few of these were offered alongside the core loan: an early indication that ASA had understood that the core microcredit loan was in fact a multipurpose loan only sometimes used for business.

We can shed light on the use of microcredit loans by reviewing what has happened since to some ASA members that we met during our 1994–95 field research.

* * *

We had last spoken to Rasheda 13 years ago, in Patuakhali. She had joined ASA at the time it was turning to microcredit. Today, Rasheda is still an ASA member, and her household still poor. She and her husband Safi Fakir, who have three children and Safi's elderly mother to care for, are uneducated and lack skills. Safi works as an agricultural laborer, and his earnings of 100 taka a day (about $1.50 at the market exchange rate) give them an average income of around a dollar a day per person for the six-person household when converted to dollars at purchasing power parity (PPP) rates.[6] That is a level that has recently come to be an indicator of extreme poverty worldwide, and used as a benchmark in the "millennium goals," a series of poverty-reduction targets that the United Nations is seeking to achieve by 2015.[7] But Rasheda and Safi also have a cow that gives about a liter and a half of milk most days, which they can sell for another 75 taka. They own a tiny patch of farmland—one-twelfth of an acre—on which they grow a little rice for their own consumption.

Rasheda hasn't escaped from poverty, but she doesn't see that as a failure of microcredit. She told us that "NGOs are very useful for the village poor. The NGOs made the life of the poor women very active. Many poor families made better progress using NGO loans. ASA bank is very good for me. I have been able to use my loans in many good works and I have become benefited."

The "good work" that Rasheda did with her loans included putting money toward buying the cow, one of several animals she has bought with the help of ASA loans over the years. Keeping a cow, an everyday matter for millions of rural Bangladeshis, with or without access to microcredit, may not be what you would think of as a "microenterprise." But NGO definitions of what counts as an approved "business use" of a loan have always been broad, taking in almost any activity in which some cash income is produced. Rasheda and Safi also used an ASA loan to release their land from mortgage. Technically, paying off a mortgage is "debt repayment," which NGOs have tended to frown on, but few branch managers would be foolish enough to try to talk Rasheda out of using her loan in this way.

Rasheda has been in ASA for 13 years, borrowing once a year. What happened to the other loans? They bought metal roof sheets for their home, a one-room, dirt-floored hut with walls made of woven leaves on bamboo supports. They stocked up on supplies, above all rice, their staple. A lot of loan money went on health care for their children: they may not have spent the loan money directly at the drugstore or the doctor's office, because the ailments may not always have coincided with the annual rhythm of ASA loans, but the loans would be used to pay back debts taken from family and neighbors at the time of the illness. The same is true of spending on festivals, entertainment, and travel.

* * *

We next looked for Kulsum Bibi. Kulsum was born during the liberation war, and when we met her in Konokdiya in 1994 she was looking after her two daughters and her father, Yusuf Ali, while her husband worked in Dhaka. Kulsum is still in the village. Her father has died, but her husband, Sadar Ali, is back from Dhaka, now in his mid-fifties, working occasionally but in poor health after many years laboring on construction sites. They had three more girls, and so far only her first daughter, Mariom, is married. Marriage is very expensive in Bangladesh, and a major strain on a household's economy. Kulsum said she was "passing [her] time with serious anxieties." She told us at once that she'd left ASA six years back, "due to financial crisis. When I found it would not be possible to make my weekly kisti at all [her husband had been ill and off work], I decided to close my ASA account. We had no regular income and still we have no regular income."

We commiserated, and more details came out. Kulsum's main problems were the irregular and unreliable income of her frail husband and the need to find husbands for the four remaining girls, starting immediately with Jasmine, now just out of school after studying up to grade eight. Kulsum commented that "among the women, those who took NGO loans, some couldn't make good progress because they couldn't use their loan properly. Now they are in trouble, like me."

Kulsum then surprised us by announcing that she had since become a member of both Grameen Bank and BRAC. She joined Grameen in 2005 and has had three loans from them, the biggest of 8,000 taka. Then in early 2007 she joined BRAC and took a loan of 5,000 taka. All of these loans were used to help repay private loans taken for Mariom's marriage. But she has four more daughters still to be wed. Meanwhile she has to find 320 taka a week to service her current Grameen and BRAC loans: her passbook shows that this has been a struggle, but now she has just 11 weeks still to pay to Grameen, and 18 to BRAC. She thought that with Allah's help—and maybe some help from her daughter and son-in-law—she might pull through.

When we put it to Kulsum that taking NGO microcredit loans had simply put her dangerously deeper into debt, she vehemently disagreed. "In this world nothing can be done without money," she said, and went on to argue that without the NGOs her choices would have been even fewer: "I would have to try to get more loans in the village, and if I failed then I would be quite unable to find husbands for my daughters. Then where would I be? It's easier to repay NGO loans [than private loans] because they make you pay back some every week."

* * *

In Narsingdi we found Mina, whom we gave as an example, in the previous chapter, of a woman who looked after her household's affairs because her husband was a weak manager. Much had happened to her. Her husband had taken another wife and deserted Mina and their son. Mina found a job helping in a pharmacy, did well, was taken on as a partner in the business—and then married her boss and had a daughter by him. As a sideline Mina delivers babies, and is known locally as "Dr. Mina." She has been in her ASA samity through all of this. She is paying down her current loan of 22,000 taka (about $320), at 500 taka a week. Most of it went into stock for the pharmacy, and the repayments come straight from its sales. Her husband has also taken a loan from ASA, and she holds a special ASA education loan that helped her son complete a degree at a local college. Her total savings and insurance deposits at ASA amount to a little under 6,000 taka. This year, she bought a life insurance policy at Alico, a foreign-owned company, and pays a premium of 4,500 taka every six months. We asked her what she thought of ASA's microcredit. "The ASA officers are friendly. I will continue with ASA so long they continue lending. All the NGOs are helpful for the poor households, because they give loans at very easy terms and conditions which you can't get anywhere else."

Serving a Basic Need

It would be a mistake to think of Rasheda, Kulsum, and Mina as examples of "moderately successful," "failing," and "very successful" microcredit users. Think of them, rather, as women whose lives have taken different paths but who have each found uses for microcredit. The Bangladesh microcredit loan, often presented as credit for microenterprise development, can in fact be used for any purpose. It owes that general-purpose character more than anything else to the frequency of the repayment installment—the kisti. Weekly kistis break loan amounts down into bite-sized pieces that can usually be found in normal household income, no matter how irregular and uncertain that may be. Repayment need not depend on business revenues, so loans need not be invested in businesses. In a careful review of 237 microcredit loans taken by 43 borrowers over a three-year period starting in 2002, I found that 112 of them (a little less than half) were used in what could in the broadest terms be described as business purposes.[8] Moreover, the business loans were taken by a small minority of the borrowers: I found that just 6 out of the 43 borrowers were responsible for three-quarters of the value of the loans used in businesses. Most were trading or retail businesses, like Mina's.

Mina, sitting behind the counter at the village pharmacy, does invest her loans in her business, pays her kistis, without difficulty, from business cash flow, and has pushed her loan value up to about $320. Hardworking, resourceful, intelligent, and cheerful, but with many hardships in her background, Mina is a prime candidate to appear in a heart-warming article in a newspaper or TV feature, a rags-to-riches story of how microcredit has helped develop a business, put a son through college, and generally hauled a family out of poverty and placed them squarely on the road to success in life. The story would be true.

But Rasheda, who'd done no such thing, has also benefited from her loans: they helped her roof her home, feed her family, buy drugs and treats, and make sure that there was always a cow in the cow house and that their small patch of land stayed under their control. Even Kulsum thought she might be able to go on finding 320 taka each week (about $4.50) to repay her microcredit loans and become eligible for more, despite her husband's poor health and irregular work.

Even now some people are shocked to learn that microcredit loans are not always invested in microenterprises, perhaps because microcredit providers have been so successful in presenting that aspect of their work.[9] But microcredit is simply a service that allows its users to get hold of modest but useful sums, usually worth no more than two or three months' household income, that can be repaid little by little out of normal weekly cash flows. Not surprisingly, they use the sums in whatever way is most urgent at the time.

From Microcredit to Microfinance

In the decade from 1996, a broad range of savings services found their way into the programs run by the big microcredit providers. To reflect this, Bangladeshis, like others around the world, were soon talking about *microfinance* instead of the narrower microcredit. There was much that had to be learned.

Savings in ASA were at first made in small, weekly compulsory amounts and could not be withdrawn until the member left the samity. That policy was either tolerated by members, who saw the savings as part of the price of borrowing, or disliked by them when they really needed access to their savings. Here is what Safia Begum, a member of Rasheda's samity told us in 1994:

> Last Bhadra month [August–September], when I had been pregnant for ten months, I felt a serious pain in my stomach. The doctor said the baby had died in the womb. I was admitted to Patuakhali Hospital where I delivered the dead baby: I was there for eight days. Much money was spent for all this. I thought I'd never recover. This was the most sorrowful and painful event in my life. But Allah saved me. I had to sell all the poultry and borrow money from the neighbors. During the illness, my nearby fellow members paid my ASA dues. I wasn't allowed to take out my ASA savings.

When medical emergencies occur, the poor in Bangladesh often have no reserves to meet the expense involved. When disaster struck, Safia got help from her fellow members, but not from her ASA savings account.

Stories like these multiplied. Then in 1995, members of some Grameen Bank *kendras* in the central district of Tangail staged protests about the bank's handling of savings. Many of them had been Grameen members for more than a decade, and their compulsory savings deposits had built into substantial sums. They felt they deserved access to them, and they didn't like the fact that they were held jointly, especially as the years went by and the composition of the group changed so that not everyone had contributed equally to the fund. The members involved in the protests refused to attend kendra meetings and stopped repaying loans.

Grameen responded, and it was an important moment for Bangladesh microcredit. Until then, the industry's leaders had maintained that saving services were unlikely to be attractive to the poor, nor be useful for them. But, following the Tangail protests, Grameen transferred the savings balances into individually owned accounts and agreed that current members could access at least some of their savings once their membership was 10 years old. It was the first step on a journey that has now put Grameen at the forefront of savings services for the poor.

By 1995 member savings, all of it then compulsory, was the single biggest source of funds for ASA's loans. ASA realized that it needed to avoid the problem that Grameen faced in Tangail, and that other microcredit providers around the world were to face. Once compulsory savings build up, savers want some access to them: and when their savings exceed the value of loans expected from the microcredit provider, clients may decide to leave the organization in order to get at their savings. How could ASA retain its members and still hold large amounts of their savings?

International advice was to move to voluntary liquid savings.[10] Besides being more useful to savers than compulsory illiquid savings, it was argued, voluntary liquid schemes reassure customers that they can get at their savings when they need them, and as a result they tend to save more. Figures from a large bank in Indonesia, the Bank Rakyat Indonesia (BRI), showed that poor villagers there had a high propensity to save when offered liquid passbook accounts.[11] In 1997, ASA went for this when it announced in March that thenceforth members would be required to continue saving at least 10 taka a week, but that they could at any time withdraw any amount in excess of 10 percent of their current outstanding loan.

ASA had been warned by one sympathetic international observer to expect an initial "great sucking sound" as members satisfied their long-stifled wish to withdraw some part of their savings, but that this would subside, to be followed by a period of growth in savings.[12] Broadly, that is what happened: withdrawals were fierce, but by late 1999, the average member was depositing two-and-a-half times as much as she had been in early 1997, before the rules were changed. But she was also taking it out again: the savings balance *per member* was exactly the same in December 1999 as it had been in January 1997. ASA had satisfied its members, and it didn't suffer from angry protests. But it had added considerably to the work in the branches and the ratio of its savings to its outstanding loans had not improved.

Finance director Azim Hossain found the experience stressful. ASA had planned branch expansion for 1998 on the basis of assumptions about savings volumes that were not met. PKSF lent ASA a little extra, but otherwise they were not in a position to get liquidity quickly from institutional sources. For once, they had to tell branches to slow down loan disbursement, putting branch managers into the rare and uncomfortable position of having to ration loans. Lessons, about planning horizons, about liquidity management, and about whether or not to listen to international advisers, were quickly learned. When it was all over, in 1999, Shafiq tried out some wry humor on me in his office: "All you experts told us that people would save more if we made the savings voluntary and let them withdraw. You, Marguerite, Imran, Bob, Graham, all of you.[13] And you were right! You were right! But we didn't realize that they'd also take all their savings out again."

But the members loved it. They now had two products at ASA through which they could turn small weekly amounts into usefully large sums. The loans still had pride of place of course: the lump sums were bigger. But they came only once a year. The sums formed in savings were smaller, but their timing was much more under the control of the member. The small amounts that they deposited each week could be extracted at any time, to deal with the daily needs the members faced. They were used to buy food when income was short, take children to the doctor when they fell ill, or buy a bargain when it was spotted in the market.

Another popular use of savings withdrawals was to make ASA loan repayments in difficult weeks, which is why ASA came to love open savings, too. Anything that made it easier to get repayments in on time was valued. So, despite open savings' difficult birth, ASA persevered with it, later making things even easier for members by allowing them to withdraw limited sums at the weekly meeting instead of having to travel to the branch office. Soon, it found a way to expand the extent to which it could harness savings to help protect its loans, by reintroducing compulsory illiquid savings in a new form.

Insuring Lives, Protecting Loans

In 2003, ASA opened a compulsory security fund for borrowers. This is, in effect, compulsory savings with life insurance included to make it more appealing. Each borrowing member is required to make a weekly deposit of 10 taka. The deposits are refundable, unless the member dies, at the end of an eight-year term, or sooner if the member closes the account and quits ASA. The deposits earn interest of around 4 percent a year, a rather modest rate with inflation now running at almost double that, but the deal is sweetened somewhat by a life insurance element. If the member dies during the eight-year term, her family receives an amount equal to six times the value of all deposits paid to date.

ASA does not have actuarial skills (skills to estimate cash flows, income and risk in insurance, and similar products) in house, and the calculations for the security fund are complicated by uncertainty over the rate at which members close accounts. It is, therefore, not yet clear how profitable the security fund will prove, and ASA is cautious about its cash flow projections. What is certain is that the plan has sucked in vast amounts of deposits. In fewer than four years, the amount on deposit grew to 4.2 billion taka at the end of 2006, easily outstripping the amount held in the short-term passbook savings. At the end of 2006, the average ASA loan was one-third matched by deposits.

The loan security fund was introduced in addition to a compulsory loan insurance plan that had been in place since the early days of microcredit. This older plan is debt relief on death, under which loans are cancelled on the death of a borrower in return for a premium of 3 taka for each 1,000 taka borrowed, paid at the disbursement of the loan.[14] This nonrefundable provision also brings in useful capital and acts as further security against loans.

ASA has not, so far, felt resistance to the security fund from its borrowers, of the sort that Grameen did in the mid-1990s movement against compulsory savings. When I ask members, as I often do, what they like and dislike about ASA, the fund rarely features in their answers. This is not because they are unaware of it: because it is paid at a fixed rate each week it is a very noticeable aspect of ASA membership. This suggests a number of things about member preferences. The first is very clear—they dislike collective plans: savings must be personal. Second—they want to be sure that their deposits are refundable, even if the term is conditional. Third, and this is perhaps a slightly more speculative conclusion, many of them actively welcome the fact that their savings hedge their loans: they don't want to be left with debt. Kulsum set her debts off against her savings when she left ASA recently, helping her make a dignified exit.

Long-Haul Savings

A fourth reason for ASA's members' acceptance of the loan security fund is that there has always been some demand from members for *long-term* savings. In Narsingdi back in 1995, Fatima Begum, one of Shamsunnahar's neighbors, had told us:

> I was a member of Shamsunnahar's samity for about a year and a half. I was a regular attender. I saved each and every week. Because I had no-one idle in my household, I didn't want to take loans. Then at the time of the third loan the ASA officer said that I must take a loan, and the other members told me that if I didn't agree to take a loan they would not allow me to stay in the samity. I left. But I would join again if they let me just save.

She saw ASA as a safe place to build up her savings over the long haul. Unfortunately for her, she was ahead of her time. Microcredit providers were interested in disbursing loans, and the few Fatima Begums were viewed as irrelevant. Few took seriously the idea that there is a market for long-term savings among the poor.

That was shortsighted. The not-quite-so-poor, middle-income Bangladeshis had shown a strong liking for a long-term savings plan offered by commercial and government banks and known as the DPS—the deposit pension scheme. Despite its name, it is not linked directly to a pension: it is a "commitment" savings device, in which the saver deposits a set sum every month for a term of 10 years, and then takes back the deposits along with interest earned. Savers saw the attraction of a scheme that served two purposes: you can use it to save up for some particular use—say, education or marriage for children, or land or home purchase—and at the same time enjoy the feeling of security that comes from the knowledge that you can cash it in if things get really difficult. Such plans have many advantages: just like ASA's loans, they break the job of building large sums down into small, regular bites that can be found from ordinary cash flow; they add discipline to the savings process, because you forgo interest if you miss payments, and they are cheap by comparison with borrowing a large sum. There was no real reason—beyond the knee-jerk idea that "well, poor people have no money, so how could they save?"—to believe that poor people would be blind to these virtues.

In the mid-1990s, some pioneers began offering an equivalent of the DPS to poorer households.[15] Others soon joined in: indeed, ASA briefly offered a version when it revised its savings products in the late 1990s, though that plan was dropped when the Central Bank made it clear that it was unhappy to have unregulated NGOs offering term deposits, fearing they lacked the financial acumen to handle the cash flows involved.

The DPS finally came to microfinance in a large-scale way through the Grameen Bank, an ironic development given that of all the microcredit providers, the bank was for long the most skeptical on savings.[16] But Grameen suffered a downturn after severe floods in 1998 dented its balance sheet, and it struggled to refinance its loan portfolio. It rebranded itself as "Grameen II" and recast all of its products for its members, including the introduction of new savings devices, such as a version of the DPS. It was popular, and attracted many new members to Grameen. Soon Grameen's balance sheet was transformed, and by the end of 2007 it held 140 taka of savings for each 100 taka it had out in loans to its members.

When microfinance providers introduced open-access, general savings plans in the late 1990s, their members began to enjoy two ways to build useful lump sums. They could take occasional bigger sums, expensively, by borrowing and then repaying little by little over a year. Or they could build sums that were much smaller but which they could get at much more frequently, through their savings. The DPS adds a third service: building large sums little by little over a long period. The shift completes the transformation of microfinance in Bangladesh, from microcredit to a full banking service for the poor.

ASA has taken note. It has reintroduced its own version of the DPS. But it is handicapped relative to Grameen because it lacks a firm legal basis for taking long-term deposits. As we shall see, this is one of several difficulties now requiring ASA to do some rethinking.

Financial Diaries: Why Microfinance Matters

The story of microfinance is most often told from the point of view of the provider. To get a fresh perspective, to find out what microfinance providers look like from the point of view of their users, I ran, in 1999–2000 and then again in 2002–5, a research exercise called "financial diaries."[17]

The diaries tracked the financial transactions of poor households at regular, frequent intervals over long periods of time. They showed that in poor but monetized economies like Bangladesh, managing money is a crucial activity for the poor, and taken very seriously. In poor households like Rasheda's and Kulsum's, for example, most income gets spent as soon as it arrives, on the basics, food and fuel. This leaves them with little cash on hand to deal with the many other things that money is needed for: buying a shirt, visiting the doctor, marrying out a daughter, or even starting a business. Short of current income, they must either go without those things or find some way of paying for them out of past or future income. Pulling off that trick—having savings that allow you to spend past income now, or taking loans that allow you to spend future income now—is the job of financial services. Poor people need those services more often than others, because they are most often without liquidity when they need it.

Where there are no microfinance providers, poor people have to manage this essential task on their own. They stash cash away at home. With friends and relatives, they run savings clubs and saving-and-loan clubs, they lend and borrow, and they store money with each other. In the village marketplace, they borrow from moneylenders or lend on interest. The two studies show that when microfinance organizations arrive on the scene, they do not replace these well-established, homemade systems, and may not even handle more than a fraction of all the transactions that poor people make. But they are very much welcomed as unusually reliable, convenient, and transparent financial partners. Finding a reliable financial partner is no small thing: it might make the difference between being fed and going hungry; between getting and not getting a job, or a husband, or a place in college; or between having an illness treated and suffering chronic disability—in extremis, between life and death. It is by supplying this basic service, more than by financing businesses, that microcredit has become so important to the poor of Bangladesh. ASA does it well, and thrives on it.

Chapter 8

Peaks and Troughs

By 2006 ASA had been enjoying many years of uninterrupted growth in its microfinance business and in the mastery of its craft. Suddenly, in 2006–7, a series of events put an end to this steady state. Bangladesh's 15-year spell of democracy also came to an end in 2006, when relations between the two main parties reached such lows that they simply couldn't engineer enough of a compromise to take part in a general election. A state of emergency was declared under an army-backed temporary administration, and a promise made to hold fresh elections before 2008 was out. Surprisingly, Shafiq found himself taking a part in the political process. The microfinance achievements of both Grameen and ASA were recognized internationally, with Grameen's Nobel Prize and ASA's unexpected appearance at the top of *Forbes* magazine's first-ever ranking of the world's best microfinance organizations. Flush with cash from its profits, ASA built itself a tower block, moved in, and established a university to fill some of the floors. Then, suddenly, expansion at ASA stopped, ostensibly to allow its new computerization program to settle in, but perhaps for other reasons as well.

Unrest

In 1991, 1996, and 2001, Bangladesh drew back from political collapse at the last moment and surprised and pleased itself and the world by holding credible elections whose results were accepted by their contestants. First BNP, then the Awami League, and then BNP again, formed democratically elected five-year governments. In 2006 this tradition fizzled out. The relationship between the government and the opposition, always extremely tense, had become poisonous in the last years of Khaleda Zia's second BNP government, especially after a grenade attack that almost killed the league's leader, Sheikh Hasina. Awami complained that the BNP government did not properly pursue the perpetrators of the outrage: they raised the suspicion that the BNP, through one of its coalition partners, was soft on the terrorist groups suspected of organizing the bombing.

The BNP government of 2001 had been in power for less than two months when the events of September 11 took place in the United States. The heightened awareness of the threat of fundamentalist terror was bound to be felt in Bangladesh, a poor Muslim country with weak institutions and a reputation for lawlessness and corruption, especially as it had once been part of Pakistan. The government had to deal with this, a task that was not made easier by the fact that the coalition through which it ruled included the Jamaat-e-Islami, an Islamist party. Some, including, vociferously, the Awami opposition, accused Jamaat of ties with fundamentalist leaders such as Siddiqul Islam, known as Bangla Bhai ("Brother" Bangla). Bangla Bhai had fought in Afghanistan and, returning home to a base in the countryside, was nastily terrorizing and sometimes brutally killing non-Muslims and even some non-Sunni Muslim groups. This had nothing to do with the old traditions of rural peasant leaders. Bangla Bhai's appeal was to a small minority of bigots, not to poor peasants in general, and he never had any sympathy from the public at large. He was more akin to the rabble of bandits who robbed and murdered in the name of left-wing causes that their very actions discredited: even today there are still Sorbahara cells, though they are seldom heard of except when the law catches up with them. In the end, Bangla Bhai was arrested and later executed.

It was common in Bangladesh for citizens and foreigners alike to reassure one another that the temperament of the country was moderate, that its Islamic traditions were so tempered by fusion with older Hindu and Buddhist habits as to be resistant to fundamentalism. People pointed out that in Bangladesh, Hindus and Muslims lived next door to each other in the same neighborhoods and shared much of their culture. "It is not like Pakistan here," you would hear. This attitude allowed the government to play down worries about extremism: it said it did so to protect Bangladesh's image internationally, whereas the opposition said it was to please the BNP's Jamaat coalition partners. Several shocks put an end to this. In May 2004 Anwar Choudhury, the popular British high commissioner (ambassador) to Bangladesh—popular partly because he was born in Sylhet and had become the first Bengali to be made head of a British diplomatic mission—was wounded and almost killed in a grenade attack. In August the same year, grenades were thrown at an Awami rally in old Dhaka, killing 20 people and narrowly missing Sheikh Hasina herself. A year later, on August 17, 2005, I was sitting on an aircraft waiting to pull away from Dhaka's Zia Airport when a cacophony of my fellow passengers' mobile phones alerted us that a bomb had just gone off in the airport. It turned out to have been one of almost four hundred explosions that were set off within minutes of each other in virtually all the main subdistricts of the country. This was an astonishing feat of coordination that had the effect of driving out complacency. It led to the creation of the Rapid Action Battalion, to closer cooperation with external security forces, and so to the arrest of Bangla Bhai and others.

Microfinance providers, and NGOs in general, were targets in some of these attacks. In the especially bad period from late summer 2004 to early 2005, eight workers of BRAC and Grameen were hurt—five of them seriously—in separate grenade attacks.[1] That turned out to be the worst of it, however, and the daily microfinance operations were never badly disrupted.

November 2006

For the elections due in 2006, the BNP-led government proposed that, once again, a temporary and neutral caretaker administration should take charge of arrangements. But the BNP was accused of blatantly interfering with promotions and retirements in the judiciary, and the senior legal figure it put forward for the post of chief adviser was seen by the opposition as not neutral at all, but someone very much in the pocket of the BNP leadership. The tussle that ensued was, as usual, played out with violence on the streets, but produced only a chaotic stalemate. At the end of the year, with no solution in sight, the formal head of state, President Iajuddin Ahmed, declared himself in charge of a special caretaker administration and appointed advisers. Their job was simply to arrange an election, but several of them, quite properly, wanted to ensure it would be meaningful, and they tried hard to bring about some kind of reconciliation between the parties to ensure that they would take part. Those efforts failed. In early January 2007, the army stepped in, pushing the advisers aside and installing their own choice as chief adviser. A state of emergency was declared and political activity banned.

At first the army-backed regime was popular. With troops on the streets, disorder declined. Ordinary Bangladeshis were pleased to see the most egregiously corrupt politicians, civil servants, and businessmen arrested, fined, or imprisoned. People were generally disposed to believe the government when it said that it would set up the conditions for a truly fair election—for example, by overhauling the disgracefully out-of-date and manipulated voter list, and issuing every citizen with an identity card. But, as time went by, discontent set in. The government lost face when it tried but failed to nudge both Khaleda Zia and Sheikh Hasina into exile. Later, when it put both of them under arrest, it was found that many ordinary people still held to their lifelong allegiance to one or other of the two parties, despite the fact that both were by then tearing themselves apart with internal disputes. Sharply rising prices also damaged the government's reputation—ordinary Bangladeshis see price stability as the first duty of government—and a big cyclone in the south in November 2007 only made things worse. The government and the army repeatedly renewed their promise to hold elections by the end of 2008, but some believe it won't happen, whereas others have lost faith that things would get any better if it did.

Shafiq in Government

In the original vision created for ASA by Shafiq and others, the NGO itself was to have withered away after acting as an organizing force for a federation of landless peasants to take over the government of Bangladesh by 1985. Twenty-one years later, in 2006, ASA did find a place in government, but not exactly as its founders had prophesized.

Shortly after President Iajuddin Ahmed declared his own caretaker administration in late 2006, four of his advisers resigned: they felt they wouldn't be able to contribute to the making of a credible election. To his surprise, Shafiq, who didn't know Iajuddin, was chosen as one of the replacements. Advisers are acting ministers, and Shafiq was given the supervision of the agriculture ministry. It is not clear who recommended Shafiq for the post. It may just be, as Shafiq himself supposes, that the president was looking for someone with proven management skills.

Some would say that there was a party political dimension to Shafiq's selection. Since the formation of ASA, he had always been careful to keep the organization clear of party politics and to say nothing in public about his own views. Nevertheless, some journalists were quick to read into Shafiq's life story an antipathy to Awami and a presumed softness for the BNP. After all, Shafiq had not strongly supported Sheikh Mujib's Awami program, had not become a freedom fighter in 1971, had expressed Maoist views and admiration for Maulana Bhasani, and was close to known BNP folk such as Azizul Haq, his old boss at BARD who had been a minister under President Zia. A precursor of this book was even used to fuel probing questions in TV talk shows featuring Shafiq.[2] Others, too, have assumed that Shafiq is pro-BNP. Some months before the 2001 election, I happened to be in Shafiq's office when a call came through from a senior BNP figure who had been, and was to become again, finance minister. He wanted Shafiq to consider bringing ASA out in favor of the BNP rather in the way that Proshika, another major NGO, was by then identified in the public mind with Awami. Proshika had arranged a massive pro-progressive (for which read pro-Awami) procession in the streets of Dhaka. Shafiq, skillfully, declined.

ASA's governing body and its staff broadly encouraged Shafiq to accept the adviser position when he consulted them on December 10, 2006, just after he got the phone call inviting him to join the caretaker administration. But, as usual, Shafiq valued his wife's opinion the most. She wanted the family to think it through, so he asked for a day to make up his mind. The family knew their quiet lives would be turned upside down, but thought they could tolerate that because they hoped that the period up to the elections would be short. The biggest concern was party political. They had to face the possibility that the Awami League would brand Iajuddin's caretaker government as an instrument of the BNP and refuse to cooperate with it, so that the election would go ahead with only the BNP fielding candidates. To be associated with such a one-sided election could damage Shafiq's reputation. Nevertheless, he decided to accept, though his misgivings grew even stronger when, within a couple of days, two ASA branch offices in different parts of the country were torched. The government's mandate was just to run the election and keep government business ticking along, but, following his misgivings, Shafiq quickly aligned himself with those advisers who thought they should go beyond this and try to ensure that both major parties would take part. The government agreed to let them try. As Shafiq tells the story, and as confirmed to me by another member of that cabinet, he was one of two advisers who played the biggest role. The lead was taken by Shoaib Ahmed, who had been in senior civil service positions much of his life. He made the contacts with the two big parties, whereas Shafiq, with his relaxed, talkative, and cheerful manner, worked the media, trying to assure everyone that there was going to be an election worth taking part in. For some, this was refreshing: here was this open-faced man, with his charming Sylheti accent, telling Bangladeshis that everything was still possible. Others wondered who this obscure, provincial NGO leader was, and why he was hogging so much television time.

In any case, it didn't work. Some senior figures in both parties were prepared to compromise enough to ensure that their parties took part in the election, but they could not create enough momentum. At least one of the two party leaders rejected the deal, precipitating an even greater crisis. In dismay, the advisers readied themselves to tell the president they would resign in unison unless he found a way to use his office to secure a deal. He couldn't, and in the end, on the night of January 11, 2007, the whole cabinet resigned and the temporary government was dissolved.

The next working day Shafiq was back in ASA. He began to sleep properly again. All through his brief time as an adviser, he had trouble putting his whirling mind to rest. He had not anticipated that the role would be at once so overwhelming and so restrictive. After the attacks on ASA's branches, the police had put men outside all three thousand of its offices throughout the country, outside Shafiq's home, and outside the homes of many of his relatives. Unable to move around without a full police escort, he further reduced his already quiet social life. His eldest son Tanvir, who had married in 2006 (an arranged marriage, just like his parents) was living at his parents' home with his pregnant wife (their daughter was born in mid-2007). He still thinks his father made a mistake accepting the post, not just because it made life uncomfortable for a few weeks—too many phones ringing, too many people hanging around, and too many sudden outings late at night—but "because my father has his own vision and mission which is quite separate from a political career."[3]

At first, Shafiq was inclined to think his son was right. After his resignation, the Awami League released a statement accusing Shafiq and his fellow advisers of acting against the country—in effect, of being traitors. He was pursued by journalists who wanted to hear his reaction to this, but he fended them off with anodyne remarks. Now that things have settled down, Shafiq is back to believing he did well by acting as an adviser: it has raised his profile and given him access to people and places that were beyond his reach before. However, not everyone, even in ASA, agrees: who knows whether all this will, in the future, come back to haunt Shafiq, perhaps to the detriment of ASA?

Shafiq was invited to the ceremony at which the president swore in the new caretaker government. The army-approved choice to become its chief adviser was Dr. Fakhruddin Ahmed, who had been heading up PKSF, the microcredit fund wholesaler. Before that he had been a reformist central bank governor, after a successful career at the World Bank. Like everyone else, I was taken by surprise: no one had connected Dr. Fakhruddin with any kind of political role—precisely what made him suitable for the post, we supposed in retrospect. Just a month earlier, I had sat in his office at PKSF discussing with him a range of initiatives that he wanted PKSF to take up in microfinance.

Nobel Elation

Toward the end of 2006, the Nobel Committee decided to award Muhammad Yunus and his Grameen Bank its peace prize. Yunus became the first Bangladeshi, but not the first Bengali, to become a Nobel laureate. The polymath poet, dramatist, composer, and social worker Rabindranath Tagore, still the best-loved songwriter in modern Bangladesh, won his prize, for literature, in 1913; and Amartya Sen, the economist, won the economics prize in 1998 for work on understanding poverty. When Yunus won his prize, Bangladesh erupted with elation previously matched only when its cricket team first beat India. It even lured Yunus briefly, but unsuccessfully, into politics. Some had wanted him to take the post that had been given to Fakhruddin, but Yunus's vision was broader: he hoped to found a political party led by honest folk with the sincere aim of developing Bangladesh. He worked on the idea for a few months but dropped it when it became clear that there would not be enough support from politically experienced people.

Yunus's prize, which he shared with the Grameen Bank, put microfinance, and Yunus's particular vision of microfinance, back in the limelight. That vision has been described as *poverty lending*: a program targeted exclusively at poor households, who, through their self-help organization into groups, and their use of microcredit to invest in microenterprise, would escape not just from the economic dimensions of poverty but also from its ignorance, humiliation, and gender abuses. That the Nobel Committee awarded Yunus the peace prize signaled that they continued to see Grameen's achievements as being about much more than just finance. The citation read that Yunus and Grameen had been awarded the prize "for their efforts to create economic and social development from below."[4]

The World's Best Microfinance Organization

A year later, it was ASA's turn to receive international recognition, though it was a lower-key matter that attracted little of the public recognition given to Nobel laureates. *Forbes,* an American business magazine, is famous for publishing ranked lists of business achievements. It decided that it was time to prepare, for the first time, a list of the world's best microfinance organizations. The criteria it used were not those of the Nobel Committee. Forbes did not recognize "social development from below," but focused on standard measures of performance for conventional financial providers like banks and insurance companies. Using data on 641 microfinance organizations from around the world, assembled by the Microfinance Information Exchange (the MIX), a respected industry watcher, *Forbes* created a composite index of four indicators.[5] They were *scale* (the size of the loan portfolio), *efficiency* (the costs of running the lending service), *risk* (how likely the loans are to be fully repaid), and *return* (profitability). Though ASA did not head any of the four rankings based on these measures individually, it came out at the top of the list overall. It became the world's best microfinance organization.

Forbes was responding to a vision of microfinance rather different from that of "poverty lending." Observers had already given it a name: the *financial systems approach,* and the World Bank tended to favor it. It sees microfinance less as an antipoverty crusade and more as a *double bottom-line business*—a business that seeks at one and the same time to make surpluses and serve a social purpose. The financial systems approach encourages microfinance providers to cover their own costs with few subsidies: ideally, funds for borrowing would come entirely from savings, commercial debt, for-profit investment, and retained earnings rather than from donors. The providers would be regulated and supervised for-profit companies rather than NGOs. There would be no need for an exclusive focus on women, and borrowers could just as easily be individuals as members of a group. Some advocates of the approach also believed that the sharp focus on targeting the poor should be softened. First, they argued that working with better-off groups as well as with the poor will improve revenues, allowing providers to expand their services to all classes more quickly. Second, they warned against lending to the "economically inactive" poor who might encounter difficulties with loans. They prefer borrowers to be Minas rather than Rashedas or Kulsums, and tend to believe that the Kulsums are best helped by nonfinancial social programs of safety nets.

This vision had gained ground because it appeared to promise two outcomes that were not there in the original poverty lending approach. The first was independence from donors, whose coffers were assumed to be limited, so that relying on them would restrict the potential global outreach of microfinance; and the second was swifter integration into the larger financial world. In the end, many thought, the poor will be best served when they are linked to mainstream finance rather than seen as an isolated special market.

The Bangladesh Accommodation

Shafiq and Yunus have always presented themselves very differently at public gatherings. Shafiq hammers on about efficiency, standardization, and sustainability, whereas Yunus prefers to talk about lifting people out of poverty. As a result, in some eyes, they came to be seen as representatives, in Bangladesh, of the two microfinance visions: ASA of the more commercial financial systems approach and Grameen of poverty lending. A well-written write-up of ASA in the Asian Development Bank's microfinance newsletter portrayed ASA as the "Ford Motor Model of Microfinance," seeming to link ASA to an icon of hard-nosed Western capitalism.[6]

But the idea that ASA and Grameen represent two wholly different visions of microfinance is wrong. When Grameen reinvented itself after near failure in the late 1990s (and introduced the commitment savings product that we described in the previous chapter), it shifted decisively toward a "financial systems" approach. It now offers the fullest range of voluntary savings products of any major microfinance provider, and finances its loan portfolio entirely from client deposits. Its larger microenterprise loans attract many middle-class, economically active borrowers. It is profitable, and it has always been regulated. ASA, for its part, still subscribes to the idea, widely held in Bangladesh, that the purpose of microfinance is indeed to eradicate, or at least to relieve, poverty.

A similarly mistaken perception has followed ASA's public skepticism about joint liability: one reads these days about the ASA model being distinguished by individual lending, whereas the Grameen model features group liability. This is also wrong. In the field, the two organizations work in the same way, as described for ASA in the previous chapter: using meetings and peer pressure wherever possible, and going directly to individual clients to retrieve repayments when necessary. Grameen, too, has said that it doesn't use joint liability.[7] Yunus has even gone as far as to say that Grameen never used it in the first place—that Grameen's approach was simply misunderstood by outside theorists.[8]

There is, then, a distinctly Bangladeshi type of microfinance, but it doesn't fall neatly into the poverty lending or the financial systems categories. Bangladeshi microfinance is certainly driven by the commitment to eradicate poverty, felt by many Bangladeshis but especially by those educated ones who, like Shafiq and Yunus, remember the devastation of their country in the wake of the independence struggle. Although this impetus has remained strong, the means to achieve its ends have become more businesslike as the years have gone by.

The feature that really does distinguish microfinance in Bangladesh most obviously from other countries is its early commitment to, and success with, going to scale. Going to scale was possible in part because the government did not have the power to control the industry in the way that stronger states did, such as nearby India, where government could both legislate and enforce measures such as caps on lending interest rates. But lack of government interference also has its downside: Bangladesh's rudimentary and increasingly old-fashioned-looking regulation of its microfinance industry is now in danger of holding its star performers back by making it hard for them to obtain the kind of legal identity that they need to expand their services. We will return to some of these themes in the next chapter, when we speculate on what's next for ASA, for microfinance, and for poverty eradication in Bangladesh.

Microfinance in Bangladesh was started by NGOs. They originated as social development organizations, and the public understanding of what an NGO is and what it should do predates microfinance. Cyclone Sidr reminded everyone of this when it pounded Bangladesh in late 2007.

Another Severe Blow

In April 1991, as ASA was starting out on its microcredit adventure, a huge cyclone swept up the Bay of Bengal. I was again at the southern tip of Bhola, the sausage-shaped island that stands in the ocean extremity of the Ganges/Brahmaputra river system, just as I had been at the time of the 1985 cyclone (chapter 5). Until we were forced back to shelter, we spent the early evening in the tiny Red Cross Red Crescent office, where a crackly radio relayed news of the cyclone's path. As in 1985, the cyclone again seemed to be coming straight for us, but then it turned east, away from my colleagues and me, away from most of ASA's field projects, and toward the west-facing coast south of Chittagong. There, it rolled over the coastal defenses—such as they were—and killed about 120,000 people.

No one can predict the formation or the path of cyclones, and for the next 16 years no really devastating ones reached Bangladesh. But on the night of November 15–16, 2007, the curiously named Sidr Cyclone crashed into the mangrove forests in southwest Bangladesh. Sidr was big, and though the mangrove took the sting out of her, she caused plenty of damage. The death toll, at fewer (perhaps much fewer) than 10,000, was small compared to the 1991 storm, and concentrated in the areas close to the forest where the tidal surge raced over the unprotected countryside. The flat, low-lying farming area that was open to Sidr once she got past the forest, was vast, and there wind damage to homes, crops, and livestock was huge. Unusually—for cyclones tend to lose power as they travel over land—Sidr was still strong when she reached Dhaka, the capital: she took out the electric power for 36 hours, shook roofs, felled trees, and broke windows in the guesthouse where I was busy working on this book.

ASA did not stop to ask what it should do. When disasters strike, NGOs' tasks are relief and rehabilitation, as they always have been. All the NGOs working at national scale, and even some local ones from unaffected areas, ran postcyclone programs. Nothing better illustrates the continuing connection, in the minds of all Bangladeshis, between NGOs and relief work, even if the NGO, like ASA, has shifted almost wholly to financial services. But compared to ASA's experiences on Urir Char in 1985 (chapter 5), dealing with the aftermath of Sidr was administratively easy. As a quasi-bank with an enormous staff and more than a million clients in the 16 affected districts, ASA was able to intervene quickly through financial measures. All restrictions on the withdrawal of savings were immediately lifted. Clients were told they could also draw down most of their security fund deposits. Swift replenishing of loan capital, repayment holidays, and outright cancellation of loans were used, depending on the severity of the situation in each region. Fresh emergency loans were made available, and, a little later, bigger loans for rebuilding homes. When the head office sent a small team down to the area to encourage local staff, it was careful to take along cash that could be given to branches to spend on first-aid materials, and more to hand over to local public administrators in a gesture of support to government. All in all, ASA claimed in a press release that went out 10 days after the storm, it was spending 1.1 billion taka (about $16 million) on its cyclone response activities. Half of this was to write off 150,000 member loans in full or in part. Much of the rest was for interest-free loans for rehabilitation.

My assistant S. K. Sinha traveled down with the head office team, and stayed on to take a closer look at some of the worst-hit places. He found, of course, plenty of muddle and confusion, poor coordination by an unprepared bureaucracy, and an alarming mismatch of resources and needs—but that had also been the case after another storm, Hurricane Katrina, had struck New Orleans in August 2005. Food and clothing were in desperately short supply in the areas that experienced the tidal wave: the wall of water simply swept everything before it, and people, if they survived, were left with just the nighttime clothes they were wearing at the time—and sometimes not even that. Sinha found people dressed in rags trying to cook rotten rice from soaked bags. Some things had worked well. A local administrator stopped the overnight river launches from setting off and probably saved thousands of lives. Mobile phones mostly continued to work, and several ASA officers used them to alert staff and clients to the approaching storm. Six days after the storm, in one village, we were able to confirm that ASA staff had already forgiven loans and paid out security funds to some deceased members' next of kin, though in another village, not so far away, the ASA members still hadn't been contacted by ASA staff and knew nothing of what ASA was readying for them.

Throughout, ASA's accounting system stood up to the test. There were none of the questions that swirled around the cyclone rehabilitation project in 1985. Sidr had shown that if you want to do something useful after a sudden-onset disaster, and do it quickly, it is better to be a self-reliant quasi-bank than a conveyor belt for donor grants.

New Heights, New Institutions

Talking recently to staff members in an ASA branch, I asked them to tell me what, in their opinion, were the most significant changes that had taken place in ASA in the previous 10 years. They obliged with a long list, mostly of new or modified services for clients, or new or modified staff benefits. When I asked them to rank the changes in order of their "significance" (leaving them to decide what was meant by that), it was the big-picture changes that they ranked highest. Financial self-sufficiency, and coming top of the *Forbes* list, they said, were important because they gave the staff pride, marking ASA as a leader in its field, and making it a permanent institution that increased their own faith in it, as well, they claimed, as that of the members. The development of ASA's work overseas, which, as we shall see in the last chapter, has taken a new and dramatic turn recently, is similarly appreciated, not just for the international recognition that it brings, but for the opportunities that staff members get to travel abroad. Also ranked high for the prestige it brought ASA—though this ranking was not unanimous—was Shafiq's spell as an adviser in the caretaker government. Right at the top of their rankings they put the ASA Tower, the microlender's new building in Dhaka. They ranked it top because they felt it was good for prestige, for publicity, and for their own self-confidence; it competes with Grameen and BRAC, who had long since built their own towers, and it's a big tangible asset.

ASA moved into the ASA Tower, built on the site it owns in western Dhaka, in July 2006. It had long repaid its first-ever bank loan, for which the site and its original buildings had been mortgaged, and it paid for the tower, which cost about $8 million, with cash from its bulging balances. Most floors are rented out, to a university, a bank, and a Saudi-owned telecom company: the tower is a revenue earner for ASA. ASA itself occupies the top two floors, crisply laid out in the modern manner with swish glass partitions, no corridors, and generous open space. Smartly uniformed guards salute visitors as they emerge from the fast elevators. Shafiq's office on the top floor looks to the northwest, away from the city, but from other windows there are views of the towers belonging to Bangladesh's other big NGOs and microcredit banks, Grameen, BRAC, and Proshika. To the southeast one can look down on the parliament buildings, empty, now, of parliamentarians, but holding Khaleda Zia and Sheikh Hasina in confinement while corruption cases against them are being prepared.[9] Also visible, though now being crowded out by Dhaka's building boom, are the gray-and-rust-red roofs of the slums, where millions of Bangladeshis, fleeing the unemployment and poverty of the villages, have settled in the hope of finding work.

The tower radically changes ASA's public image. For a long time ASA had enjoyed its reputation as a supremely cost-conscious organization not given to exhibitionism. Observers often remarked (and senior staff privately grumbled) that ASA had only four cars, the smallest ratio of SUVs-to-staff of any major Bangladeshi NGO. But ASA found it needed to project a more up-to-date image if it was to be taken seriously in a world where microfinance had completed its move from the pages of development journals to the boardrooms of Wall Street.

The university in the lower floors of the tower is ASA's own. Universities were long a state monopoly, but in 1992 the first BNP government had passed an act providing for private establishments. Educational entrepreneurs soon discovered there was strong demand for them, and many, of varying quality, were opened. They catered for the middle-class families whose ranks were being swelled by Bangladesh's rapid economic growth. ASA University opened in the spring of 2007, offering courses in business, law, and English. It is a nonprofit enterprise owned outright by ASA but has been able to cover its costs and produce a surplus within a year of its foundation. A little of the surplus goes into subsidized tuition fees for poorer students, especially the children of samity members.

It may be a model for other new institutions to be established, owned and run by ASA. Building institutions that would deliver nonfinancial services to the poor is now much discussed in ASA. Although this has echoes of the "development as delivery" approach of ASA in the 1980s (chapter 5), the model would be quite different. Back then, services were paid for by donors, and ASA largely followed methodologies, in legal services, health and nutrition, and so on, that had been developed by other NGO–donor partnerships. Permanent infrastructure was not, then, a feature. This time, ASA would be the financier and owner, the services would be designed to cover their costs, and they would be delivered from institutions housed in built form. Feasibility studies have begun on establishing a medical college, and discussions continue about a series of hospitals at the district level, and about high schools. These plans remain at an early stage and are part of a wider discussion about ASA's future direction that we shall look at again in the following chapter.

An End to Growth

In a long-delayed modernizing move, ASA finally computerized its whole operation, from branch to head office, between 2006 and 2008. There were historic reasons for ASA's nervousness about computerized bookkeeping. The organization's early microcredit success, as we have seen, was based on the very simple manual systems that Shafiq had designed. In 2006 they were still working well: the district offices had computers, but all they did was to consolidate the manual reports that came from the branches into electronic format for sending on to the head office. Shafiq felt no pressing need to change this, not just because he knew that full computerization was likely to be a messy business with months of irritating hardware problems and software debugging, but also because by computerizing he was symbolically relinquishing the very personal control of detail that he had maintained for so long. He was not familiar with computers: unlike some modern CEOs, he does not have one on his compulsively clean desk. He was prepared to spend heavily on the task, to ensure a good outcome, but worried that he would be taken for a ride by unscrupulous consultants. In the end, he awarded a contract to his cousin, one of a new generation of capable computer engineers that Bangladesh's technical universities were beginning to turn out. Asifur Rahman brought his huge team of 60 engineers into the heart of ASA: many of them younger, with better education, better English-language skills, and better pay than even the most senior of ASA's existing staff. The two groups rubbed shoulders awkwardly.

The rollout plan for the computers was pure ASA. It was done all at once, with virtually no piloting. A total of 3,300 machines were simultaneously shipped to the branches, where Asifur's additional staff of 160 field engineers set them up. It was only then decided that each branch should have an assistant branch manager (ABM) with special responsibility for computers. To achieve the instant recruitment of 3,300 ABMs, ASA simply promoted 3,300 loan officers. To replace 3,300 loan officers, though, would take time, especially in an employment market in which competition between microfinance providers was making steadily more difficult. So, for the first time since the turn to microcredit in 1991, Shafiq suddenly called, in late 2007, for a six-month halt to branch expansion.

This was a dramatic move: the growth of the branch network had been accelerating to keep up with the ever-growing flow of resources from profits, and was running, at the time, at about 10 new branches a week. Computerization, it seemed, had jolted ASA more profoundly than any decision since the shift to credit in 1991. Or were there other reasons behind the sudden halt to expansion? At the close of the six-month pause in the spring of 2008, the ABMs and the replacement loan officers were in place, and the computer system was working well. But ASA chose not to start opening new branches again, and in my last interview with Shafiq in August 2008, he told me that ASA no longer has any plans to expand its branch network. ASA, evidently, is undergoing a major change of direction.

Chapter 9

Renewing the Pledge

Despite its enormous success, ASA faces some uncertainties. There is anxiety that microfinance's breakneck pace of growth may mean that the market for its core product, the small, general-purpose loan, is nearing saturation, raising questions about what will then happen to ASA and to the industry as a whole. Some in ASA worry that microfinance hasn't yet brought about the miracles that it promised, especially in poverty eradication. The impact of microfinance on poverty is famously hard to measure, but interviews in Manikganj, where ASA started out 30 years ago, with families who took part both in ASA's early social mobilization and the later microfinance samities, suggest that microfinance's effects are large, even though they are multiple, often indirect, and not at first obvious. Another field trip, to talk to members of a social mobilization NGO that is still at work, shows how villagers are able to deal with, and get the best from, both kinds of organizations. Meanwhile, ASA has begun to develop a new market serving business people, and although there is debate about how best to achieve that, it looks set to become ASA's biggest change of direction since it moved to microfinance in 1991.

March 2008

The 30th anniversary of the midnight pledge in the gardens of the Uthuli rest house passed unnoticed in ASA Tower. Nevertheless, I decided that it would be a good moment to go back to the villages in Manikganj to find out what local people had to say about ASA's 30 years' work among them. I had not been there since 1994, when, as recounted in chapter 4, I went to uncover memories of the early days of the social mobilization work. At the time of that visit, ASA's microcredit was new. Now, after more than a decade and a half of it, I wondered what the villagers would have to say. Would there be the same story of initial enthusiasm and hope worn down by a string of disappointments, as had largely been the fate of the social actions program?

I was interested in these questions because I had detected a new mood in ASA Tower: a growing sense that another change in direction will be needed, and cannot be long delayed. The idea that change is called for comes partly from microcredit's astonishing success, and partly from an unsettling feeling that it hasn't been successful enough.

On the one hand, microfinance's stunning growth may be nearing its limits. There are now several providers in all but the most remote villages, so the still fast-expanding supply may soon outstrip the remaining demand. When I asked Shafiq what, if anything, keeps him awake at night, he needed no time to think through his answer: *overlapping,* the multiple membership of several credit-giving organizations by a single household. He sees difficulties ahead for ASA, and maybe a train crash for the industry as a whole, as indebtedness among clients builds up and repayment falters.

On the other hand, there is growing uncertainty about the fruits of microfinance. To some extent this is a morning-after effect of the Nobel Prize. The renewed publicity that accompanied the award reminded Bangladeshis again and again that microfinance, their country's most famous invention, is the single best antidote to poverty. In that case, ask the letters to the newspapers, why does Bangladesh still suffer so much poverty? Exactly where are all these empowered women and their successful microenterprises? ASA's executive vice president Sushil Kumar Roy, chatting to me in his office, addressed this:

> My hopes for microcredit have been only partially fulfilled. More than half of our borrowers don't experience continuous development. Many make progress only to slip back into poverty. We need to understand why they go on and on taking small loans. . . . Of course, there are all sorts of factors at work here—politics, natural and family disasters, and so on—but I can't help thinking that the NGOs haven't quite got microcredit right yet.[1]

With senior staff members in this kind of mood, it looks as if ASA needs to find a response to the saturated market for its core product that will at the same time revitalize its sense of mission. It needs, somehow, to renew its pledge.

Manikganj 30 Years On

My first stop in Manikganj was at the college where, in 1978, local professor and ASA sympathizer Sushil Bhowmik, who had been a participant in the original pledge, had made a room available for use by Shafiq as ASA's first office. Bhowmik died in 2007, and ASA has remembered him by funding a new building at the college, which my ASA traveling companions inspected. One of them was Darbesh Ali, of all the seniors still left in ASA perhaps the one with the fondest memories of the days of "social actions." His home is in the area, and he worked there for BRAC and then for ASA. He was still able to recognize, among the elderly villagers we came across, some of the young men who had joined the first ASA samities. He quickly led us to Azgar Ali and Nizamuddin, men now in their 60s who joined their ASA samities in the late 1970s. As Azgar remembers it, ASA officers "taught us many things," especially "how we must have unity, how we must fight against corruption, how we must struggle for better wages and to get government land meant for the poor, how we mustn't marry off our daughters before they are sixteen, how we must save and how we must have good leadership."[2]

Darbesh jogged his memory, and he confirmed that the ASA officers tried to teach them to read and write. They also set up their own local arbitration court (*shalish*) and scored at least one success when they forced a landlord to apologize to a laborer he had beaten, though "often we weren't able to do much more than comfort those that had been aggrieved." Sadly, Azgar's samity ended like so many others: after a failed attempt to petition for rights to use two acres of local government land, members began to lose heart. They stopped attending and saving regularly, opening themselves up to the risk of the savings fund being embezzled. Part of it was, so they divided what remained among themselves and abandoned the samity.

But our purpose was not to hear more stories of those early social action samities but to find out what everyone thought about how they compare with the modern microfinance ones. Azgar and Nizamuddin took us a few dozen meters across the village to meet Sondar Sharma, chairperson of today's ASA samity, which has 26 women members. A small crowd collected, but a little to my disappointment this carefully engineered encounter between old and new samity members failed to produce much of a debate. The two worlds, perhaps, are just too different. The women listened politely to the tales the old men told, but it seems that conditions in their village have changed so much that the ideals of the first samities cannot resonate with them. Azgar reminded the women that a local wealthy landowner still occupies government land that should, by rights, be used by the poor, but the women shrugged: the economy is so diversified now that getting hold of land is less important than it was. They thought that the local rich elite would certainly like to keep the poor in their place but they no longer had the means to do so: landowners no longer monopolize job opportunities, because the husbands and sons and daughters of the modern samity members no longer look for farm laboring work but work in transport, or as traders in the local market, or go off to Dhaka or even to the Middle East for employment. In any case, the poor are as clever as the rich now: their children are educated, and many of them earn as much as the sons of families with land. The stories about poor, illiterate people being duped into giving away their rights or their land by putting their thumb marks to legal documents they didn't understand struck them as quaint—once-upon-a-time stories their grandfathers might recount. "Anyway," said Sondar, "everyone, rich and poor, wants to live in peace if they can: no one would listen to you if you tried to get people to fight each other." For their part, Azgar and Nizamuddin had no criticisms of the microfinance samity, and the questions they asked about it were thoroughly modern: Does ASA deduct anything from the loan before they give it to you? What interest rate do they charge? Asked why ASA hadn't done all this for them in their day, their answer was bland (and spot-on): "Well, ASA didn't have the money to do it." But surely, I asked, there must be some people in the village—perhaps conservative religious folk—who criticize your samity? "Of course there are," said Laili, the samity treasurer. "No one listens to them."

We went off for lunch at the quayside on the Jamuna River, where Shafiq had tried to develop fishermen's cooperatives for CCDB, and then came back to a different village, Nehando Nayachar. We settled ourselves comfortably in the courtyard of a prosperous-looking homestead and quizzed Zigir Ali, his wife, one of his sons, and his daughters-in-law. Zigir had been a member of an early social mobilization samity, but his memories of it have dimmed, and Darbesh had to work hard to pull them out. As a young married man he was poor, trying to bring up a family on day laboring wages: like many in those days, they couldn't always manage three meals a day, sometimes not even two. Now, asked to describe his economic condition, he demurs, but his wife, Fulmeher, says "We've become middle class now." It's her samity, the microfinance one, that they keep talking about when we ask about samities, not his old social action one. Fulmeher repeats much of what we had heard from Sondar Sharma and her members, and adds further details. She points out, for example, that these days people wouldn't fight exploitation through direct action because that would open them up to harassment by police and local officials: rather, they'd have to fight the exploiter through the courts. And she says that it's not just that the poor are less dependent on the rich for work, they are also less dependent on them for credit, and this makes a big difference, because the poor no longer need to preserve a good relationship with the wealthy to ensure they have somewhere to go when they are desperate for money. These days, she says, we go to the microfinance groups or to their members.

This gave us the chance to talk about her samity and its loans and savings, and what part it played in the family's present prosperity. They have four well-built, timber-and-tin-sheet rooms arranged around the courtyard. We are invited into one of them and find a modern color TV, DVD player, a fridge, and nicely carved timber furniture. All four of the rooms, and most of their contents, are new, and all were paid for by their two sons, one by remittances from Saudi Arabia and the other from income he earns as a truck driver. The truck driver lives at home still, and the family keeps in touch with the son in Saudi Arabia through the three mobile phones in the household. When I say that it looks as if their prosperity is all based on the hard work of their family, and has little to do with ASA's loans, Fulmeher laughs. "Don't you know how much it costs to pay the bribe for a permanent driving job with a good company? 30,000 taka. And we needed 160,000 taka [$2,300] to send the other boy to Saudi. Where do you think that all came from? And how do you think we put them through school, or found husbands for our daughters?"

I needed to follow this up, for I knew it couldn't be as simple as it sounds: ASA's loans just aren't that big. But their answers made sense. The 160,000 taka for the Saudi trip was made up of 50,000 from the boy's parents-in-law (effectively, it was the dowry his wife brought him), 20,000 from selling the family's savings in gold jewelry, some loans from cousins and neighbors, and the balance from a string of ASA loans taken by Fulmeher, her daughter and daughters-in-law. Subsequent ASA loans then repaid the private loans and helped the household rebuild its savings. The microcredit borrowing gave continuity and stability to the whole sequence of transactions. The daughter-in-law confirmed that the 50,000 her parents provided came from the same kind of gearing of microcredit loans. Zigir's family now holds a formal insurance policy on his life, into which they deposit 500 taka a month, a DPS at the local farmer's bank, also 500 a month, and they have recently opened one of ASA's newly reintroduced long-term savings plans. All these are funded by the remittances from the son in Saudi Arabia.

Heading back to Dhaka in the car, I asked Darbesh for his comments. He pointed out, rightly, that Manikganj is, by Bangladesh standards, no longer poor: he could show me many areas where there is little tradition of migrant work and where the poor are still heavily dependent on farm day labor and are still exposed to exploitation. He also told me something that set me off a few days later on another trip.

Still Struggling

Darbesh reminded me that social-empowerment programs, very similar to what ASA used to do all those years ago, are still working in Bangladesh. He told me that they are enjoying a new lease of life, having come back into fashion with donors: not just the smaller, private donors of the kind that used to fund ASA, but major, bilateral ones like DFID (Department for International Development, official British aid).

The obvious one for me to go and look at was Nijera Kori ("We Do It Ourselves"). This was partly because it is one of the best known, in and outside Bangladesh, and partly because its website is charmingly frank in its hostility to microcredit. The NK website says that not doing microcredit is "what has set Nijera Kori apart from perhaps every other NGO in Bangladesh."[3] The site goes on: "Nijera Kori believes that microcredit cannot and does not reach all sections of society—especially neglected communities and people, who need it most." True, although the reader is made to feel that that may not be such a bad thing: "Nijera Kori realizes that microcredit, as a financial institution, has succeeded in creating dependencies and vulnerabilities among communities that have used it."

They are right when they say that not doing microcredit is rare among NGOs, especially among NGOs that work in the countryside. The World Bank found, in a study done in 1995 and repeated in 2003, that when they asked focus groups in the villages what they most wanted from NGOs, the number of people who put credit at the top of the list had risen from 21 to 81 percent: people tend to like what they know they can get, perhaps.[4] The very expression *NGO* has come to mean "microcredit bank." NGOs active in the countryside had to work hard to publicize themselves if they didn't do microcredit, or they were liable to be misunderstood. A rickshaw puller I hired some years ago told me that his wife belonged to three NGOs—Grameen Bank, ASA, and GSS (Gono Shahajo Shangstha, an NGO then promoting collective action against injustice, like ASA did and NK still does). I asked him what Grameen did:

RICKSHAW PULLER:	They give taka and take taka [*taka dei, taka nei*].
AUTHOR:	And what about ASA?
RICKSHAW PULLER:	They give taka and take taka.
AUTHOR:	And what about GSS?
RICKSHAW PULLER:	[pause] Well . . . they don't give taka.
AUTHOR:	OK, so what do they do?
RICKSHAW PULLER:	[pause] Well . . . they will give taka and take taka, I suppose.

But it was history that most strongly drew me to NK, for it is run by Khushi Kabir, one of the angry youngsters who worked in BRAC in the aftermath of the liberation war, became radicalized by their exposure to life in the villages, and encouraged Shafiq Choudhury to pursue his ideas for a new kind of grassroots-led NGO. Khushi Kabir was a member of ASA's first governing body, and although she soon left ASA, she has stayed true to the original ASA ideals.

Nijera Kori's objectives today, as set out on its website, sound very much like ASA in the late 1970s. Rather than temporarily ameliorating rural poverty and destitution by delivering services, NK is concerned with "the struggle to create a society free from oppression and deprivation, through the establishment of the fundamental rights of the people."

To achieve that, NK has developed a strategy "to make people conscious of their rights and assist them to develop the collective strength necessary to establish those rights," and to carry out that strategy, NK's staff members "are more like social activists who must live among and interact closely with the poor whom they try to mobilize." NK works with both men and women, and although they meet in separate weekly groups, the staff members try to bring them together when they engage in social actions on issues such as land rights, gender equality, violence against women, fundamentalism—and "moneylending and microcredit."

I put it to Shafiq that though he had moved ASA away from development as struggle in the mid-1980s, partly out of fear that donors would not support such work, NK, 20 years later, is being generously funded by one of Bangladesh's big-four donors to carry out exactly the same kind of work—*gheraos,* mass protests, and confrontations with corrupt officials and land-grabbing elites. His reply was a mix of sentiment and realism: "I like that work, I still like the awareness building activities and the agitation: from my heart we started this similar work... Khushi is committed...."

On the other hand, he is quite sure Khushi is on the wrong track. He pointed out that although some donors are prepared to support such work, it can be done only on a small scale: one cannot imagine a donor-funded effort big enough to reach more than a tiny fraction of Bangladesh's poor. Besides, "*Nijera Kori* is doing what it does, good, but when the poor people demand health services or demand credit or education, then *Nijera Kori* cannot really respond strongly, that is why I feel bad about it."

Direct and Indirect

A few days later, in a village just outside Comilla, not far from the BARD campus where Shafiq had started his professional life, I found some NK members. I had deliberately avoided NK's best-known work areas, down in the south, for they are closely associated with a specific struggle—against large-scale shrimp cultivators who drive poor farmers out of their land and livelihoods. I wanted to see NK's work rubbing shoulders with ubiquitous microcredit. Did any of their members really think that microfinance was bad for them?

Almost all of the NK members I spoke to on that trip were also using microfinance. None saw any contradiction in taking membership in both sorts of organization, and an NK worker who we chanced upon confirmed that NK workers do not actively campaign against microcredit. His view was straightforward: NK doesn't itself do credit because it doesn't mix well with their main activities. One tends to push out the other.

All the NK groups in that village—there are 11, some male, most female—practice group-based savings. Indeed, this seems to be the activity that the identity of the group depends on: groups that had stopped saving were said to be closed. These savings plans are much shrewder than the ones that ASA had promoted in its early days. Though there was talk of the savings being available in case any social action needed support, the NK savings are mostly being accumulated for investment. The investment is done carefully to minimize the risk of the savings being captured. For example, rather than put the money into a joint enterprise, members prefer to use it to lease a piece of land and then rent it out to an outsider, by the season or year, with the rental income taken in cash and immediately divided among the group members. The returns seemed modest: I told them I thought they'd get more if they put the cash in a fixed deposit at a bank, and that there might be less risk if they did so. They didn't agree: the better rates at the bank are available only on individually owned accounts, so there'd be the risk that a quarrel or change of membership in the group would tempt the account holder to capture the money. They convinced me that they are better off holding their wealth in an immovable land lease.

The NK groups in that village seemed to function at three levels: finance, discussion, and social action. Underpinning the groups, helping to bring them together, regularly, around a shared asset, is the savings. Then there are the regular discussions with the NK field worker: on the day I visited they had talked about bird flu, and what they should do if they found a sick bird. And finally there are the occasional issues that lead to some kind of joint action. There had been a case of acid throwing in the village: a boy had assaulted a girl who had refused his marriage proposal by disfiguring her face with acid. NK members had led the local reaction to the crime, organizing a procession of several hundred people to the authorities, making sure that they did what they otherwise might have chosen not to do, or been bribed or cajoled not to do—arrest the boy. He is now in jail. NK's central office had then joined in: they raised money for plastic surgery and found the girl a job in Dhaka.

In another social action, the village's NK groups had got up a procession and *gherao*'ed the authorities, surrounding and jeering at them as they tried to dismantle the huts of migrants from a distant village who had squatted on the nearby river embankment. Unlike the reaction to the acid throwing, which represented an obvious threat to their own village, helping these unrelated squatters seemed an act of pure benevolence. It was, an NK member told me, and it was led more by the NK workers than the members. Nevertheless, such support can have its own rewards, said NK member Lutfar, offering her own case as an example. Her father had lost an arm in an accident caused by electrical equipment that had not been properly maintained by the authorities. Requests for compensation were ignored until an NK-led procession, in which the embankment-dwellers joined, intimidated the authorities into making a gratuitous payment of 10,000 taka.

This sum was only a fraction of what was needed for her father's treatment, and to finance the rest, Lutfar, her mother, and her sister-in-law had raised another 90,000 taka from various microcredit NGOs, now being repaid from rickshaw income from Lutfar's son and nephew, and from Lutfar's business peddling saris in the villages. When I asked her to reflect on the two kinds of NGO—NK and the microcredit providers—her answer was thoughtful but straightforward: "Well, both helped me with my problem with my father, so I like them both. You see, one helped me directly, with the procession and all that, and the others helped me indirectly, with the loans. We need both kinds of help."

The Donors' Dilemma

Back in Dhaka, I did some research into donor thinking. Britain's DFID is one of the four big donors responsible for the bulk of aid to Bangladesh: the others are Japan, the World Bank, and the Asian Development Bank (ADB). As Bangladesh's long march to prosperity has continued, the proportion of the country's development budget supported from overseas has fallen from over 85 percent in the 1980s to less than 45 percent in the late 1990s, but donors remain important.[5]

When ASA was doing social mobilization, the big bilateral and multilateral donors had not gotten into the habit of financing NGOs. DFID had mainly supported infrastructure projects such as the road and power networks. But it had a poor opinion of the government's record in providing basic services to the public, and this eventually led it to fund NGOs directly. Some of this support went to microcredit funds—DFID supported BRAC and Proshika—until the rise of PKSF made that unnecessary, but more went, and still goes, to NGO partners for work in education, health, and water supply, for example. But the donors didn't want to undermine an already weak government by building too strong an NGO sector, and this led them to seek cleverer ways of working with government. One line of thought was that receiving governments would improve their performance if they took full "ownership" of (that is, full responsibility for) aid policy and expenditure. Accordingly, DFID briefly experimented, in just one sector, with *direct budget support*—handing money to the Bangladesh government and leaving it to decide how to spend it. DFID withdrew quickly from this when they found, as they diplomatically put it, that the Bangladesh government was handicapped by "capacity constraints" that made it hard for them to "capture the full benefits" of this kind of support. In other words, they dropped it because it was being siphoned off by corrupt politicians.

Further rethinking was in order, and the arrival of Tony Blair's government in the United Kingdom in 1997 gave this thinking a boost. In common with other donors, DFID had come to believe that it was not so much lack of money but lack of sound institutions and good governance that stopped countries like Bangladesh from developing more rapidly and fairly. But how to improve another country's institutions and governance was not obvious. Sending civil servants to attend courses in western colleges didn't seem to have had much impact. So when it was proposed, the idea of working on the "demand side," by finding ways to help ordinary Bangladeshis to put pressure on their own government to improve things, appeared promising. This was especially attractive because it chimed with the renewed commitment to poverty eradication within the aid community: DFID was a leader in putting poverty at the center of aid, and the adoption of the millennium development goals by the members of the UN in 2000 strengthened this with its focus on indicators of poverty such as income, school attendance, infant mortality, and so on. Fomenting demand for better schools and clinics from poor people themselves, if it could be done, might help to reach the MDGs faster.

And so *voice* became central to DFID's aid. DFID wrote in their 1998 strategy paper for Bangladesh, "If poverty is to be reduced in Bangladesh, it is necessary that the poor themselves become a stronger voice in society."[6] *Voice* in this context means direct participation in decision making by ordinary citizens. The aid givers could not promote voice directly, but local organizations could be helped to do it.[7] This led back to the NGOs, only this time NGOs were seen not as alternative service delivery channels, but as components of "civil society": local bodies that articulated the aspirations of ordinary citizens and enabled them to be heard at all levels of government. Happily, there had been a steady increase in the number and strength of NGOs working on policy issues and on *rights*: environmental and social rights, women's rights, children's rights, and rights to justice or information, for example. Most of the international NGOs had joined this group, subcontracting their project work in the villages to local NGOs. An observer pointed out that Bangladesh had an unusual combination of a weak government but a strong civil society.

In this way DFID came to support NK. Reviews done for DFID to try to determine whether their investment has been fruitful have been mixed.[8] Donors like to be able to measure the impact of their work. This proved hard to do with NK, not just because it is difficult to make judgments about how the NK-related experiences of people like Lutfar helped her, or changed the situation in which households like hers live, but because—as both sides admit—the work style of NK, which needs to be sensitive to people and their problems as they emerge, and to events as they arise, doesn't fit very easily with the hard-edged devices that DFID uses to track and measure progress.[9] There's a little bit of Shafiq's old problem here: "What will the donors say? They will ask, 'Only one social action, two social actions…how are you earning your money?' " Still, DFID staff members believe that simply by battling on year after year, fighting for the rights of ordinary poor citizens, NK and others like it have helped to shape public opinion and the behavior of officials. But NK, with about two hundred thousand members scattered over the country, reaches only a small proportion of the population, and the costs to DFID of managing its relationship with NK do not look like a bargain to the donor's auditors. For these kinds of reasons DFID is now creating and funding stand-alone *challenge funds*, which award contracts to promising initiatives at arm's length from the donor itself. If NK continues to draw DFID support, it will most likely come through *Manusher Jonno* ("For the People"), a fund that DFID and some like-minded donors have established.

Microfinance and Poverty

Although microfinance, compared to the kind of work that NK does, has many elements that are precisely measurable, the problem of assessing its impact on poverty appears to be just as hard. If researchers had been able to come to clear conclusions about the impact that microfinance has made on poverty in Bangladesh, those letters to the newspapers that we noted at the start of the chapter would get crisp replies, and Sushil Kumar Roy and his colleagues in the tower could adjust ASA's products accordingly, and move closer to "getting microfinance right." But measuring the effects of microfinance isn't easy, whether we are trying to understand the extent that microfinance improves incomes, or promotes microenterprises, or has some other effect on poverty or on poor people, such as improving their health or advancing their education or helping them to exercise their rights or to influence local or national politics.

In the late 1990s, Shahid Khandker undertook a large survey in Bangladesh for the World Bank, and many hoped it would settle the issue.[10] It showed that households with someone in a microcredit group increased their expenditure on food and other goods and services more than households that lack such a member but are otherwise similar. Presumably, they had increased their income. They were also better able to *smooth consumption* (a technical term meaning that savings and credit help you to have something to eat always, rather than just when you happen to have earned some income). This didn't sound like "the end of poverty," and some practitioners were disappointed.

But measuring impact is as contentious as it is difficult. Another researcher, Jonathan Morduch, ran an analysis of the data that Khandker had gathered and found the consumption smoothing but not the consumption increase.[11] Other studies showed that microfinance had a beneficial effect on some nonincome aspects of poverty, such as the education and health of member households and women's influence in the home and freedom of movement in the village. But it wasn't clear which aspects of microfinance were responsible for these effects: they may have been due to loans, or they may simply come about when poor women are "organized" into groups, as yet other studies suggested. The matter remains contentious.

The present book, with its focus on understanding the behavior of those who offer and those who use microfinance services, may be well placed to make some informed guesses about what is going on.

Most Bangladeshi microfinance is what we have called the *core product*: the small annual loan repaid in weekly installments. As we saw in chapter 7, precisely because they are so easy to repay, households use these loans, which are rarely worth more than two or three months' household income, for whatever purpose is most urgent at the time. Although much of the credit, by value, may get used for some kind of income-generating purpose, investment in *businesses*—permanent and profitable enterprises—is done by a minority of borrowers and the small microcredit loans more often supplement, rather than transform, the businesses. This helps explain why surveys do not pick up big effects on microenterprise development, and register only mild effects on household income. But as we asserted in chapter 7, having a reliable financial partner is of immense importance for poor people, because it helps them manage a resource that, by definition, poor people have in short supply—money. That may be why all surveys pick up microfinance's effects on consumption smoothing, a phrase that understates the importance that access to liquidity can play in the fortunes of the poor.

Many of microfinance's most important effects are indirect, and surveys like the one by the World Bank cannot detect them. For example, Rasheda was always able to borrow from her family when she needed to buy medicine for her children because they could rely on her repaying them when the next ASA loan came along. In Manikganj, Zigir and his family never used microcredit to run a business, but as the foundation for a complex structure of transactions that led to vastly increased income from his two employed sons and propelled them into the ranks of rural well-to-do. In their case, microcredit did not achieve this miracle on its own—it had to be matched to hard work and shrewdness and to informal sources of credit—but at the same time the achievement itself would have been impossible without the continuity that microcredit gave to their financial life. In Comilla, NK member Lutfar saved her father's life with the help of microcredit loans, something of immense value to her that would show up in no survey of income or microenterprise growth.

But there remains, as Darbesh Ali reminded me, a particular problem for the *very* poor. Their access to microfinance has been limited, so their chances of benefiting from both its direct and indirect effects are constrained.

The Very Poorest

In its earliest days, ASA was not especially committed to working with the very poorest people in Bangladesh. Its first groups were formed of able-bodied working men who could be urged to confront oppression, not of deserted mothers struggling to bring up a child without male support in the household. The microcredit movement, though, did claim to be working with *the poorest of the poor*: the phrase became a popular one with NGOs, endlessly repeated in their grant applications to donors and their annual reports. It therefore came as something of a shock to NGO watchers and the public when, in the mid-1990s, Dr. Yunus of Grameen admitted that his bank found it hard to retain *very* poor members.[12] Researchers argued about the numbers, but at least 10 percent of rural households, and perhaps as many as 20 percent, had cash flows that were so frail—so small, irregular, and unreliable—that they couldn't make steady weekly repayments 52 weeks a year. The slightest upset, a brief illness of the breadwinner, for example, caused them to fall into payment arrears and, often, to quit their microcredit group altogether.

Microcredit insiders knew this all along, of course. Hardheaded ones like ASA, as we have seen, advised its staff not to take the very poor for this precise reason. Loan officers soon learned how to deal with weak payers: somehow or other, get them to pay back their current loan until their debt is no bigger than their savings, then "allow them to leave" the samity. This formula provides at least some dignity on both sides: I have met many ex-members who, from ASA's point of view, were eased out because they were poor payers but who, from their own point of view, left honorably, without leaving debt behind. Kulsum, when she left ASA six years ago, was one of these.

After Yunus's surprise admission, there was considerable interest in finding ways to make microcredit more friendly to the very poor (or "hardcore poor," "extreme poor," or "ultra poor," as they were variously called), and many programs were tried. Some sought to work intensively with very poor households to bring them up to a level at which they could benefit from regular microcredit. BRAC's "Challenging the Frontier of Poverty Reduction" (CFPR) initiative goes beyond that, seeking not just to prepare very poor people to make good use of microfinance, but to establish a fresh approach to working with very poor people in which microfinance is just one element.[13] Although BRAC is one of the three biggest microfinance providers in Bangladesh (70 percent of its staff members work in microfinance), the NGO "doesn't want microfinance to be its driving culture,"[14] Imran Matin, its research director, told me. It wants to be known as a development organization. This makes it more sympathetic than ASA to researching intricate routes to poverty alleviation.

In CFPR, for example, very carefully selected "ultra-poor" women work with a team of BRAC staff members who try to identify and find solutions to the full range of constraints they face: not just their financial difficulties but their health problems, their skills deficit, perhaps their weak integration into their village society, and their own lack of self-confidence. While this is going on, they receive a subsistence grant, and in due time a package of assets to get them going on some activity that they feel they can make a success of: it might be poultry raising or crafts production or the like. They may or may not end up a member of a microfinance group, run by BRAC or by another credit provider. CFPR illustrates the BRAC view that, as Matin said, in order to take the struggle against poverty further, microfinance must be seen as a resource now widely available for incorporation into new, "smarter" programs. All this, of course, costs money, and CFPR is well supported by donors.

Another novel aspect of CFPR is that among the many tools that BRAC has developed to help the very poorest are "village poverty alleviation committees"—essentially groups of the wealthy elite in the village plus some NGO staff members—who are encouraged to oversee the progress of CFPR participants. They are to look out for the poor in times of crisis or emergency, and see to it that they have basic sanitation and water. They give cash support whenever it may be needed to ensure that the CFPR participant's family is eating or can get medical attention. This is an interesting reversal of the target group approach (chapter 4) that BRAC's own earlier research, especially the book *The Net*, had done so much to popularize as the main organizational principle of NGO work. That approach saw the interests of the poor and the elite as irrevocably opposed, as did Harvey Perkins, ASA's mentor. But poverty, says Matin, is about more than just the poor, and the fight against poverty must involve more than just the poor. In an echo of what the villagers of Manikganj told me, Matin points out that the "village elite," so often demonized by social activists, turns out, in the end, to be made up of ordinary people with ordinary jobs: perhaps drivers or field workers for BRAC or NK.

Other microfinance NGOs who have looked at the problem of including the poorest, have tried to adapt microcredit to fit the very poor, rather than adapt the very poor to fit microcredit. Grameen, with its beggars program, is the best known of these. ASA was another. In ASA's "hardcore poor program," the poorest were offered smaller loans and more flexible repayment schedules, subsidized from income on regular loans. But ASA's strength is in simple products that can be offered, profitably, en masse to millions of clients. It never really put its heart into special services for the extreme poor. Shafiq recognized this when he told me, in a recent interview, that such work is better left to others. The hardcore poor program is being downplayed. ASA will not emulate BRAC's CFPR program, and not only because ASA has no wish to take donor money again. ASA's talents lie in doing simple things on a large scale, not in developing the specialist staff skills that BRAC needs to make a success of CFPR.

ASA's best hope of working with the very poorest is to continue to develop its products to make them usable by a wider, including a poorer, range of households, and later in this chapter we will look at some ideas that should help achieve that. Meanwhile, simply gaining entry to a microfinance group is now much easier for the very poor than it used to be because of growing competition between providers. In the drive to get members at all costs, providers are willing to recruit members from a wider range of economic backgrounds including the very poor, have adjusted group sizes to ensure that members can join as soon as they apply rather than having to wait until there is a vacancy in a group and have changed loan disbursement procedures so as to give a loan as soon as a member joins. They are also happy to welcome back many members who had previously dropped out of their own groups or those of another provider: it was Shafiq himself who pointed out to me that many of those now joining ASA are "returners." But the very ease with which even the poorest can now get microcredit raises worries that they may use it unwisely, leading to repayment failure or overindebtedness. This takes us back to Shafiq's concerns about "overlapping" and his fear that "there will be a train crash. Which train will crash, and where it will crash, we don't know. We will make sure it isn't ASA."

Avoiding the Train Crash

The possibility of a microfinancial crash in Bangladesh cannot be entirely ruled out. The core microfinance product is now widely available throughout the country, through many hundreds of providers, of whom ASA is one of the big three that hold the bulk of the business. Away from extremely remote areas, most households have at least two or three providers serving their village or slum, and many households have opened accounts in more than one NGO. Imran Matin of BRAC says that the "first-generation gains" of microfinance have been realized, in that most poor Bangladeshis now have routine access to a basic banking service that is often more reliable than the educational and health services that they commonly encounter. Nowhere else in the world has this yet happened.

Before the turn of the century, commentators were already warning that the basic microloan market was nearing saturation. They prophesied that multiple accounts would lead to sharply declining repayment rates as borrowers became cavalier about the ease with which they could draw credit. They also warned of an unhealthy increase in indebtedness among the users, as they borrow from one provider to repay the next, noting the potential similarity to what can happen in credit card markets when they first reach saturation. In 2003, South Korea was to go through those convulsions. As the BBC reported: "The average South Korean now owns at least four credit cards, but alarm bells are ringing, as household debt has nearly doubled over the past five years.... Record numbers of Koreans are in arrears on their credit card payments."[15]

It isn't hard to find examples in Bangladesh of microcredit users in arrears on payments to multiple providers. In Gazipur in central Bangladesh, S. K. Sinha recently interviewed Johura Begum and her husband Shamsuddin, a couple whose children have grown up and left home, and who are now struggling to stay alive on the very small income that Shamsuddin earns as a day laborer on the very few days that his increasingly poor health allows him to work.[16] Johura has been a member of Grameen Bank since 1986 but in the last five years she has taken additional memberships in no fewer than six microfinance NGOs, including ASA—as well as getting taken on as a borrower in a second Grameen branch. The loans she has taken have paid for food, for medical treatment for Shamsuddin, without which he may not have survived, and for the marriage costs of their second son. But all this has left them with microcredit debts totaling 62,000 taka (about $900) that require 2,600 taka in weekly repayments, far more than they earn in any week. Sinha calculated, from their passbooks, that over the last few months they have been repaying an average of 340 taka each week: less than an eighth of what is due. The NGOs have responded variously: some, like ASA, keep up the weekly pressure for repayment and settle for a token payment, while others visit the couple rarely, having concluded that it simply isn't worth chasing these debts. In the end, some loans will be traded off against the couple's savings, some formally canceled, and some forgotten: the couple may manage to repay most of what they owe to one or perhaps two providers who will then allow them to borrow again. If Shamsuddin dies, the providers will cancel the debts and will not chase Johura.

Aware of the business risks if too many cases like Shamsuddin and Johura's occur, but unequipped with any industry-wide mechanism to curb growth, the microcredit NGOs have been indulging in what some see as a race to the cliff edge, with each organization determined to secure the largest possible share of the market before it starts to shrink. PKSF, with its massive funds, fuels the process. Rather than shun areas already heavily populated by competitors, organizations have been rushing to establish branches wherever a rival has one.

When, in late 2007, ASA decided to impose a six-month pause on the expansion of branches to allow time for the recruitment of staff members needed for its program of computerization, there was a feeling in the tower that this wasn't such a bad thing, given the possibility of a "train crash." Shafiq was then more worried about the consequences of all-out competition than at any other time in our conversations. A survey that branch staff members had recently completed had made Shafiq feel that "the scenario is very horrifying," with too many borrowers multiply indebted, and missed payments on the rise. A circular went out to the staff advising caution: lower the amount by which loan values can rise each loan cycle, reduce the numbers of members per staff to allow the staff more time to sort out problem borrowers, and do all this even at the cost of losing some members. This was briefly reversed when the six-month pause ended in the spring of 2008, but by the middle of the year Shafiq decided that prudence should prevail: no more branches will open for the foreseeable future.

The crash may not be too severe, and ASA can certainly avoid it. Happily, microfinance's core product loans are not as dangerously liable as credit cards to create overindebtedness. Microfinance lenders require that borrowers repay some 9 percent of the capital value of the loan each month, with no fresh credit available until most of the loan is paid down, whereas many credit card companies will allow their clients to build debt much more rapidly. The financial diaries revealed only modest debt levels among microcredit borrowers, partly because, as Rasheda pointed out, they are repaid week by week, unlike debt from village moneylenders. When poor people choose to pay off moneylender debt by borrowing from microlenders, as they often do, it is not just because the NGO debt is cheaper (which it usually is) but because microfinance loans' disciplined repayment schedules make them easier to repay. Moreover, microfinance clients tend to build up savings—even the desperate Johura and Shamsuddin had 12,500 taka in savings accounts at the eight NGO branches they were in contact with, more than 20% of their outstanding debt.

Improving the Core Product

There is plenty of scope for ASA to improve the core product. Its success in opening up its savings accounts to allow members to choose different levels of weekly deposits, and to take withdrawals in any amount in any week, shows that it has learned how to broaden its principle of standardization to offer equally disciplined but more flexible services. The new computers make that even easier, as they reduce the bookkeeping burden on the loan officers and provide better real-time data to managers worried about the risk of fraud. It is time, therefore, to bring a similar level of flexibility to ASA's loans. The most obvious first step would be to offer a range of loan terms. A choice of terms of, say, 3, 6, 12, or 24 months will improve existing clients' chances of matching their borrowing to their needs. It should also attract, or help retain, poorer clients who find it difficult to maintain repayments over a full year because they have seasonal dips in income: they could choose shorter terms that avoid the need for repayments in the downtimes. Grameen Bank has experimented with allowing borrowers to refresh their loan back up to its full capital value after six months of repayment. Our financial diary research showed that many Grameen borrowers treat that as an opportunity to borrow from the bank at six monthly, rather than annual, intervals, and it soon became popular. Mahenoor, from the poor district of Shariatpur, found that she liked "getting new money every six months. A year is too long. When loans are a year, you feel bad because you have spent the money and then you need to wait for many months before you can pay it off and can take a new loan. Sometimes it doesn't seem worth it. But if I get new money every six months it is really helpful for school fees, clothes, poultry and so on."[17] Mahenoor's comments suggest that there is also room for allowing borrowers to pay down loans before their full term: doing so might well increase borrowing enough to compensate for the additional work involved, and is the kind of improvement that computerization should be used to facilitate.

A choice of terms and options to prepay or refresh loans would make borrowing more manageable for many clients, not just the poor. ASA can build on that with improvements to the quality of customer service. At present, for example, microfinance clients in Bangladesh do not receive documentation of the products they use. They learn about the terms and conditions of the services from their loan officer by word of mouth. This is part of the old paternalism that accompanied early work with groups of poor village people, and for a long time it was justified on the grounds that most poor villagers can't read. That is changing: indeed, all microfinance clients now have a literate person in the immediate neighborhood, if not among the children in their own household. The lack of clarity about product rules causes endless confusion and frequent disputes in microfinance group meetings, but loan officers tolerate it out of fear of the alternative—well-informed clients willing to challenge them. Such old-fashioned attitudes must go, and ASA, the least bureaucratic of the providers and the most able to change course quickly, has an opportunity to get ahead of the competition by starting to shift to less unequal staff–member relationships. A senior officer of an NGO that works in both human rights and microfinance recently told me about their plans for new, rights-based work in ensuring that poor people get improved access to information. A good place to start, I suggested, would be by giving your microfinance clients access to unambiguous information on your savings and loan product rules.

Some ASA staff feel that ASA's commercial success could become an embarrassment. Profits from core product lending are large, but since 1991 they have been plowed back, just as quickly as possible, into new branches. But with the moratorium on branch opening, profits may simply pile up. "We must find a way" some fret, "of returning these profits to our members." One way of doing that, they argue, is through lowering the interest rates on loans or raising them on deposits or both. Dropping the interest rate on loans is certainly another way of making the core product more attractive, and, with ASA's rates at the industry's national average but a little above Grameen's, ASA is well placed to exercise that option at an appropriate time. But the idea of modifying rates as a way of returning profits to members is not popular with ASA's senior management, for good reasons. Interest rates are not set in a vacuum, but in an environment populated by many competitors. They should be changed as a way of moderating or stimulating business and keeping abreast of the market as it evolves, and not as a way of rewarding samity members.

ASA already returns some of its surpluses to samity members in the form of grants for hospital treatment for a limited range of serious illnesses. The payments are generous, usually enough to cover major surgery, but the budget is kept under control by rationing: the provision is capped at so many grants each year for each district, so not every ASA members enjoys this service. The program grew from the branch staff's observations of one of the dilemmas of general purpose credit services: that credit may be used in expensive ways that, before the coming of the microcredit providers, were seen as not within the expectation of poor villagers. Often the expenditure is for medical services, and this is one of the main causes of multiple indebtedness to several microfinance providers.

Johura and Shamsuddin were in exactly this situation. Asked to list the ways in which she had used her NGO loans, and then rank them in order of importance, Johura unhesitatingly put medical treatment at the top of her list. Without loans for health expenditure, said Johura, "we would not get rid of our serious aliments and consequently we would die." In a nearby village, also in Gazipur, an NGO microfinance group told us about a member, Biroja, who had had to leave their group. Biroja had been a good member, borrowing and repaying on time, but after her children left home and her husband died, she needed hospital treatment. Her erstwhile group members told us that to pay for her treatment, "She had to borrow in the village and she used her samity loan [20,000 taka, about $300]. She was cured and now she is back home. But she couldn't repay her samity loan on time so they cut her name. She is no longer in the samity and cannot get loans. She is living in a pitiable condition."[18]

The financial services approach to this problem is medical insurance, and insurance is a growing sector of microfinance internationally, with many advances being made.[19] At present, ASA has no plans to offer health insurance, but it is edging toward it in a number of ways. One is the hospitalization grants already mentioned. Another is the loan security fund, which managers sometimes allow to be tapped in emergencies. A third could emerge if current discussions about establishing medical institutions come to fruition. ASA may find it possible to make samity membership even more popular by including an insurance element in the security fund payments that provides members with cover for catastrophic medical treatment at an ASA-owned institution. That would allow members like Johura and Shamsuddin and Biroja to deal with their medical emergencies and maintain their rights to ASA's financial services, and it would help reduce the incidence of multiple membership that Shafiq found so horrifying.

Moving Upmarket

The core product market can be deepened, with a wider variety of products, including health insurance, in greater volumes, for years to come, even if the growth of the branch network slows or stops entirely. Meanwhile, it is already clear that ASA will make a determined attempt to open up a big new market among customers a notch or two wealthier than the typical core product samity member. That brings us to Madhuri Begum.

We met Madhuri Begum in Dhaka in late 2007. She's a formidable character intent on escaping from the rural poverty she was born into in her village in southern Bangladesh. The first step was migrating to Dhaka, 13 years ago, dragging her less ambitious husband with her: he now labors in a sawmill. Madhuri sews, and has made her skill the foundation of her success as a businesswoman. When she got to Dhaka, she immediately began to sew clothes for her slum neighbors. Soon she became a microcredit client of one of ASA's main competitors, and took three loans, all used to buy fabric. But she thoroughly disliked joint liability and hated "the meetings! They were a waste of my time. I had to sit around while everyone quarreled and the 'sir' shouted at us."[20]

So she left. A few months later she joined an ASA samity, but didn't enjoy that experience either: "They didn't honor me. I had the best business. I had two full time workers by then sewing for me. But all they would lend me was 7,000 taka! 7,000 taka! Think of it! That was no good to me. But they gave other women much more, and they had no businesses at all."

Disillusioned with microcredit, she started saving at a conventional bank, out of her business income, and patiently built a balance of 30,000 taka. She withdrew it and made a five-month rent advance on what she calls her "factory," the large, one-room, brick-walled, tin-roofed shed where we interviewed her. But she had underestimated the capital she'd need to keep her workers busy, so she started asking questions about microcredit again.

Hearing that ASA now gave bigger loans, she joined another ASA samity, and had better luck: they gave her a loan of 20,000 taka and then another of 25,000. Then she heard about a new ASA product, the small enterprise loan (SEL), given to entrepreneurs who are not obliged to join a samity and attend its weekly meetings. She started negotiating with ASA, and in due course a loan officer inspected her "factory" and lent her 40,000, which she is repaying in 12 monthly presigned checks drawn on her commercial bank account. For the first time during our interview, she broke into a smile: "I'm now a proper businesswoman and not just a group member. Now they have to treat me with respect. I don't need to waste time at meetings. Soon I will need a loan of 300,000 taka."

But though her SEL loan is only three months old, ASA has already had trouble collecting repayments. The loan officer presented the presigned checks at Madhuri's bank, only to find the account had insufficient funds. When we asked Madhuri about this, she shrugged. "Well, some customers were late paying me. So what? That's not my fault, is it? Does ASA seriously think I'm not going to pay?"

Johir, the loan officer, told me he was at a loss as to how to deal with Madhuri. Nothing in his career with ASA had prepared him for this. We went with him to his next SEL client, and rang the bell at a middle-class apartment. Johir looked miserable. The client patronized him, and insisted on talking English to me, knowing that Johir wouldn't be able to understand. The power ploy worked, and Johir was put firmly in his place.

As this story reveals, ASA, like all the major microfinance providers in Bangladesh, has already begun to work with a class of client somewhat better off than the typical core product samity member. Recently, as in Madhuri's case, it has been willing to work with them as individuals, outside the framework of the samity. In common with its competitors, ASA sees this as a market for business loans, not consumer loans. The perspective is consistent with microfinance's traditional focus on "productive" credit: money management and consumer lending are simply not "developmental" enough to suit the microfinance mission, even though, as we have seen in the previous chapters, much of the core product lending is in fact of that sort. We can safely predict that in the end microfinance providers will offer consumer loans. But first they have to learn to make business loans work properly.

Observers have long been urging microfinance organizations to start serious business lending. They note that the commercial banks are too stuffy to deal with small businesspeople (though that is changing), but group credit doesn't suit these clients either because loans are too small, and compulsory weekly attendance at meetings too costly.[21] They argue that lending to this class of small businessperson would not only help to develop the microenterprise sector nationally, but would also create jobs for poorer workers.

ASA would very much like to develop this business, which, though growing, still accounts for only a tiny proportion of its borrowers and less than 15 percent of its outstanding loan portfolio. But it's not ready yet, in several important respects. It hasn't obtained the right legal identity, nor has it developed the right technology, the right staff, or the right style of branch premises. Of these, executive vice president Sohel Mahmud Sagar thinks staff preparation is the most critical. Commenting on the "Johir problem"—ASA staff being patronized by business clients when all of their experience has been in dealing with samity members whom they can patronize—Sagar thinks it is simply a matter of getting used to it. He advocates target setting as the best way to force learning, requiring every branch manager throughout ASA to identify five small businesspeople, lend to them, and bring the resulting experience to meetings with their peers and seniors.

Thinking Like a Bank

Others think it will take more than that. Until very recently, all ASA's business loans were simply samity-style lending with rather bigger loan values. Only with the SEL loans, started in 2003, has ASA begun to learn how to underwrite individual business loans, and skills are still rudimentary. Shafiq believes ASA will need an entirely different presence to deal effectively with business lending: smart-looking premises that will impress the borrowers in the same way that educated young loan officers can impress the poorer samity members. Nor does he think that an NGO is the right legal identity for a business lender: business people will see them as soft, semicharitable organizations with little power to enforce contracts.

Moreover, notwithstanding the very high levels of profitability that the core product lending has produced, ASA would need much bigger quantities of capital to finance a large-scale shift into business lending. Grameen's success with deposit taking since its remake as Grameen II in 2001—it now finances its entire growing loan portfolio from deposits, some from *kendra* members and some from the general public—has been an eye-opener for ASA. Before he stopped borrowing from PKSF, Shafiq saw no reason to envy Grameen the bank ordinance that allows it to raise deposits from the general public. Now, mobilizing deposits to fund business loans is just one of several reasons to favor the acquisition of formal bank status.

Not that ASA itself will be transformed into a bank—or at least not yet. NGO status remains suitable for handling ASA's core product in the samities. In Bangladesh, NGOs may own for-profit businesses. When the NGO BRAC set up a licensed bank, BRAC Bank, there were legal challenges, but they were overcome, and BRAC Bank has entered the SME (small and medium enterprise) lending market. ASA has already tried to acquire a bank that was for sale, but failed. It will try again, or it may establish its own bank and use it as a vehicle for a major shift into deposit taking and business lending.

Updating the Pledge

In my very last interview with Shafiq,[22] I asked him what ASA's pledge would look like, updated for 2008. The answer comes in three parts. First, ASA promises to go on supplying a high-quality general savings and loan service to its millions of poor samity members and to continue to improve its range and quality. Second, the organization will harness its talent for creating cost-effective reliable basic services to develop small-business lending for hundreds of thousands of potential new clients in Bangladesh. Third, as we shall see in the final chapter, ASA promises to export it skills and its services on a massive scale to millions of poor people outside Bangladesh.

Chapter 10

An International Brand

When rural-based Maoist rebels triumphed in neighboring Nepal, ASA took no notice. It was too busy preparing for a new venture: ASA International. Much of the energy in ASA Tower now comes from its preparations for expansion into overseas markets. Even in the branches out in the countryside, lowly managers are poring over their English language textbooks, hoping to learn enough to get themselves selected for a spell working for ASA China, ASA India, or ASA Nigeria. Although ASA has been working overseas since the mid-1990s, it did so as a consultant, paid by international NGOs or United Nations projects to help develop microfinance internationally. But NGOs and multinational organizations are no longer the main investors in microfinance. Increasingly, money is coming from private sources: some of them pure profit-seekers, and others, the social investors, hoping for social as well as financial returns. ASA owns a share in a company that manages a multimillion-dollar fund, and its role is to make ASA's core product work wherever there are large populations of poor people who might find it useful. ASA and its founder Shafiq, could hardly be more pleased: they have a challenging but clearly defined job of enormous size that suits their talents perfectly.

March 2008

In 1996 Maoist rebels in Nepal, a country separated from Bangladesh by a narrow strip of Indian territory, began an insurgency aimed at replacing what they saw as an unjust and repressive social order with a socialist republic. For some time they were not taken seriously. They were based in the countryside, had few arms, and appeared incoherent and amateurish. But by successful raids on police stations they built up a formidable stockpile of weapons, and more and more areas came under their control. One of their aims, to abolish the monarchy, came unexpectedly closer when the royal family suffered a shoot-out in the palace in 2001 in which the king and other members of his family were killed. The dead king's brother then came to the throne, but in putting himself at the head of repressive measures against the rebels, only made himself more unpopular. With a large part of the countryside behind them—willingly or unwillingly—the rebels began to negotiate with the government, and in March 2008 confirmed their readiness to stand in national elections. These were held the following month, and the Maoists won handsomely.

Shafiq saw few parallels with Bangladesh and appeared unmoved by the success of a rural-based social revolution, with so many echoes of ASA's early days, in a country so close to home. Such insurgencies can be successful, he told me, only in countries with poorly developed infrastructure. In Bangladesh, after many years of investment, there are roads and telecommunications everywhere, leaving few places isolated enough for an insurgency to get going.

In any case, Shafiq and ASA had other things on their minds.

Marching Orders

ASA has been helping smaller Bangladeshi NGOs to follow its methodology since soon after its turn to microcredit. There are now about 30 that borrow money from ASA to fund their work, and ASA's investment in them totals close to $5 million. But work-sharing collaboration with other NGOs within Bangladesh has been less common and less successful, for reasons that the reader can by now guess: ASA has a set way of doing things and doesn't have the temperament or the time to get involved in variations to its work that are not going to be adopted ASA-wide.

That was the fate, for example, of a collaboration in the mid-1990s with an American international NGO, Save the Children USA.[1] The idea sounded good: Save, as it is known, had developed an innovative health program in a few villages in the south, but concluded that it would work much better if the villagers were able to improve or at least stabilize their incomes through savings and credit. Wisely, Save didn't set up its own microfinance program—the better NGOs had by then come to understand that short-term microbanking set up just to service other work rarely succeeds. Instead, it invited ASA to work alongside its own team, with the two NGOs interacting with groups that would serve both as ASA samities and as forums for Save's health work. It didn't last, largely because ASA, predictably, treated these groups no differently from its other tens of thousands of samities. From the point of view of the local Save workers, ASA's approach was too commercial—it led to some of the most vulnerable people in the village, many of them in poor health, quitting the group for failure to repay their loans on time.

But the association with Save led to new opportunities for ASA. Recognizing ASA's true strengths, Save commissioned it to advise on microcredit in programs it was running in Tajikistan and Afghanistan (from 1995), and Jordan and Ethiopia (from 1996). Again, ASA didn't find it easy to work in programs that had priorities other than microcredit, and in the end the collaborations were only partly successful. However, the experience overseas set ASA up to compete for other international contracts in which the focus would be wholly on microcredit. Some of these proved more successful and longer lasting.[2]

They came about when Henry "Hank" Jackelen, a jovial Brazilian–American banker and microcredit enthusiast who was working for the private sector development program at UNDP (United Nations Development Program), came through Bangladesh looking for help to kick-start microcredit in a range of developing countries. What Save's local field staff had found difficult—ASA's hard-nosed approach—is exactly what appealed to Hank. Back in 1991 he had written, with Beth Rhyne,[3] an article called "Towards a More Market-Oriented Approach to Credit and Savings for the Poor"[4]—and that's precisely what he found and liked in ASA. ASA competed for three of UNDP's "MicroStart" contracts and won two of them, to give microcredit a boost in the Philippines (from 1998) and to get it going in Nigeria (from 2000).

Joining the United Nations

ASA handled these contracts astutely. It had learned from its earlier ventures overseas that ASA-style microcredit would not take root in another culture until the senior local managers of the program had become convinced advocates of the ASA approach. Nigeria turned out to be the easier challenge. There, microcredit was a novelty, and UNDP had picked a local partner ready to be convinced. There was ample funding on offer, encouraging the partner to listen carefully to ASA. Shafiq, who looked after the contract himself and made several trips, found himself regarded with awe.

The Philippines was harder. There, microcredit was already well established, largely based on a version of Grameen's methodology adapted to local conditions, and its leaders were more experienced and more confident in their own way of doing things. ASA worked with several partners, and not all collaborations were successful, but by the end of an initial three-year program, clients served by the partners grew from about twelve thousand to forty thousand.

Since then, several of the partners have turned into large-scale providers.

The case of the Filipino microcredit provider CARD showed that ASA's penetration into the Philippines was more than skin deep. CARD, under its ebullient founder Aristotle Alip, had been one of the first NGOs to introduce the Grameen methodology to the country (Aris had also introduced it to Vietnam).[5] Confident in its own approach, it did not apply to take advice from ASA under the UNDP program. But after some disappointing results at CARD, Aris went to Bangladesh to see for himself whether ASA's approach might improve things. What he saw convinced him. He found ASA's methods simpler and more cost-effective than Grameen's. He liked the way that ASA's structure focused every staff members' attention on results, telling me in a recent interview that "ASA is not just a system, it's more 'a way of life'—an attitude about how to get things done."[6]

What appealed to him most was ASA's shift away from joint liability to greater reliance on well-trained loan officers to ensure good loan collection rates, as we described in chapter 7. Some of CARD's problems had arisen from too great a dependence on joint liability, in turn resting on too great a belief in the solidarity of the groups. Aris asked ASA and UNDP to extend the consultancy and bring CARD in as a partner. They did, and CARD turned, not without difficulties, to an approach more in line with ASA's, seeing borrowers less as cooperative members of self-help groups and more as individual clients borrowing on their own account.

One result of this is that, internationally, the ASA and Grameen approaches are seen as more distinct than they really are in the villages of Bangladesh. In Bangladesh, where Grameen, too, has abandoned any form of joint liability, clients report only small differences between the two. But the international understanding—that ASA has pioneered a fresh, new, individual approach to microfinance—has done ASA no harm at all. It has allowed it, unwittingly, to develop a "brand."

Aris found Shafiq easy to work with. Shafiq's frankness cuts through polite half-truths and discussions get quickly to the heart of the matter. In 2002–3, when CARD was facing difficulties with its introduction of the ASA methods, Aris was spending only part of his time at CARD, devoting the remainder to work in government, where he was an undersecretary in the social welfare ministry, and to consultancies. Shafiq, who had responded quickly to a call for help from Aris, flew into Manila and told him to get back to CARD full time. The reputations of both organizations were on the line, said Shafiq: "You should live or die with CARD."[7] In return, Shafiq promised whatever help was needed. It was forthcoming, and CARD is now a good advertisement for the ASA brand in the Philippines.

Independently of its UN contracts, ASA soon found itself in demand to coach other microbanks. Among the most spectacular of these is Bandhan, based in West Bengal, just across the Indian frontier with Bangladesh. By following ASA methods closely, and taking ASA staff on as consultants, Bandhan began to emulate, or even outstrip, ASA's rate of growth, reaching a million clients in 500 branches within six years of its foundation. When *Forbes* put ASA at the top of its list of microfinance operators, it put Bandhan second.[8]

ASA handles all of its international consultancy work in-house. It could easily have given contracts to the swelling band of consultants that has grown up as microfinance has expanded around the world, but it chose not to. Instead, it sends its own staff, so what the world sees of ASA is not polished international jet-setters but men of modest Bangladeshi backgrounds and basic English language skills, lacking fluency in the latest microfinance theories but single-mindedly committed to getting on with the job, and happy to work long hours as long as they can find somewhere to sleep soundly and cook some Bengali food. Having come up through the ASA ranks, they are used to being reposted from branch to branch throughout Bangladesh, and they are encouraged to see Nigeria or Sri Lanka as just the next place to get on with their normal work.

As time goes by, they are more and more at home in the wider world.

Shafiq Discovers Equity

The Save and UNDP projects were all funded in the traditional way, by donors. ASA earned a consultancy fee and a good reputation. As late as 2004, Shafiq would have wanted ASA's overseas work done in no other way. Then, in January 2005, he met Dirk Brouwer, a Dutch banker with a background in corporate finance. Dirk had left Merrill Lynch in 2002. He came away with enough money to set up his own business, but took a year-long break first, traveling in developing countries. He discovered microcredit, liked it, and saw opportunities to work with it. He thought about setting up an outfit to fund and train microfinanciers, and discussed ideas with a number of international microcredit figures from Latin America, Africa, and Asia, including Shafiq. Not much progress was made despite a raft of meetings because it was difficult to establish clear, doable goals that suited all the players. But Dirk took instantly to Shafiq, finding him refreshingly direct. Shafiq, clearly, was a microcredit wizard—but he knew almost nothing about finance. "He barely knew what 'equity' means," Dirk told me, "but he's an incredibly fast learner."[9] The two got on well, and since then have hatched a scheme to carry ASA's core product to millions more poor people worldwide.

The plan was to set up a commercial fund that would be invested in microfinance, though ideas about exactly how the money should be used have been, and still are, changing. Microfinance investment funds have become one of the most startling and fastest growing features of microfinance as it has expanded worldwide. More than anything else, they signal how thinking about microfinance is evolving. It is still widely seen as a development methodology for fighting poverty, backed by those whose business it is to look after such things—public and private donors, NGOs, developing country governments, and international organizations like the United Nations. But it is rapidly acquiring a second identity, as a fast-growing branch of international commercial finance. It has become what Wall Street types call an *asset class*. That is how *Forbes* magazine saw it when it put ASA at the top of its microfinance organizations rankings.

International funds for microfinance—*microfinance investment vehicles*, or MIVs—have been by far the fastest growing source of finance for microfinance in the last few years.[10] This is partly because older investors, such as public developments banks, have started to route their money through MIVs rather than passing them through governments or through set-ups like Bangladesh's PKSF (chapters 6 and 7). Individual investors, too, these days, put three or four times as much money into MIVs than they send directly to microfinance retailers, and that proportion may be growing. According to the World Bank (2008) most of these are social investors, who have a "double bottom line," as the jargon has it—they want their investments to show a social as well as a financial return.

But among institutional investors, there are many with a traditional for-profit motivation, such as pension funds, now coming into MIVs. This is especially the case since the financial world was startled when a canny Mexican microcredit organization, Compartamos, which had been good at raising investments and grew its lending business very quickly, sold a big chunk of itself through an initial public offering on the Mexican Stock Exchange.[11] Pent-up interest in microcredit as a commercial investment pushed its share value through the roof, turning its NGO backers and managers into millionaires overnight. It also drove the microfinance industry into a frenzy of self-examination, because it was the high interest rate on Compartamos's loans to poor rural women that contributed to the MFI's profitability and attracted the investors—and those women received no share of the bounty when Compartamos went public.

Traditional banks are scrambling to catch up, and many of the biggest names—Citi, Standard Chartered, Deutsche Bank, for example—are wholesaling loan funds to microcredit organizations. According to the latest figures I have, they lent more than half a billion dollars in that way in 2006, and the pace has certainly quickened since then, not least in Bangladesh, where BRAC and a number of the midsized lenders like BURO have borrowed heavily. That 2006 figure would be roughly 15 percent of the total funds available for microfinance in that year, reports the World Bank.

ASA International

Dirk and Shafiq and their organizations, Sequoia (from the Netherlands)[12] and ASA, opened their fund in late 2005, calling it CMI (Catalyst Microfinance Investors), and set up a company, owned equally by the partners, to manage it. The fund is to have a life of 10 years, at the end of which it will be sold, perhaps, if it is successful enough, by a placement on the London Stock Exchange or other international capital market. They immediately attracted some investors. At first the business plan was to place equity into promising young microfinance organizations in countries with big populations of poor people—India, China, Vietnam, and Cambodia, for example, though Africa was not ruled out—and introduce them to ASA's systems. Some partners were found in this way, including Lak Jaya in Sri Lanka, whose growth rate sprang to life as soon as it adopted ASA-like methods. But in general the recipe was too restrictive: there are not enough such organizations, and those that do exist often don't want to share power with an aggressive new investor with a mind of its own like CMI.

A rethink was needed, and the plan changed to a preference for *greenfield* sites: the setting up of brand-new microcredit lenders rather than trying to find a foothold, through debt or equity, in existing ones. Under such a circumstance, it makes sense to stress the ASA "brand," so, where possible, the new ventures will use the name ASA, and be part of an international grouping, "ASA International," a name that has already been registered. Notwithstanding the preference for greenfielding, in practice, as experience is showing, there will be a mix of arrangements, depending on the legal environment in each country and the state of development of its microfinance. The situation in the three biggest potential markets illustrates this. In Nigeria, ASA's old UNDP partner is applying for a bank license and may change its name to ASA Nigeria. In India, work has started with the purchase of a non-bank financial institution (NBFI) and a network of branches opened up in West Bengal, next door to Bangladesh.[13] In China, they have recently secured permission to buy a majority share in a finance company, but so far in just one province.

Meanwhile, the fund has filled up to its forecast $125 million, with American and Dutch pension funds among the biggest investors. In addition, the banks are trouping into ASA to suggest that the managers leverage the fund's capital with their loans. The Gates Foundation has offered to lend $20 million at 3 percent a year for the 10 years of the fund's life.

ASA (Bangladesh) is contracted by the fund management company to be the exclusive provider of technical inputs into all these ventures. This is a massive task, but Shafiq is happy with it, telling me, "I am glad, Stuart. I thought maybe I had made a mistake, becoming a fund manager. But now I can concentrate on managing the growth of these new banks."[14]

Under the arrangement between ASA and Sequoia, the Dutch firm will do all the tricky setting up—the legal issues, the fine print of the contracts, the getting of visas, and the shaking of hands with bureaucrats. Shafiq has concluded that, internationally, ASA's home-grown staff members are at a disadvantage in such tasks. What the Bangladeshis can do is run a microcredit show, make it profitable, and scale it up in double-quick time. ASA will send its own managers to establish the new ventures or remodel existing ones, so that local managers can be exposed directly to the ASA work ethic. In some cases, ASA will set up training centers in the receiving countries to speed up the process.

That is the wager that Dirk Brouwer and Sequoia are making on behalf of the fund's investors. Essentially, they are betting that ASA's classic core product, which we have examined closely in this book, is going to appeal to multimillions of poor households in countries that are similar to Bangladesh in having big populations with unreliable access to credit. In making this bet, they are covering new ground in two important ways. First, most foreign investment in microfinance has gone elsewhere. Noting that Latin America, Eastern Europe, and Central Asia account for most of it, a World Bank report says, "Africa and Asia, where poverty and potential microfinance demand is highest, receive only six and seven percent of foreign investment, respectively."[15]

That may change: much more may flow into Asia and Africa. But the second respect in which new ground is being covered is more interesting. Most investment in microfinance has been based on the assumption that loans go to small business holders, something that is often true in markets in transition economies in Eastern Europe, Latin America, and Central Asia. In those markets, loan sizes, both in absolute terms and relative to GNP, are bigger than in Bangladesh. By backing ASA, CMI is betting that convenient general purpose credit, based on the core Bangladeshi product with its low loan values and frequent repayment installments, will be attractive to tens of millions of households who may not own or run businesses. Just as ASA did at home, the first product to be rolled out will be credit, backed by as much compulsory savings as is compatible with local law. Only where or when ASA can get a license to mobilize deposits will the full range of savings services come on line.

* * *

Just as its core product, the small general-purpose loan, is running up against its limits in its home territory, ASA is gearing up to get it going in the vast spaces of China, India, Nigeria, and elsewhere. If the assessment of the core product presented in this book is right—a useful service that may not always transform poor people's lives but rarely fails to help them—ASA's internationalization is something to celebrate.

As Dirk sees it, he has a profitable product—the ASA methodology—to sell. As Shafiq sees it, "A lot of Latin American and other microcredit organizations are also going towards commercialization, but I say no! We are going in a new way. We can show to the whole world that by serving the very poor it can be profitable."[16] Watch out for ASA's distinctive green and yellow signboard in a village or slum near you.

Notes

Preface

1. Matthew Swibel, *The World's Top Microfinance Institutions*, December 20, 2007, http://www.forbes.com/2007/12/20/top-microfinance-philanthropy-biz-cz_ms_1220intro.html (accessed May 16, 2008).

2. I first went to Bangladesh in April 1983 and lived there from December 1984 until March 1999. I was familiar with the work of ASA in the field from the time of the 1985 cyclone. I met Shafiqual Haque Choudhury, the founder of ASA, in 1993. In 1995 I wrote, for ASA, *ASA: The Biography of an NGO*, published privately by ASA in Dhaka. From 1996 to 1999 I served on the governing body of ASA. After 1999 I traveled frequently to Bangladesh.

Chapter 1

1. Md stands for the Prophet Muhammad, and is often prefixed to Bengali names of Arabic origin, such as Choudhury's.

2. Under the British, *zamindars* were given outright title to their land on which they were to pay a fixed tax. They collected tax from their tenants in ways that were sometimes brutal, sometimes fair if paternalistic. For a vivid fictional description of the *zamindari* system at the end of its life, and an account of its abolition, see Vikram Seth's novel *A Suitable Boy* (New York: HarperCollins, 1993).

3. For a discussion of how Islam came to Bangladesh, see David Abecassis, *Identity, Islam and Human Development in Rural Bangladesh* (Dhaka: Dhaka University Press, 1990), on which this account is partly based.

4. For Sufism in Bengal, see Muhammad Enamul Huq, *A History of Sufism in Bengal* (Dhaka: Asiatic Society of Bangladesh, 1975).

5. A haji is someone who has performed the haj—the pilgrimage to Mecca, which is a duty for all Muslims who have the means to achieve it.

6. For more on the Fara'izi movements, see A. F. Salahuddin Ahmed, *Bengali Nationalism and the Emergence of Bangladesh* (Dhaka: ICBS 1994, distributed by Dhaka University Press, Dhaka), and Lawrence Ziring, *Bangladesh from Mujib to Ershad: An Interpretive Study* (Dhaka: Dhaka University Press, 1992).

7. This view is not shared by all authors: some books present the Fara'izi movement as one of ignorant fundamentalism.

8. Indigo was not a native crop, but was introduced by the British partly as a way of raising income by means of taxing its production.

9. Asif Dowla (personal communication, May 2008) notes that economics professor Muhammad Yunus was experimenting with *tebhaga* systems for irrigated land near the university in Chittagong when he first encountered the villagers to whom he was to give the loans that marked the start of the Grameen Bank experiment.

10. Taj Ul-Islam Hashmi, *Peasant Utopia: The Communalization of Class Politics in East Bengal 1920–1947* (Dhaka: Dhaka University Press, 1994).

11. *Ittefaq* (Revolution), a leading Bangla-language daily, Dhaka, April 4, 1957.

12. This section owes much to discussions with Nurur Rahman, now of the Bangladesh Agricultural Working People's Association (BAWPA) and former leader of *Bangladesh Khetmojur Samity* (Labor on the Land), a peasant movement inspired in part by Bhasani, in whose movement Nurur worked at one time. See Rahman's *Report on the 17 Peasant and Agricultural Workers' Associations of Bangladesh* (Dhaka: PACT–PRIP Bangladesh, 1992).

13. Besides Bhasani and Huq, H. S. Suhrawardy, from Calcutta, was another major force in Muslim Bengali politics. He had been a Muslim League chief minister of undivided Bengal in the British period (like Huq), and tried hard to avoid Bengal's partition in 1947. He is not given prominence here because he was not seen as a peasant leader in the way that Bhasani and Huq were. He died in 1963.

14. My account follows that of Muhammad Ghulam Kabir, *Changing Face of Nationalism: The Case of Bangladesh* (Dhaka: Dhaka University Press, 1994).

Chapter 2

1. Azizul Haq, interview with author, Dhaka, September 10, 1994.

2. Asif Dowla (personal communication, May 2008) tells me that the Mogul (Muslim period) *taccavi* system was based on grants for disaster relief: the British changed this to loans.

3. *Daily Star*, Dhaka, January 10, 2008.

4. J. Allister McGregor, of the University of Bath, United Kingdom, *Credit, Debt and Morals: Local and Universal Models in Development Practice in South Asia*, based on a paper presented to the European Network of Bangladesh Studies in the Netherlands in 1994, unpublished and currently under revision. Several of the examples of colonial concern with credit in this chapter are taken from McGregor's paper.

5. See A. M. M. Shawkat Ali, *Agricultural Credit in Bangladesh* (Dhaka: Centre for Development Research, 1990), for a good general survey.

6. Nicholson Report, 1885, for the Madras Administration.

7. A. M. M. Shawkat Ali, *Agricultural Credit in Bangladesh*.

8. Unions cover a number of villages and are run by an elected *union parishad*. A union might these days have a population of 20,000 to 40,000.

9. Quoted in Hasnat Abdul Hye, *Cooperatives, Comilla and After* (Comilla: Bangladesh Academy for Rural Development, 1993), from which the later quotation from Khan in this chapter also comes.

10. For more information, contact CCULB (Cooperative Credit Union League of Bangladesh), phone: (880) 2-9899739, fax: (880) 2-8813781.

11. Clarence Maloney and A. B. Sharfuddin Ahmed, *Rural Savings and Credit in Bangladesh* (Dhaka: Dhaka University Press, 1988).

12. Fritz Bouman first named the ROSCA: see his later review of them in F. J. A. Bouman, "Rotating and Accumulating Savings and Credit Associations: A Development Perspective," *World Development* 23, no. 3 (1995): 371–84. A book by Shirley Ardener and Sandra Burman, eds., *Money-Go-Rounds: The Importance of Rotating Savings and Credit Associations for Women* (Washington: BERG, 1995), illustrates the way the device is used around the world. My own book, Stuart Rutherford, *The Poor and Their Money* (Delhi: Oxford University Press, 2000), reviews how the poor manage money and discusses ROSCAs at length in this context.

13. See two articles by Md Maniruzzaman, "ROSCA: A Self-Sustaining Non-formal Financial Institution," *Bangladesh Observer*, June 23 and 24, 1993.

14. Asif Dowla tells me (private correspondence, May 2008) that the staff at Grameen Bank's head office run a ROSCA.

Chapter 3

1. Whether the 1971 conflict was a struggle for independence or for liberation became, later, a matter of dispute. See Moudud Ahmed, *Democracy and the Challenge of Development* (Dhaka: Dhaka University Press, 1995).

2. According to Rounaq Jahan, *Bangladesh Politics: Problems and Issues* (Dhaka: Dhaka University Press, 1980, revised 2005), the government in 1973 had no less than five armed organizations: in addition to the army, navy, and air force, the Awami League had another and its labor front yet another. Jahan wrote in 1980, "Clashes amongst these *Bahinis* are quite frequent" (p. 130, n. 28 of the revised 2005 edition). Between June and November 1973 there were armed attacks on 52 police stations.

3. However, at that time the army was in serious disarray, and was not brought back to discipline until the regime of General Zia in the late 1970s.

4. *Bari* is often translated as "homestead." Strictly speaking, it is an area of land raised above the flood plain on which one or more households—usually but not always related—build their houses.

5. Translations from Bangla of interviews with Bangladeshi villagers and slum dwellers are mostly by S. K. Sinha, though some are by the author. The interview with Yusuf Ali, by the author and S. K. Sinha, took place at his home village in Patuakhali in November 1994.

6. Binayak Sen, Mustafa K. Mujeri, and Quazi Shahabuddin, *Operationalising Pro-Poor Growth*, a report written for the donors AFD, BMZ (GTZ, KfW Development Bank), DFID, and the World Bank (Dhaka, October 2004), http://www.dfid.gov.uk/pubs/files/oppgbangladesh.pdf (accessed May 16, 2008).

7. At first the acronym stood for Bangladesh Rural Advancement Committee, but now the organization is known simply as BRAC.

8. For a description of the war written soon after it finished, see chapter 3 of Jahan, *Bangladesh Politics*.

9. See Stuart Rutherford, "Learning to Lend" (London: Save the Children, Overseas Department Working Paper No. 5, 1993).

10. Muhammad Yunus, *Grameen Bank Project in Bangladesh: A Poverty Focussed Rural Development Programme* (Dhaka: Grameen Bank, 1982); quoted on the Grameen Bank website in abridged form at http://www.grameen-info.org/index.php?option=com_content&task=view&id=19&Itemid=114 (accessed August 18 2008).

11. Manzarul Alam, interview with author, Dhaka, February 19, 2008.

12. Shereen Rahman, interview with author, Dhaka, February 18, 2008.

13. See Ali, *Agricultural Credit;* Maloney and Sharfuddin Ahmed, *Rural Savings;* and F. Cruz, *History of the Credit Union Movement in Bangladesh* (Dhaka: CCULB, n.d., before 1995).

14. A way of rescheduling debts in which a fresh loan is issued but is used in part (or even in whole) to repay a delinquent earlier loan. See

Maloney and Sharfuddin Ahmed, *Rural Savings*, p. 119, for case studies of BRDB rollover loan behavior.

Chapter 4

1. Susanta Adhikari, interview with author, Dhaka, October 1994.

2. In Bombay the main influence on Shafiq was Malcolm Buck, a teacher at the Centre for Development Studies.

3. Grameen Bank itself was well aware of the tension between conscientization and the need to help the poor with financial and employment programs. For a book that discusses these problems in the context of the bank, see David Bornstein, *The Price of a Dream* (New York: Oxford University Press, 1996).

4. See Lawrence Lifshultz, *Bangladesh: The Unfinished Revolution* (London: Zed Books, 1989).

5. This and all other quotations from Shafiqual Haque Chowdhury in this chapter are from a series of interviews with the author in his office in Dhaka in August, September, and October 1994.

6. Golum Chowdhury was a governing body member until 1983, then left. He returned to ASA later as an employee. He left and became involved in several other NGOs.

7. The spelling Chowdhury (as opposed to his father's Choudhury) came about simply as the result of a transcription error by the registrars.

8. In *ASA in Transition* (Dhaka: ASA, 1994), coauthored with Mustafa Kamal, now ASA's head of research, p. 7.

9. Quotations from Mongol Sheikh, Akhtar, Shusil Bhowmik, and Poran Ali in this chapter are from interviews made in the field by the author and S. K. Sinha during several trips to Manikganj and nearby villages in September and October 1994.

10. This may not have much to do with ASA. There have been rickshaw driver associations in many local bazaars for many years.

11. To *gherao*: literally to surround; a mass of people surrounding a government officer or office can be very intimidating.

12. Several of the quotations from interviews with Shafiqual Haque Choudhury in English, such as this one, from an interview in Dhaka in August 1994, are presented verbatim, from recordings made by the author.

13. Kamrul Hassan later went to the Institute of Social Studies in the Hague to complete an MA and wrote a dissertation in 1990 titled "Participation of the Rural Poor in Rural Newspaper: Role of NGO in Grassroots Communications for the Empowerment of the Rural Poor."

14. Kamrul Hassan, interview with author at his home in Dhaka, October 2, 1994.

15. Called *ASA Barta* up to 1984.

16. The reports referred to in this and the following paragraph were both edited by Anwarul Islam. *ASA Annual Report 1982–83,* (Dhaka: ASA, 1984), and *The Counterlinkage, ASA Activity Report 1985* (Dhaka: ASA, 1986).

17. BRAC, *The Net: Power Structure in Ten Villages* (Dhaka: BRAC, 1980). Two other important early books on BRAC's work are Martha Chen, *Quiet Revolution: Women in Transition in Rural Bangladesh* (Rochester, Vt.: Schenkman Books, 1983), and Catherine Lowell, *Breaking the Cycle of Poverty: The BRAC Strategy* (Dhaka: BRAC, 1992). For a fiery defense of the empowerment work done by one of BRAC's great rivals, the NGO Proshika, see Bosse Kramsjo and Geoffrey D. Wood, *Breaking the Chains: Collective Action for Social Justice among the Rural Poor in Bangladesh* (Dhaka: Dhaka University Press, 1992).

18. *The Counterlinkage.*

19. See Davies' Web site "Monitoring and Evaluation NEWS," http://mande.co.uk/ (accessed May 16, 2008). In the mid-1990s Rick worked on his PhD in Bangladesh, and developed an innovative monitoring device for CCDB, the NGO that Shafiq had worked for.

20. K. M. Jahangir Alam and Manfred Statzer, *Is Unity and Social Action Enough to Develop the Poor?* (Dhaka: ASA, 1984).

21. Ibid.

22. Harvey L. Perkins, *ASA: Hope for the Landless* (Dhaka: ASA, 1985), pp. 10–12.

23. Ibid, pp. 18, 21–22.

Chapter 5

1. The reforms to the drug policy were initiated by Shafiq's friend and fellow crusader Zafrullah Chowdhury, for whom Darbesh Ali had also worked. Zafrullah Chowdhury set up the People's Health Center, designed to improve health services to the poor. D. Melrose, *Bitter Pills* (Oxford: Oxfam, 1982), tells the story of the campaign for drug reform. Ershad may have warmed to the radical drug policy as a way to gain favor in "progressive" circles. Some of the same reasoning may also have been behind his decision to grant Prof. Muhammad Yunus a special ordinance to put the Grameen Bank on a sound legal footing.

2. I interviewed Jahangir in October 1994, and he confirmed that my account is broadly accurate.

3. Shafiqual Haque Choudhury, *ASA in Transition* (Dhaka: ASA, 1995), pp. 7–27 and 28–43.

4. UNICEF stands for United Nations Children's Fund.

5. I went to Bangladesh for ActionAid in late 1984 and remained its Bangladesh country director until 1991. In 1985 I set up, in Dhaka, Bangladesh's first urban microcredit program, and developed a microcredit program in Bhola District that grew to 25,000 clients. I was therefore well placed to see ASA's work in credit in context. Later, in 1996, I founded *Safe*Save, a microfinance provider that works in the slums of Dhaka; see http://www.safesave.org (accessed May 16, 2008). For more on my views on microfinance, see www.thepoorandtheirmoney.com (accessed August 10, 2008).

6. *Bangladesh Observer.*

7. Francis Rolt, *On the Brink in Bengal* (Dhaka: Dhaka University Press, 1993) is an entertaining tour of the geographical and social periphery of Bangladesh.

8. These rivers are known in Bangladesh as Padma and Jamuna.

9. Unpublished report of which I saw a photocopy.

10. Graham Wright (of *MicroSave*) calls such uncomfortable hybrids between grants and loans "groans."

11. Anwarul Islam (ed.) *The Counter Linkages, ASA Annual Report 1986–87* (Dhaka: ASA, 1987), p.3.

12. M A Rub (ed.) *ASA Annual Report 1988–89* (Dhaka: ASA, 1989).

13. *The Counterlinkage, ASA Activity Report 1985* (Dhaka: ASA, 1986).

14. Shirin Akhtar, interview in Narsingdi district at an ASA branch office with the author and S. K. Sinha, February 1995.

15. In Bangladesh, where the judiciary was not fully separated from the executive until late 2007, district commissioners acted as magistrates, as they did in British times.

16. *ASA in Transition*, p. 45.

Chapter 6

1. Quotations from interviews with Shafiqual Haque Choudhury in English in this chapter (except for the last one) are presented verbatim, from recordings made by the author during interviews in his office in Dhaka between August 1994 and April 1995.

2. Opinion expressed by an ASA staff member who asked not to be identified; interview with author, September 20, 1994.

3. The Yunus paper had been widely quoted and the appearance of some of its text in ASA publications is a good example of how his influence was disseminated. Muhammad Yunus, *Grameen Bank Project in Bangladesh: A Poverty Focussed Rural Development Programme* (Dhaka: Grameen Bank, 1982); quoted on the Grameen Bank website in abridged form at

http://www.grameen-info.org/index.php?option=com_content&task=view&id=19&Itemid=114 (accessed August 18, 2008).

4. Kamrul Hassan, *Around the Year '92* (Dhaka: ASA, 1993), p. 1; *Across the Days 1993* (Dhaka: ASA, 1994), p. 2.

5. Shafiqual Haque Choudhury, *ASA in Transition* (Dhaka: ASA, 1995), p. 45.

6. For views of the potential of Grameen expressed in that period, see Mahabub Hossain, *Credit for Alleviation of Rural Poverty: The Grameen Bank in Bangladesh* (Dhaka: International Food Policy Research Institute and Bangladesh Institute of Development Studies), and Andreas Fuglesang and Dale Chandler, *Participation as Process—Process as Growth: What We Can Learn from the Grameen Bank* (Dhaka: Grameen Trust, 1993). For a much more pessimistic view stressing the limits to development through the financing of off-farm businesses, see S. R. Osmani, "Limits to the Alleviation of Poverty through Non-farm Credits," *BIDS Journal*, 18, no 4 (December 1989).

7. According to one estimate, the proportion of women in the ASA workforce fell from 50 percent to 27 percent as a result of this process. It has never since recovered. Women staff members at senior levels are especially rare. In November 2007 I attended a monthly policy-making meeting in the ASA headquarters where the 50 senior-most staff of ASA gathered: none was a woman.

8. These accounting routines are available, in full, in English, in a number of ASA publications, such as Mostaq Ahmmed, *Key to Achieving Sustainability* (Dhaka: ASA, 2002).

9. This helps to explain why so few of ASA's staff are female. There are female loan officers and branch managers, however. They may work in their own areas and live at home, or board locally.

10. Two short essays by Pankaj Jain remain the best summaries of the efficiencies of the ASA microcredit system: *Managing Fast Expansion of Microcredit Programs* (Dhaka: ASA, 1997) and *Maturing of Micro-credit Movement: Some Pointers from ASA* (Dhaka: ASA, n.d.).

11. This was the origin of my *ASA: The Biography of an NGO*, published privately by ASA in 1995. This present book reuses much of the material researched at that time.

12. DANIDA (Danish aid) granted ASA 2 million taka in 1990 and again in 1991, and almost 10 million in 1992. Along with earlier grants this made a total of 17 million taka, and DANIDA thus became ASA's fifth-biggest donor up to that time, after Miserior (92.8 million), CEBEMO (84.5), HEKS (67), and DIA Netherlands (23).

13. All quotations from Shah Alam in this chapter are from interviews by the author and S. K. Sinha during a series of visits to his branch area in Konokdiya starting on October 3, 1994 and continuing until April 1995.

14. *Jibon Gorar Notun Pat* (New Ways to Change Your Life) (Dhaka: ASA, 1994), 5th ed.

15. All quotations in this chapter from Shamsunnahar and her acquaintances Rahima Begum and Helena Begum (no relation), and from Joygam Bibi (and from their husbands) are from interviews by the author and S. K. Sinha during two visits to villages in the Gazipur area in late October 1994.

16. For more about work by Grameen in Patuakhali at that time, see Sanae Ito, "The Grameen Bank: Rhetoric and Reality" (PhD diss., Institute for Development Studies, Sussex University, 1999).

17. Though common in Bangladesh, the use of landowning qualifications is misleading. A householder may be landless today but inherit five acres from his father tomorrow. Besides, landholding can easily be disguised or concealed. For this reason many fieldworkers (sensibly, in my view) pay only lip service to the rule. It is not uncommon to find members whose land ownership exceeds the limit.

18. Mina, interview with author, Narsingdi, October 1994.

19. Anne Marie Goetz and Rina Sen Gupta, "Who Takes the Credit? Gender, Power, and Control over Loan Use in Rural Credit Programs in Bangladesh" (Brighton: IDS working paper, 1994); and Naila Kabeer, "'Can Buy Me Love'? Re-evaluating the Empowerment Potential of Loans to Women in Rural Bangladesh" (Brighton: IDS working paper, 1998).

20. Farooque Chowdhury, ed., *Micro Credit Myth Manufactured* (Dhaka: Srabon Prokashani, 2007).

21. *Around the Year '92*, p.1.

22. Details of PKSF are available at http://www.pksf-bd.org/ (accessed May 16, 2008).

23. The deal was not easy to negotiate and was helped along by Patrick Vath, an adviser working for the USAID-funded Financial Sector Reform Program.

24. Shafiqual Haque Choudhury, interview with author, ASA office, Dhaka, February 17, 2008.

Chapter 7

1. The ASA data used in this chapter are from ASA Head Office records. I am very grateful to finance director Azim Hossain for preparing data for me.

2. Quotations from ASA staff and members dating from the 1994–95 period in Patuakhali, Gazipur, and Narsingdi are from interviews with the author and S. K. Sinha between August 1994 and April 1995.

3. For a discussion of the social costs of joint liability, see Richard Montgomery, Disciplining or Protecting the Poor? Avoiding the Social Costs of Peer Pressure in Micro-credit Schemes. *Journal of International Development*, 1996, 8(2): 289–305.

4. Shafiqual Haque Choudhury, interview with author, ASA office, Dhaka, February 28, 2008. Other quotations from Choudhury in this chapter are from the same series of interviews in February and March 2008, unless otherwise noted.

5. Shahedara Parvin and Kurt Healey, *ASA in Micro-Finance 1996* (Dhaka: ASA, 1997), p.7.

6. PPP converts currencies according to their relative purchasing power. For example, although a U.S. dollar is worth about 70 taka at the market exchange rate, 70 taka in Bangladesh buys about four times as much as a dollar does in New York. The PPP rate for a dollar–taka conversion is therefore around 17 taka.

7. A description and discussion of the millennium development goals (MDGs) is available at http://www.un.org/millenniumgoals/.

8. Stuart Rutherford, *Uses and Users of MFI Loans in Bangladesh*, *MicroSave* Grameen II Briefing Notes No. 7, 2006, available at http://www.microsave.org.

9. The fact that borrowers do not always invest in businesses sheds light on the arguments put forth in S. R. Osmani's paper (see chap. 6, n. 2).

10. Madeline Hirschland, ed., *Savings Services for the Poor: An Operational Guide* (Bloomfield, Conn.: Kumarian Press, 2005), provides a good account of the need for voluntary savings services.

11. For a work published during that period that discusses BRI, see Paul Mosley, "Indonesia: BKK, Kurk and the BRI Unit Desa Institutions" in David Hulme and Paul Mosley, eds., *Finance against Poverty* (London: Routledge, 1996).

12. This comment came from Graham Wright, of the microfinance advisory service *MicroSave*. Wright is familiar with microfinance in Bangladesh, having lived there for several years and having assisted Bangladesh microfinance providers, notable BURO, to develop their services.

13. Marguerite Robinson is a researcher and writer whose work on savings, and microfinance in general, has been very influential. She has written a multivolume work, *The Microfinance Revolution: Sustainable Finance for the Poor* (Washington, D.C.: World Bank, 2001). Imran Matin

is now head of research at BRAC, Bob Christen now leads the Bill and Melinda Gates Foundation work in microfinance, and Graham Wright works at *MicroSave* (see previous note). Wright, Christen, and Matin were in Bangladesh at the time, working on a study of ASA's savings: see G. A. N. Wright, R. P. Christen, and I. Matin, "Introducing Savings Services into ASA, a Microcredit Institution," *Small Enterprise Development*, 12, no. 3 (September 2001): 20–32.

14. In 2008 the price was raised to 10 taka per 1,000.

15. I discovered one pioneer in a few villages in central Bangladesh in the mid-1990s. Social Development Society, a locally registered NGO, was offering a long-term commitment savings plan to villagers. Unfortunately, SDS came to a sticky end, but the midsize microfinance provider BURO took it up and made a success of it.

16. At "BankPoor 1996," a precursor to the microcredit summit held in New York in February 1997, Muhammad Yunus was still telling participants at the conference that savings would be of little use to the poor and that the focus should remain firmly on credit.

17. The financial diaries were carried out in Bangladesh in 1999–2000 (managed by David Hulme and Stuart Rutherford) and in India in 2000–1 (managed by David Hulme and Orlanda Ruthven) as part of a research program by the Institute for Development Policy and Management at the University of Manchester, U.K. The Bangladesh diaries are discussed in Stuart Rutherford, *Money Talks: Conversations with Poor Households in Bangladesh about Managing Money* (Manchester: IDPM, 2002). Later, Daryl Collins (assisted by Jonathan Morduch and Stuart Rutherford) ran a set of diaries in South Africa, and Stuart Rutherford (assisted by Md Maniruzzaman and S. K. Sinha) ran a special set of diaries in Bangladesh specifically to look at the performance of Grameen Bank and other Bangladesh microfinance providers: his report is *Grameen II: The First Five Years* (Nairobi: *MicroSave*, 2006), available at http://www.microsave.org. Collins, Hulme, Morduch, Rutherford, and Ruthven are preparing a book on the diaries, *Portfolios of the Poor* (Princeton: Princeton University Press, 2009).

Chapter 8

1. "Brac, Grameen Bank under Bomb Attack," *Daily Star*, February 27, 2005, http://www.thedailystar.net/2005/02/17/d5021701011.htm (accessed May 16, 2008).

2. The book was Stuart Rutherford, *ASA: The Biography of an NGO* (Dhaka: ASA, 1995).

3. Tanvir (Ashraful Haq Chowdhury), interview with author, ASA University, February 27, 2008.

4. The Nobel Prize citation can be found at http://nobelpeaceprize.org/eng_lau_announce2006.html (accessed May 16, 2008).

5. Updates for the MIX Market are available online at http://www.mixmarket.org/ (accessed May 16, 2008).

6. Nimal A. Fernando and Richard L. Meyer, "ASA—The Ford Motor Model of Microfinance," *ADB Finance for the Poor*, 3 no. 2 (June 2002).

7. The statement appears at http://www.grameen-info.org/bank/ataglance/GBGlance.htm (accessed May 16, 2008).

8. Interview of Muhammad Yunus by Jonathan Morduch and Stuart Rutherford, Grameen Bank, Dhaka, December 15, 2002.

9. Since this passage was written, Sheikh Hasina has been released and has gone to the United States for medical treatment, and negotiations for the release of Khaleda Zia are ongoing.

Chapter 9

1. Sushil Kumar Roy, interview with author, ASA office, Dhaka, March 4, 2008.

2. Quotations in this chapter from ASA and Nijera Kori members and staff and other villagers are from interviews with the author and S. K. Sinha during visits to the Manikganj area (on November 6, 2007 and January 22 and March 3, 2008) and to the Comilla area (February 23 and 24, 2008).

3. See http://www.nijerakori.org/index.php?option=com_content&task=blogsection&id= 5&Itemid=28 (accessed May 16, 2008).

4. Hassan Zaman (team leader) et al., *Economics and Governance of Nongovernmental Organizations in Bangladesh, World Bank Country Study* (Dhaka: Dhaka University Press, 2007), p. 21.

5. *Bangladesh Country Strategy Plan* (Dhaka: DFID, 1998), p. 4.

6. Ibid.

7. Kirsten Westergaard, *NGOs, Empowerment and the State in Bangladesh* (Copenhagen: CDR Working Paper 92.2, 1992), is one of several articles that reviews the prospects for empowerment NGOs to influence the state.

8. A sympathetic but realistic review can be found in Naila Kabeer, *Making Rights Work for the Poor: Nijera Kori and the Construction of Collective Capabilities in Rural Bangladesh* (Brighton: IDS Working Paper 200, 2003).

9. I interviewed Khushi Kabir at Nijera Kori's offices in Dhaka, and DFID officers at their Dhaka offices, in February 2008.

10. Shahid Khandker, *Fighting Poverty with Microcredit* (Washington, D.C.: World Bank, 1998).

11. Jonathan Morduch, *Does Microfinance Really Help the Poor? New Evidence from Flagship Programs in Bangladesh* (Boston: Harvard University Press, 1998). Morduch selected from the data only the poorer households—those with less than a half acre of farmland (a criterion for microcredit group membership in most organizations). But Mark Pitt then had yet another go at the figures, setting the landowning limits at a different level (three-quarters of an acre) and found that this strengthened the original conclusions. See his *Reply to Jonathan Morduch's "Does Microfinance Really Help the Poor? New Evidence from Flagship Programs in Bangladesh"* (Providence, R.I.: Brown University working paper, 1999).

12. Dr. Yunus made this statement at a conference in Dhaka in 1996 organized by the NGO Proshika's Institute for Development Policy Analysis and Advocacy in Bangladesh. See the book that came out of the conference: Geoffrey D. Wood and Iffath A. Sharif, eds., *Who Needs Credit? Poverty and Finance in Bangladesh* (London: Zed Books, 1997).

13. A good recent description and analysis of the plan can be found in Munshi Sulaiman and Imran Matin, "Making Microfinance Work for the Extreme Poor, Evidence and Experiences from Bangladesh," *ADB Finance for the Poor*, 9, no. 1 (March 2008).

14. Imran Matin, interview with author, BRAC, Dhaka, March 9, 2008.

15. See http://news.bbc.co.uk/2/hi/business/2719929.stm (accessed March 30, 2008).

16. Johura Begum and Shamsuddin, interviews by S. K. Sinha, Gazipur, June 22–27, 2008. Sinha tracked the couple's receipts and payments each day for a week and examined their passbooks.

17. Mahenoor Begum, interviewe with the author and S. K. Sinha in Shariatpur during the Grameen II research, December 11, 2004.

18. Interview by the author and S. K. Sinha with a microfinance group, Hrishipara, Torgaon, Gazipur, February 22, 2008.

19. Microfinance organizations in Bangladesh have been contributing to the development of health insurance, but it has proved difficult. Grameen Bank, for example, has been working on programs since as far back as 1995.

20. Madhuri Begum, interview with author and S. K. Sinha, Dhaka, November 2007.

21. BRAC Bank, for example, a commercial bank owned by the NGO BRAC, is aggressively moving into financing small and medium enterprises, but is having difficulty persuading the Bangladesh Bank (the central bank) to allow it to open as many branches as it would like.

22. ASA office, August 11, 2008.

Chapter 10

1. Helen Gallagher, Save the Children's Bangladesh country director at the time, helped me reconstruct this story (private correspondence, April 2008).

2. Doubts about whether microcredit programs can be exported to second countries had been expressed in the literature. See, for example, David Hulme, "Can the Grameen Bank Be Replicated? Recent Experiment in Malaysia, Malawi and Sri Lanka," *Development Policy Review*, (January 1990): 287–300.

3. Elisabeth Rhyne, who works for Accion (an international, for-profit microlending organization), has written widely on microfinance.

4. Henry R. Jackelen and Elisabeth Rhyne, "Towards a More Market-Oriented Approach to Credit and Savings for the Poor," *Small Enterprise Development*, 2, no. 4 (June 1994): 4–20.

5. CARD has recently produced a brief history of itself: Jaime Aristotle B. Alip, *A Chain of Change* (Manila: CARD, 2007).

6. This interview took place in Dhaka, March 4, 2008.

7. Quoted by Aristotle Alip during the March 4, 2008 interview with the author.

8. Sukhwinder Arora, *Bandhan: Lessons from a New MFI Serving One Million Clients in Seven Years* (Lucknow: *MicroSave*, 2008: http://www.microsave.org). This is one of a series of papers looking at fast-growing microfinance providers; the companion paper on ASA is written by Stuart Rutherford.

9. Dirk Brouwer, interview with author, Dhaka, November 13, 2007.

10. See Xavier Reille and Sarah Forster, "Foreign Capital Investment in Microfinance: Balancing Social and Financial Returns," Focus Note 44 (Washington, D.C.: CGAP, 2008).

11. For two views on the Compartamos story, see Richard Rosenberg, "CGAP Reflections on the Compartamos Initial Public Offering: A Case Study on Microfinance Interest Rates and Profits," Focus Note 42 (Washington, D.C.: CGAP, 2008), and Robert Cull, Asli Demirguc-Kunt, and Jonathan Morduch, "Microfinance and the Market," *Journal of Economic Perspectives* (forthcoming).

12. Not to be confused with Sequoia Capital, a U.S.-based company that also invests in microcredit.

13. Where it is in direct competition with Bandhan, the MFI that ASA coached and that most resembles itself.

14. Shafiqual Haque Choudhury, interview with author, ASA office, Dhaka, March 8, 2008.

15. Reille and Forster, *Foreign Capital Investment.*

16. March 8, 2008 interview.

Index